TERRORISM AND GLOBAL POWER SYSTEMS

TERRORISM AND GLOBAL POWER SYSTEMS

SHAHWAR JUNAID

OXFORD
UNIVERSITY PRESS

OXFORD

UNIVERSITY PRESS

Great Clarendon Street, Oxford OX2 6DP

Oxford University Press is a department of the University of Oxford.
It furthers the University's objective of excellence in research, scholarship,
and education by publishing worldwide in

Oxford New York

Auckland Cape Town Dar es Salaam Hong Kong Karachi
Kuala Lumpur Madrid Melbourne Mexico City Nairobi
New Delhi Shanghai Taipei Toronto

with offices in

Argentina Austria Brazil Chile Czech Republic France Greece
Guatemala Hungary Italy Japan South Korea Poland Portugal
Singapore Switzerland Thailand Turkey Ukraine Vietnam

ISBN 0 19 597788 2

Second Impression 2005

303.62
JUN

Typeset in Times
Printed in Pakistan by
Kagzi Printers, Karachi.
Published by
Ameena Saiyid, Oxford University Press
Plot No. 38, Sector 15, Korangi Industrial Area, PO Box 8214
Karachi-74900, Pakistan.

To
all those
who have protected me
so that I may write freely

CONTENTS

INTRODUCTION

Terrorism has become a factor that commands serious consideration in global politics and strategic planning at the national and international level. This book covers the rising tide of terrorist activity during the period 1980 to 2002 and looks at the factors involved in making terrorism an option for bringing about political, economic and cultural change. It examines global power systems in order to determine how an environment in which terrorism becomes an option for bringing about political change, is created.

In order to examine the origin and use of terrorism as a tool of political, social and economic change, the factors, situations, circumstances and systems that give rise to the need for change have to be discussed. Part II of this book deals with a number of factors that have contributed to the escalation of terrorist activity in recent times. Part III considers issues of national and international security from a global perspective. Underlying security concerns have a profound impact on the psyche of communities and nations. Unresolved issues demand new solutions in view of a history of failure at resolution. In such situations, the use of unusual methods, including militant activity and the systematic use of terror, may be considered legitimate means for achieving results. It may be a good idea to examine such rationalizations in order to consider strategies to deal with this phenomenon and consider the extent to which state terrorism contributes to such rationalizations.

Shahwar Junaid

PART I

EXAMINING THE PHENOMENON

1

THE FUNDAMENTALIST PSYCHE

In the final analysis, the followers of all religions that are practised in the world are 'fundamentalists'. Religions are based on beliefs and rituals that are fundamental to the identity and enforcement of the faith. Many beliefs and rituals are rationalised through elaborate theological arguments. One way of defining the mindset that is created through such rationalizations is to consider those generalized tendencies and trends in religious thought that inspire a range of activities and lead to the creation of systems that are considered necessary for the perpetuation of the faith.[1] Sometimes these systems and practices are extremely simple in essence and deed: for example, the performance of Hajj, a pillar of Islam, as a unifying ritual that brings Muslims from all parts of the world together, is expected to be an empowering experience. It is expected to allow the faithful to establish links and renew a sense of belonging to the larger community. The political possibilities of this gathering cannot be ignored.

The scale of participation in Hajj these days requires a certain amount of discipline and insistence that individual, sectarian and national expression conform to a universal norm within the religious community, on the occasion of Hajj. Taken in the right spirit this makes sense. It also makes sense that the good feeling, the search for a meaning to life and desire to purify the soul, of whatever the individual feels the need to purify himself of, seems a more attainable goal when the psyche of so many is involved in the same endeavour at the same time. The basic purpose and meaning of the act needs to be understood and appreciated, not romanticised. It can be an awe-inspiring spectacle. It can also be a transforming experience for some. Similarly, 'Jihad' has re-emerged as an important concept for the achievement of common objectives, binding Muslim societies worldwide, in the second half of the twentieth century.[2]

The rituals of Catholicism serve to remind followers of that faith of its fundamentals and origin. In fact, the pomp and ceremony of ritual is a visible reminder of the power of the Church. The continuity of ritual allows adherents to relive history, briefly, but on a regular basis. The Pope, as the fount of Roman Catholic wisdom, is a man who trains long and hard for the job and then works at it all his life. Through an elaborate system of delegation of religious authority, a veritable army of trained clergy manages millions of people. A very practical system has been put in place. The people, the flock, share a sense of community, and there is a focal point of authority. Similarly, in Judaism, there are beliefs, rituals and customs, exclusive, or shared with other religions, that have both a practical purpose as well as a spiritual and historical significance.

The pillars of one faith need not encroach upon the beliefs of another nor should they be used to intimidate or inspire fear. In its own way each religion seeks to order civilisation and society by taming the beast in man. Yet some of the most vicious battles have been, and are being fought because of religion and in the name of religion. Today, more than ever before, there is a need to understand the origin of violence in the name of religion, in its various manifestations as the consequences are too grave to ignore. It is not a recent phenomenon. Every battle being fought in the name of religion today has a precursor in history.

Violence has been a weapon used by institutions and governments, as well as individual revolutionaries, throughout history in every epoch and throughout the world. Violence has been used to subjugate populations, assert power, or create an illusion of power in order to achieve political objectives and gain control of resources. Power has also been sought in the name of religion, to gain control over the spiritual life of a population. In the fourth century BC, a Greek historian Xenophan, wrote of the effectiveness of psychological warfare against enemy populations. The Roman emperors Tiberius and Caligula executed people in order to discourage opposition to their rule, but the first recorded acts of violence in the name of religion were perpetrated over 2000 years ago by an extremist offshoot of a Jewish sect, the Zealots. The Zealots were active in Judea during the first century AD. They resisted Roman rule by attacking fellow Hebrews suspected of aiding the Romans. They did this through pre-meditated and well planned assassinations that took place on festive occasions and in crowded places, to inspire fear. Between 1090 and 1272, the

'Assassins', who belonged to a sub-sect of Shi'ite Islam, used similar methods. They would emerge from their mountain hideouts to kill the leaders and scholars of another sect (Sunni) as part of their campaign to acquire power for what they considered to be the true faith. They also fought the Christian Crusaders who had invaded a part of what is known as Syria today. During the late 1400s, the Spanish Inquisition used torture and execution to punish what it considered religious heresy, thereby asserting the authority of the Church and consolidating its position at the highest level within state structures.[3]

Ideologically, the French Revolution (1789-1799) was about liberty and human rights. Regardless of the methods used and the historical process that led to change, the Revolution managed to abolish serfdom, slavery, inherited privilege and judicial torture. The evolution of a new social contract between the rulers and the ruled led to new opportunities for those who had been excluded from the exercise of power on account of social status or religion. Terrorism, during the French Revolution, was an indication of regression to practices that were current during the wars of religion in the seventeenth century when terror was an instrument used to subjugate local populations, regardless of their status as combatants or otherwise.

During the 'Thirty Years War', the fight in Europe was between believers and apostates, Protestants and Catholics. As a result, entire communities were devastated and displaced. This led to efforts to establish a code of conduct that would make a distinction between combatants and non-combatants and would protect the civilian population by limiting the impact of war and political violence to warring parties. The Treaty of Westphalia of 1648 upheld the principle that peace required toleration of differing religious beliefs. The American Constitution rests in part on Europe's acceptance that civil peace on the continent required the separation of religion from the state. This differs from the Islamic view because Quranic law, the 'Shari'ah', the codified law as practised and defined by the last of the prophets—Muhammad (SAW), gives Muslims a code of conduct covering every aspect of human activity. Minorities, those following other faiths and living in a Muslim state, are protected under Shari'ah law. According to most sects of Islam, Shari'ah is subject to interpretation and redefinition by appropriately qualified religious authorities to cover situations that arise as a result of scientific developments and socio-cultural transitions of a fundamental nature.

By inventing the new ideological category of 'enemy of the people' during the French revolution, the Jacobins, who denounced their contemporary Girondins[4] for lacking zeal, again blurred the distinction of combatant and noncombatant and renewed justification to the use of murder as a political weapon (Reign of Terror). Thereafter, terror continued to be a major component of European history when left/right and nationalist tensions, fuelled by economic hardship, reached a boiling point. Between 1870 and the First World War, anarchists attacked the establishment in a number of European countries, including Spain, Russia, the Austro-German empire and America, by eliminating the top leadership there,[5] but their activities were not inspired by religion. Nor were those of the nihilists in Russia at the turn of the twentieth century. In subsequent years there was a rise in political violence. Apart from terror unleashed by anarchist elements, there was an increase in state, or, establishment terrorism. There were violent 'ethno-separatist' movements as well as other movements resisting colonial rule. Communal violence in the subcontinent on the eve of the departure of the British colonists and thereafter (1947), was inspired by a combination of forces. Irreconcilable differences between the practitioners of Hinduism and the practitioners of Islam re-emerged as an irresolvable irritant with the departure of the neutral overseer in the shape of a colonial government. The dislocation caused by the partition of territory in the subcontinent, and the creation of Pakistan and India, led to economic loss, social hardship and great psychological stress.[6] In this environment, terrible crimes against humanity were committed in the subcontinent.

The attribute of activism in those who are committed to the spiritual principles of a faith can create a strong sense of solidarity. When such activism is organized to oppose injustice within society, the implicit and explicit use of force for achieving political objectives can become the fountainhead of terror. Terrorist activity can be ideologically motivated. It can also be sponsored by the state to impose the writ of government and rationalized as a tool of war during religious or ethnic struggles for political supremacy. According to the United States Department of State, between 1968 and 1987, the number of international terrorist incidents increased by more than 600 percent. On 23 July 1968, a group of terrorists from the Popular Front for the Liberation of Palestine hijacked one of Israel's El Al airliners in Rome and forced its pilot to fly it to Algeria. This event marked a new phase in the revival of resistance to Israeli occupation of Palestinian territories, just as years later the 'Intifada' marked another phase of resistance in the area. The roots of such revolt lie in communal tyranny and the political, social and economic inequities that systematic oppression produces in dispossessed populations.

The Crusades of the Middle Ages took English troops thousands of miles from home in a bid to conquer the Holy Land and bring it under the fold of Christendom. Not so different after all from the successful attempt of the British and the Jewish community to annex the same territories in the name of religion half a century ago. Interesting observations emerge from analysis of the recent history of the Jewish people, the region, the creation of Israel and its subsequent policies towards the original inhabitants of the area.[7] Some policies, which are generally considered repugnant in developed countries, appear to have been accepted as the norm in these territories by the international community, possibly as a result of their guilt over what happened to the Jews during the Holocaust, in a war between Christians. The Muslims had nothing to do with their travails. This was, basically, the final solution of the West to the problem of Jewish statehood. The polity in the region was too weak to resist encroachment.

After the signing of the now defunct Washington peace accords, the Middle East was poised on the brink of a compromise, which many found difficult to swallow.[8] The conditions necessary for the success of the peace accords did not exist and it did not take long for the peace process to collapse once the hard-line government of Ariel Sharon was in power. After the renewal of the 'Intifada' and the re-occupation of the West Bank by Israel in 2002, Palestinians have been facing harsh retaliatory measures again, and in the end, they will face the same kind of untenable sell-out that took place during the 1940s if Muslim states do not unite to support them. Meanwhile, political will developed by adversity has found many outlets: multi-sectoral organizations with political, social and militant wings, each working relatively independently of the other, have emerged in the area. Religion is an important source of strength for these organizations.

Religion has emerged as a powerful binding force worldwide. As a result of the experience of joint guerrilla operations conducted in many parts of the world during the 1970s and 1980s with US forces, Muslim militants have acquired knowledge of tactics and technical expertise in modern warfare. Combining fighting skills with single-minded faith in the cause they espouse, they have emerged as dangerous opponents. Those who thought they were training mercenaries are learning that they made a mistake, for the skills they imparted can be used in many ways.

'Hamas' was set up as a welfare organization to help needy Palestinians. Its character changed in 1987 with the beginning of the Intifada,[9] although it continued to maintain a very important and effective welfare and relief component. In early September 2003 even the relief and welfare wing of Hamas was proscribed. Much of the credit for the concept and organization of the Intifada goes to Hamas. Its intervention in the area was welcomed by the Palestinians, who needed leadership and a blueprint for civil action in the area. On occasion its activities have embarrassed the Palestine Liberation Organisation (PLO), which eschewed violence, began negotiations for peace through the multilateral peace process, and which regularly deplores retaliatory violence in the Occupied Territories now. Hamas remains extremely powerful and voices the demands of those who do not want to accept the 'Declaration of Principles'. A number of questions come to mind in this connection:

Is Hamas the organisation of the underdog, the dispossessed? Is it a militant organisation, or should it be called a fundamentalist movement because its members openly adhere to the tenets of Islam—the perceived ritualistic requirements of the faith—and feel this reinforces and strengthens the identity of the community as well as its ability to fight. The link between religion, the mobilising and unifying potential of religion, and the translation of this potential into political power has to be examined in order to answer these questions.

Egypt's Muslim Brotherhood[10] also began as a welfare organisation. It has adherents amongst the poorest socio-economic groups in society, people who have nothing to lose except their life, and professionals who have everything. Both types consider their life well spent if they die for the 'cause' as they will then be considered martyrs. This has put the fear of God in the Egyptian government. Sheikh Omar Abdel Rehman, jailed in the United States on charges of conspiring to blow up the World Trade Center, was retried *in absentia* in Egypt, after being acquitted twice, on charges that he and his followers had participated in a 1989 demonstration to overthrow the Egyptian government. Forty-six others were also retried with him.

On 8 February 1994, the Jama'a Al Islamiya[11] claimed responsibility for planting bombs at three Egyptian state bank buildings. It accused the bank of usury, calling the buildings '...usurious monuments, which have become huge treasuries for the loot plundered by senior officials from the toiling masses...' This is a familiar theme that finds support among the less privileged in many countries. Unless the fruits of modernisation and political compromise filter down to the less fortunate in society, they are likely to flock to organisations that assist them in practical terms, give them a sense of belonging and also demonstrate a capacity to shake, if not change, the status quo.

In Algeria[12] much of the initial support for the Islamic Salvation Front (FIS), the so called Party of God, is known to have come from young Algerians who had despaired at the corruption and inefficient economic policies of the ruling party, the National Liberation Front, that had run the country for a quarter of a century with the backing of the army. Moderates, who did not support the extreme policies of the FIS, have not cooperated with the military government either, due to its failure to initiate economic change.[13] The Algerian authorities admit the existence of more radical groups than the FIS, which was voted into power but not permitted to rule, and say that it (FIS) was never as extreme as it was portrayed. Meanwhile, the Algerian people have been facing severe civil strife. A perceptive observation on the emergence of politico-religious organisations came from an Israeli foreign minister. During a visit to Albania he said, '...fundamentalism is not a new religion. It's an old protest against poverty and corruption...'

In Pakistan an operation to clear the Jallozai Afghan refugee camp[14] of a number of radicals led to the discovery of an elaborate defense system with underground tunnels accessing houses in the camp containing a sizeable supply of food and ammunition. The fact that the group involved (Takfiri), trained for the Afghan war, was active and entrenched well inside the settled areas in Pakistan (Nowshera) and hostile to the state, should raise questions about the wisdom of training and using informal forces such as the Taliban. It is short sighted in the extreme and does not serve the interest of Pakistan and the states of the region. It is not possible to exert control over such trained militant groups for an indefinite period.[15]

Long before the spectre of so-called 'Islamic fundamentalism' raised its head, violence in the name of religion was rampant in parts of the Western world. A quick look around the globe provides us with information about pockets of political activity where the use of violence for seizing and maintaining power in the name of religion has ravaged communities for decades now. A classic case is that of

Roman Catholic Northern Ireland.[16] The root of the issue was economic exploitation of the worst kind over centuries. The struggle, widely known to be one between Roman Catholics and Protestants, led to a level of violence where more people were killed by Protestants during the first six months of 1993, than were ever killed by the traditional aggressors in this war, the Catholics. This is the case in other parts of the world as well, where moderate and extreme groups are at war. A peace settlement, brokered by the British government with American help, with Sinn Fein, now includes an agreement for the disarming of organization members. However, this has not been able to prevent demonstrations of hostility and lapses into violence. Both, the government in Dublin and that in London condemn violence, as does the Pope, yet it is believed that the local clergy sympathise with the combatants in their community and take sides accordingly. It is generally not publicised, but the Bosnian Serbs were fully backed by the Orthodox Christian elders, during the war in Bosnia-Herzegovina.[17] The intervention of the Orthodox Church was able to secure Russian support for the activities of the Serbs against the Bosnian Muslims. Those who are familiar with the Balkans know that some of the most secular and mild Muslims in the world live in these areas. The fundamentalists in the area were the Bosnian Serbs and their allies.

The fundamentalist mindset is not exclusive to a race, community, nation or region. Nor does it occur at a given level of mutation of religious thought, or social and political development in society. A combination of these, as well as historical factors, economic interests and security concerns, create an environment in which individual and collective behaviour that can be characterised as 'fundamentalist', surfaces.

REFERENCES

1. Marty Martin C., and Scott Apple (eds.), *Fundamentalism and the State*, Chicago: University of Chicago Press, 1984, pp. 20-25.
2. Calvert, John, 'The Islamist Syndrome of Cultural Confrontation', *Orbis*, Spring 2002, Vol. 45, No. 2, pp. 333-349; Jennifer Stern, 'Pakistan's Jihad Culture', *Foreign Affairs*, November/December 2000, Vol. 70, No. 6, pp. 116-126.
3. Jenkins, John Philip, 'Terrorism', *Encyclopaedia Britannica*, 12 November 2002, http://search.eb.com/eb/article?eu=73664.
4. Ibid.

5. Herf, Jeffrey, 'What is old and what is new in the terrorism of Islamic Fundamentalism?' *Partisan Review*, Winter 2002, pp. 2-3.
6. A legal process led to the creation of two states, Pakistan and India, on 14-15 August 1947.
7. Ibid., see note 5 above.
8. 'Washington Peace Accords', *The News* (Islamabad), AFP (Gaza City), 5 May 1996.
9. 'Fundamentalist Threat', *The Muslim* (Islamabad), AFP (Cairo), 12 May 1996.
10. Report, *The Muslim* (Islamabad), APA (Cairo), 22 November 1993; 'Muslim Brotherhood Threat', *The News* (Islamabad), *Reuters* (Cairo), 2 September 1994.
11. 'Attacks on Tourists', *The News* (Islamabad); *Reuters* (New York), 25 May 1994.
12. Fisk, Robert, 'Report From Algiers', *The Independent* (London), 2 February 1994; 'Military Operations against the FIS', *The News* (Islamabad); *Reuters* (Paris), 6 February 1994; *The News* (Islamabad); *Reuters* (Tunis), 8 February 1994.
14. Editorial, *The Muslim* (Islamabad), 2 July 1994.
15. Zeb, Rizwan, 'War Against Terror: Lessons for Pakistan', *Journal of South Asian and Middle Eastern Studies*, Spring 2003, Vol. 25, No. 3, pp. 53-73.
16. Ghiles, Francis, Report, *The Financial Times* (London), 2 February 1994.
17. 'Europe-Bosnia-Herzegovina', *The Economist* (London), 24-30 June 1995, p. 54.

2

WARS OF RELIGION AND POWER

During the 1990s what is generally perceived to be a war between obscurantist religious groups and progressive modernism entered a new phase worldwide: there were riots between different religious communities in Indonesia that had lived peacefully, side by side, for centuries.[1] The attacks on Christian minorities in India that took place at about the same time did not appear to be the work of the usual Hindu extremist groups that had also been responsible for earlier attacks on Muslims.[2] At about the same time genocide and atrocities were perpetrated by the Serbian authorities on the Muslim population in Kosovo, 90 per cent of which was forcibly displaced—children and able-bodied men were the special targets of death squads there. There was no doubt in the minds of relief workers who entered Kosovo after NATO intervened, that official Serbian policy had been to kill, terrorise, impoverish and displace a well established and economically secure people. Through the proceedings of the trial of former Serbian President Milosevic at the International Court in The Hague, the world has gained some insight into the mindset of those responsible.[3] The fears that motivate intrigues for ascendancy, outright elimination, or the ruthless suppression of individuals and peoples have a great deal to do with power politics and history. Even where religious differences are cited as the cause, the primary concern is often the future disposition of power, not proselytising. This is not very different from the reasoning of the Nazis in eliminating the Jewish people from territories under their control. Jews were being eliminated, not Judaism.

Whether such actions are motivated by religion has always been debatable: the fears that motivate outright elimination or ruthless suppression, of individuals and peoples. During the late 1940s, for a few years, a small nursery school for displaced children of certain families from a number of countries was set up in Britain. The marked differences between the abilities of children of various races were keenly observed and noted. Two children, from different parts of the world, became the subject of special interest.[4] When they showed exceptional intelligence, the Special Service men in charge seriously discussed their future. Among other things, they agreed, 'Keep them apart...the thing to do is not to let them breed...imagine what would happen if...there were more of them.' Their remarks indicated that their primary concern was the future disposition of power, and that their attitude and actions were not motivated by religion or a desire for racial purity.

Sometimes a people self-destruct instead of acquiring power, when using religion as a rationale. The attitude of the Taliban[5] towards the disposition of women and their role in society was not sanctioned by Islam. They were well aware of this and frequently said they would moderate their policy towards the education of women and their inclusion in civic life once their government was administratively and economically secure. Basically, the suppression of women and their confinement was a convenience for the regime.[6] Contrary to common belief, girl children are cherished by ordinary Afghans, if not for anything else then as the future mothers of their nation. In Afghanistan, ten years of communist influence had created a society in which many women in urban areas were studying, working and could generally look forward to a productive life. At the same time, orphans of the civil war in Afghanistan were being educated in orthodox seminaries in Pakistan and elsewhere, where there was no exposure to women or family life and all manifestations of modernity were viewed as the work of Satan.

Subsequently, in Afghanistan, 'Ijtehad', the interpretation of the injunctions of the Holy Quran in the light of changing times, was replaced by a superstitious, rough and crude justice that was reminiscent of the *Jahiliya* period, prior to Islam: in one instance, a brick wall was dislodged on an eighty-three year old man accused of immoral conduct. The man had denied wrongdoing and when he survived the ordeal, it was said to be a sign that he was not guilty.[7] The amputated hands and feet of thieves were hung at crossroads in Kabul.[8] While Islam enjoins that believers take heed (ibrat) of the consequences of evil, this kind of exhibitionism was seen only after struggles for power and the control of resources and territories began in certain parts of the Muslim world (between Muslims).[9] In other parts of the world Muslim rulers and conquerors alike used compassion and humane conduct to win over populations.

The tactics used to control the population in Afghanistan during the Taliban rule had everything to do with power and little to do with Islam. It was a form of state terrorism used to subdue a volatile and brutalized population, through a unique interpretation and application of Islamic religious tenets. Initially, the Taliban enjoyed the full support of the United States establishment, which encouraged US oil companies, such as UNOCOL, to conduct preliminary surveys for laying oil and gas pipelines there. It was only later, as a result of severe international criticism of their policies, that Washington imposed economic sanctions on the Afghan Taliban. Shortly after the events of 11 September 2001, the United States declared war on the Taliban,[10] although, at the outset, even Britain[11] and France expressed reservations and their experts were of the view that proof of the Taliban's complicity in the incident would not stand scrutiny in a court of law.

There is a fallacious assumption current amongst many western analysts that both Muslim, and other religious fundamentalists, are motivated by purely theological concerns and an implacable belief in the superiority of the particular religion, or branch thereof, that they subscribe to. As understanding of this particular twentieth century manifestation of the phenomenon grows, sociologists and politicians are beginning to accept that there is much more to such movements than religion. A closer study reveals that pragmatic economic and political concerns have been important in spawning them and will eventually serve as a moderating force. The basic question is how these economic and political concerns can be addressed in order to make religious extremism unprofitable.

Developments in 1994 saw western nations adroitly manoeuvring the Arabs and other Muslim countries into opening channels of communication with Israel.[12] The 1994 Casablanca moot sponsored by the United States, Russia and Morocco, as well as many other US initiatives, including agreements between Jordan and Israel, and the lifting of the Arab states' ban on trade with companies that had links with Israel, were a prelude to the emergence of Israel as a nation in the Middle East. The establishment of full diplomatic relations between Israel and the countries of the region and an amendment in the Palestinian Constitution accepting the continued existence of Israel, constituted significant moves[13] that had everything to do with strategic adjustment and nothing to do with religion. The rejection of the Middle East peace process by the government of Ariel Sharon, United States' support for Ariel Sharon's policies,[14] the subsequent call by some Arab states for severing ties with the Israeli government, also had everything to do with strategic adjustment and little to do with religion per se. Those of an orthodox persuasion need to analyze such moves and recognize them for what they really are: political stratagems.

In 1998, subsequent to these developments, it was predicted that in the not too distant future, fundamentalists of many religions, including Islam, could be left waging war between themselves for political supremacy, against those belonging to other sects of their religion and against those they consider less committed to their cause. In Pakistan this has already happened. A quick look at the so-called fundamentalist movements around the world confirms that, for the most part, Muslim activists tend to become embroiled in wars against those who are more liberal in their interpretation of Islam and easy going in the observance of the rituals and outward manifestations that some consider an essential part of the faith.[15] This observance of rituals is generally considered a means of separating the wheat, that is the true believers, from the chaff, that is those who were merely born into the faith. This is a manifestation of caste within religion, and it is as rigid as any caste system that ever existed.

Understanding of this reversal of hostility—from that directed towards the west, and alien theologies or cultures, to hostility directed towards other Muslims, whether they are individuals or loosely Islamic authoritarian regimes and corrupt rulers—could lead to better comprehension of the origin of purist, back-to-the-roots religious movements. A basic feature of these movements, often run by theologians who are also sophisticated social and political strategists, is their well organised social welfare component, which is directed at alleviating the misery of those who exist on the fringe of economic and political systems.[16] The unemployed, those with no source of income, no recourse to the law, the dispossessed, those who are too poor and powerless to attract the attention of governments, these are the people who are easily absorbed by fundamentalist movements, and constitute their rank and file.

One striking development in 1994 was the victory of the Islamic Welfare Party of Erbakan in Turkey, a country which has been considered a bastion of secularism since 1922 and straddles Asia and Europe. The Turkish Islamists, thereafter ousted on account of their Islamic credentials, have had to rename their Party.[17] In July 2002, Mr Bulent Ecevit, the Prime Minister of Turkey, delayed the dismissal of his weak government and the announcement of a date for holding general elections. Expressing fears that the re-named Islamic Party would again win a majority in the Parliament,[18] he delayed the dismissal of his weak government and the announcement of a date for holding elections. The Turkish Islamists were always cautious in their approach towards reform.[19] Their movement was spurred on by the refusal of the European Union to consider Turkey for membership until it improved legislation on human rights, amongst other things. In 1994, the Islamists captured 19 per cent of the vote in twenty-nine major municipalities and four hundred smaller ones. This placed them a close third to the True Path Party and the Motherland Party. Fortunately, the West to date has avoided labelling these new Turkish Islamists, as fundamentalists, but the appearance of the headscarf on Turkey's campuses is a daily reminder that religious practices are surfacing in civil life. The present situation remains very different from that of the Turkey which battled urban guerillas, believed to be communists or communist sponsored, during the 1960s and 1970s.[20]

Turkey's approach to relations with Iraq may have been influenced by socio-political changes that took place in the country during the mid-1990s. After 1998, US/UK attacks on Iraqi military installations took place from bases in Europe, not Turkey.[21] UN sanctions on Iraq had crippled the economy of Turkey's south-eastern region as Iraq used to import goods worth up to US$2.5 billion annually from this region. Ankara also used to receive about US$300 million annually in transit fees from Iraq's oil exports through its territory. Turkey has paid a heavy price, as the Arabs have, for remaining loyal to Western policy on Iraq. In spite of UN sanctions, traffic began to move between Turkey and Iraq during 1994. Up to seven hundred trucks carrying humanitarian supplies began to move into Iraq each day with food and medicines. In return they got cheap Iraqi diesel. Now trade is conducted through a hundred kilometres of Western protected Kurdish territory in northern Iraq. Transit fees are paid. Once again, interests other than religion, are at work.[22]

The emergence of conservative Islam as a political force, with power gained through due political process, is not a new development in Muslim countries. In Algeria, Jordan, Kuwait and Sudan, elections have been won by such conservative political groups through the electoral process. Conservatives are likely to surface as a political force in Indonesia, Bosnia and Chechnya, among other countries. It may not be wise to block, indefinitely, the transfer of authority to groups that have won power through due electoral process. Failure to do so has led to chaos and conflict in Algeria.[23] It may be a better idea to make attempts to understand and work around the socio-political deprivations that create the constituency for such groups.

In Pakistan, the state frequently expresses the view that the nuisance value of fundamentalists has always exceeded their strength as a political force. By 1993, the combined share of the votes culled by these parties had shrunk to 7 per cent from 13 per cent in the previous general elections. However, it would be wrong to underestimate their influence within the polity.[24] Most religio-political parties are now aware that one reason for their limited success in Pakistan is the common man's fear of extreme orthodoxy and the inability to comply with the demands of orthodox practices. The links that government has established between conservative groups and a number of violent incidents also inspire fear. Added to this is the fear created by the activities of repressive regimes, such as the Taliban in Afghanistan, which are linked to many militant groups in Pakistan.[25] A number of overtly sectarian religious groups that have emerged in the past twelve years are a product of infighting in the Muslim world, from which they derive their finances. They would vanish if their patrons were warned off and their money supply cut off. The handling of developments subsequent to the events of 11 September 2001 has had a ricochet effect in many parts of the world, however. The hunt for terrorists amongst Muslims has led to the closing of ranks in many Muslim countries where populations have been under official pressure to modernize and secularise. In a number of cases this has led to a rise in nationalism, in other cases it has led to bonding with Muslim freedom movements in other parts of the world.[26]

Meanwhile, there are reliable reports that a number of Arab countries maintain links with the more powerful orthodox elements in the region in an effort to balance close ties with the West. Qatar is home to a $178 million US prepositioning supply base—the largest in the world outside the US—supporting 10,000 troops and 5000 vehicles, but there are also reports that the country is 'hedging its bets' by cooperating with orthodox elements operating in the region. The United States is reported to be concerned about the 'sympathy' shown by a number of traditionally pro-West countries in the region towards alleged terrorist elements there. Explanations have been sought and steps taken to create public opinion against such moves.[27]

A number of nations, religious orders, institutions and concerned groups have made efforts to promote inter-cultural and inter-religious dialogue. Dialogue must, however, be seen to be in the interest of all parties concerned to be sustainable. Where this has not been the case, structured dialogue on religious issues has been viewed with distrust and resentment. On 28 June 1999, the Secretary General of the United Nations spoke at the Oxford Centre for Islamic Studies, in Oxford, England, to encourage efforts being made to promote inter-cultural and inter-religious dialogue. Laying emphasis on the need for understanding between people of various faiths, the UN Secretary General said, '...Sometimes the groups in conflict have very similar cultures. Some even share the same language. Such was the case with the Serbs, Croats and Bosnian Muslims in the former Yugoslavia, and with the Hutus and Tutsis in Rwanda.' He went on to quote from a speech by President Khatemi of Iran, who had said 'the Islamic Revolution of the Iranian people...calls for a dialogue among civilizations and cultures...'[28]

After the declaration of the United States' so-called war on terror and the setting up of a coalition of states to fight it, what is generally perceived to be a worldwide struggle between obscurantist religious groups and progressive modernism entered a third phase. Proposals for a dialogue between peoples of different faiths and ethnicity slipped into the background and a struggle for survival began. During the second phase, there had been riots between religious communities in Indonesia and attacks on the Christian minority in India. At the time, parallels were also drawn between the mentality that led to the organized destruction of the Babri mosque in Ayodhya and the genocide of Kosovar Muslims by Serb forces. However, NATO intervention in Kosovo undercut accusations of religious bias that had surfaced in Europe after the Bosnian conflict. The withdrawal of Israeli forces from Lebanon and the interest of the Clinton administration in furthering the Middle East peace process[29] went a long way towards reducing tension in many parts of the world.

Information systems have created communities that transcend international borders, and the message they broadcast at the time was that the West was inclined to help communities under pressure, regardless of religious belief. The significance of this, and a number of other developments, was not fully understood and given the consideration it deserved in future strategic planning by major world powers and multilateral institutions. As a result, insecurity and other root causes of terrorism were not addressed. Analysis reveals that as a result of various measures taken by the United States and its allies, in reaction to attacks on US territory in September 2001, violence was not contained. After an initial lull, there was an escalation in the intensity of violence (such as suicide bombings) and the frequency of violence in the struggle between communities with different interests.

This increase in the intensity of violence occurred during a shorter time frame than anticipated. Hostility between communal groups had a negative impact on Muslim interests worldwide. It is significant that during the first week of May 2002, the front page of most newspapers in Pakistan carried two main items: one item was about a suicide bombing in Israel. Israeli citizens were the targets. Another item on the front page covered a suicide bombing in Pakistan.[30] Expatriates were the targets in this instance. Expatriates, including diplomats and foreign workers, had come to be seen as the constituency of an unpopular regime that had not contributed to the common weal but had contributed to an alliance that battered and hounded Muslims worldwide.[31] It is generally believed that many innocent people have suffered in a revengeful, rather than target-specific anti-terror exercise by powerful states and institutions. This perception in Pakistan is detrimental to the future of foreign direct investment and joint enterprise. It is also significant for those industrially developed states that seek additional markets for goods and services and new areas for capital investment. This situation benefits no one.

Another perception is that in the frenzied aftermath of 9/11 Muslim nations and Islam have become fair game for a variety of ambitious groups and institutions worldwide that want to cultivate Western governments.[32] Many adventurers have hitched their wagons to the hunt for so-called terrorists, just as a previous generation of adventurers, who were installed by the West in states around the globe, made a living out of fighting communism. In this new phase of global power adjustment, sharp lines have been drawn between religious, secular, as well as ethnic groups around the world, from Fiji to Madagascar, in the United States and Europe, in the Middle East and South Asia. This is a profound setback for those who have always worked for the peaceful coexistence of communities.

Fears that fuel ruthless suppression or outright elimination of individuals and peoples on the basis of religion or ethnicity have a great deal to do with national and regional history. Although proselytising, religious differences, and intrusion in matters concerning religion, may be cited as the cause of conflict, the underlying concern of combatants is often the future disposition of power through various means, including the control of the hearts and minds of populations.

This is not very different from the situation in Germany during the 1930s, which arose from the rationale of the Nazis for eliminating the Jewish people from territories under their control. Jews, as a force within society and the economy, were the enemy to be eliminated, not Judaism. Israel has attacked symbols of Palestinian nationhood[33] in order to destroy the growth of a collective entity with economic and political presence in the region, and thereby seeks to prevent the emergence of yet another Muslim nation on the map of the world. In a sophisticated game of musical chairs that blocks possibilities for peace, first one and then another Israeli politician, declares unwillingness to negotiate for peace even though mass demonstrations are often held by Israeli citizens in favour of the withdrawal of Israeli forces from Palestinian territory and for the establishment of a Palestinian state.

Two important casualties of the so-called global war on terror were multi-culturism and the rule of law. The third, equally significant casualty has been democratic practice. A series of actions that are considered patently extra-legal, by experts as well as many of its citizens, were undertaken by the United States at the national and international level in response to attacks on its territory.[34] In member states of the international coalition formed to fight terrorism, the natural allies of anti-terror forces were the armed forces and police personnel. In a number of cases, retrograde elements in law enforcement agencies saw this as a chance to garner international support in order to strengthen their hold on state institutions and government machinery. Many cases have been cited in which such elements are reported to have created sectarian trouble and encouraged communal violence to discredit political, as well as religious, organizations and promote authoritarian rule. The situation in Indonesia and Pakistan, among other countries, is disturbing.

In countries such as Pakistan, where the concept of parliamentary democracy was first introduced during colonial times,[35] the idea is deep rooted and defies repression. The nation has a unique political culture and a history of resistance to military rule. There is no basis for the comparison of Pakistan's political culture with that of Turkey, which was a small part of the much larger Muslim Caliphate, carved out through war and where a tradition of supreme authority existed prior to the emergence of the present form of government. Similarly, in Iran the concept of supreme authority reposed in a single individual existed prior to the Islamic Revolution. In the sparsely populated Gulf strong tribal links and patriarchal forms became the basis for present systems of government. These have evolved as prosperity has created new needs.

Intra-religious power struggles are often encouraged by vested interests to reverse hostility from the West, or alien theologies or cultures, to other Muslims including individuals and groups of other sects. Understanding of the origin of purist, back-to-the-roots religious movements, can provide clues to the evolution of their culture and future line of action. Concerns such as the disposition of power, which will guarantee the right to practise their religion, are equally important for minority as well as majority groups. Studies have revealed that pragmatic economic and political concerns are important factors in the rise of such movements and can eventually serve as a moderating force. It may be worthwhile for the international community to consider if economic and political concerns can be addressed in such a way as to make religious extremism unnecessary, and unprofitable, as a tool for gaining political power and economic control.

In order to remove the need for confrontation and minimize the risk of conflict between various established and emerging power groups in society, it is essential to take a number of steps: when conservative political organizations and parties acquire power through due political process, they must be recognized as a legitimate political force. By bringing such forces into the mainstream of national life their potential for constructive action can be explored and harnessed, and their theories of political and social organization tested.

REFERENCES

1. 'Communal Disturbances in Indonesia', *The Nation*, APA (Jakarta), 25 July 1998.
2. Report, *The Nation, Reuters*/AFP (New Delhi), 16 August 1999.
3. Proceedings of the Balkan War Crimes Tribunal, May-October 2002. BBC Online, coverage. London: Transcript. The Hague: Office of the Tribunal, 2002; James Rubin, 'Countdown to a Very Personal War.' *Financial Times Weekend* (London), 30 September to 1 October 2000, p. 1.
4. Royal Archives, United Kingdom: Shahwar Junaid. 'Terrorism and the State', *The Nation* (Islamabad), 1 October 1998: Horsley, Sir Peter. 'Sounds From Another Room' [s.n.] GB.

5. Editorial, *The Nation* (Islamabad), 7 March 1999.
6. Ermacora, Felix (UN Special Rapporteur on Human Rights Abuses in Afghanistan) 'Statement on Human Rights Abuse in Afghanistan.' *The News/The Nation* (AFP, Islamabad), 20 December 1994.
7. Qaiser Butt, 'Special Report', *The Frontier Post* (Peshawar), 22 September 1995; Report, *The Nation*, (APP), 18 February 1997.
8. Rahimullah Yusufzai, 'A Parting of Ways', *The News* on Friday, 15 September 1995.
9. Ibid., see 8 above.
10. Report, *The Nation* (Islamabad), AFP/Reuters, 21 November 2001.
11. Blair, Tony, British Prime Minister. Press Briefing. *BBC Online*, November 2001.
12. 'Casablanca Summit', *The Nation* (Islamabad), APA, 26 September 1994.
13. Report, *The News* (Islamabad), APA/Reuters, 15 October 1995, Hassan Ibrahim, Secretary General of the Ministerial Economic Unity Council, The Arab League, Cairo. *Emirates Today*, 2 May 1995; Report, *The News* (Islamabad), AFP, Occupied Jerusalem, 2 January 1994.
14. Special Report, *The Nation* (Islamabad), 2 July 2002.
15. Mahatir bin Mohammed, *Terrorism and Islam: Vital Speeches of the Day*, Vol. 68, No. 16, June 2002, pp. 484-487.
16. 'Income Distribution Gap' and 'Special Report' *The Muslim* (Islamabad) PPI, 13 September 1994.
17. Report, *The News* (Islamabad), AFP, Ankara, 25 February 1998.
18. Report, *Dawn* (DPA), Ankara, 14 December 1997.
19. Report, *The Nation*, (AFP) Ankara, 15 September 2002.
20. 'Turkey', *The Economist* (London), 20 December 1997.
21. Jentleson, Bruce W. and Thomas Paterson eds. *Encyclopedia of US Foreign Relations*, Vol. 4, 1992, Oxford University Press, New York, pp. 225-227.
22. Ibid., see 19 above.
23. Report, *The News* (Islamabad); *Reuters*, Algiers, 21 March 1994.
24. Ismail Khan, Special Report/Peshawar, *The News* (Islamabad), 13 May 1996.
25. Ibid., see 23 above.
26. Report, *The News* (Islamabad); *Reuters*, 28 September 2002.
27. Report, *The Nation* (Islamabad) AFP, 28 March 2001.
28. Annan, Kofi, Secretary General, United Nations. 'Speech on inter-cultural and inter-religious dialogue', Oxford Centre for Islamic Studies, Oxford, England, 28 June 1999.
29. The Middle East, *The Economist*, London, 16 August 1997.
30. Report; *The Nation* (Islamabad); *AFP/Reuters/APP*, May 2002.
31. Ibid., see 29 above.
32. Report, *The Economist*, London, 4 May 2002.
33. Report, *The Nation* (Islamabad); *Reuters*/Occupied Jerusalem, 15 May 2002.
34. Eisendrath, Craig, 'US Foreign Policy After September 11'. *USA Today* Vol. 130, No. 2684, May 2003, pp. 12-14; Foner, Eric, 'Changing History', *The Nation*, New York, 23 September 2002.
35. Greenber, Stanley, and Robert O. Boorstin, 'People on War', *Public Perspective*, Vol. 12, No. 6, November-December, 2001, pp. 18-22.

3

THE NEW WARS

Changes that were to take place in the international political arena during the 1990s were planned as far back as the early 1970s. In anticipation of the collapse of the Soviet Union, the concept of a multicentred world with regional power bases was floated for comment in 1976. During the 1980s there was discussion about the possibility of the breakdown of communism. In the Western hemisphere this was expected to usher in fundamental changes at the international, regional and national level. It was expected that the elimination of bipolar hostility would reduce competition to influence smaller nations. The possibility of nuclear conflict was also expected to recede. There was to be a re-location of power outwards, from traditional centres of world power, to regional hubs.[1]

Moves to promote democratic values and institutions were expected to lead to the acceptance of basic human and civil rights as the worldwide norm. The success of movements for democracy in Eastern and Central Europe was thought to augur well for freedom movements elsewhere. The introduction of the free market system and globalisation of financial services was expected to lead to an increase in foreign direct investment in less developed countries. This was to take the place of dwindling concessionary development assistance as the industrialised countries were no longer interested in maintaining their influence through financial intervention in other parts of the world once the communist threat was eliminated.[2]

It was expected that economic interdependence between nations would eventually make peace more profitable than war over territorial disputes. A combination of economic and political development was expected to lead to a more equitable distribution of the benefits of capital investment between states and within communities. Profound changes have occurred in the distribution of power within economic, political and security systems across the globe but these changes have given rise to a host of new tensions within national borders and between states. They have not produced the results that were expected by analysts.[3] In order to review developments and assess the direction of future change, it is necessary to consider the strategy of power groups that brought about global change and take stock of the new wars that have to be fought worldwide.

Apart from nations, alliances between nations, international and regional institutions, global power groups now include multilateral financial institutions and transnational corporations. It is debatable whether the industrialised countries were ever serious in their pursuit of the altruistic goals of democracy, universal and individual human rights, and global economic progress. An assessment of the nature of their alternative agenda is called for. A review is needed of the measures that were, and were not taken, in order to bring about change in the political, economic and security environment of the Post Cold War era.[4] The weaker nations of the world are less able, than ever before, to influence international events. However, with a clear worldview, they may be able to adjust their own policies to safeguard national interest.

Within three years of the disintegration of the former Soviet Union and the heralding of an age of democracy, the newly independent states were quietly allowed to slip back into the hands of those domestic hierarchies that had controlled them under communist rule. According to reliable surveys, there have been two divergent and paradoxical trends during the 1990s: the continued growth of electoral democracy and the stagnation of liberal democracy, an indication of a decline in freedom. The regularity with which effective democracy is found in the high-income countries has prompted studies, which have determined to a significant extent, that economic factors influence the existence of stable democratic political institutions.[5]

The number of formal or electoral democracies in the world grew from 76 in 1990 to 117 in 1995 but the percentage of liberal democracies declined from 85 to 65 per cent of the total during the same period. This remains a fluctuating percentage. Russia, Kazakhstan, Turkmenistan, Tajikistan are included in the countries in which the electoral process has been called a charade to obtain international legitimacy and economic rewards. The impact of ideological democracy is acknowledged to be superficial in these countries. In Sri Lanka, India, Pakistan, Poland, Peru, Brazil, and Turkey among others, the quality of democracy has declined.

The military has been used to help regulate and support political institutions in a number of countries.[6]

About eight years after the heralding of a new age of freedom and democracy, only a few political variables had changed for the majority of the world's population: less than 10 per cent of the world's total population participates fully in institutionalised political, economic, social and cultural activities that have an impact on their lives. US and Russian forces were still poised at hair trigger alert against each other in 2002.[7] Political and economic manoeuvring remains at an all time high. Countries that were of strategic importance for countering communist influence have been abandoned. The only smaller states that carry weight are those with natural resources that can be exploited, a strong economy that can influence world trade or those with the leadership and the political will to conduct an independent foreign policy.

Comparisons are frequently drawn between the situation in many states in East Asia and that of Pakistan forty years ago and today: when making such comparisons, there is a need to remember that conditions, both domestic and international, were created for the development of East Asia with the assistance of the industrialised countries of the West. Possibly, this was done to counter the anticipated emergence of the People's Republic of China (PRC) as a global power.[8] In East Asia, foreign assistance was provided in key sectors and transnationals not only exploited local markets but also entered into joint ventures with local entrepreneurs and produced goods for export to third countries. The economies of South America and South Asia were never of the same strategic level of importance and many South American economies floundered after initial success with economic liberalisation. The result has been acute political instability and an increase in poverty there.[9]

A review of developments that have taken place over the past fifteen years (1987-2002) shows that economic and political power has been centralised within specific institutions and within specific states in regions by deliberate design. A number of economic objectives of the more influential industrialised states have been achieved through the cooperation of multilateral trade bodies and financial institutions that are active in the poorer countries of Asia and Africa. In the existing global environment, power over nations that have become dependent on foreign assistance and credit has been centralised within Multilateral Financial Institutions (MFIs) and sources of commercial credit. These operate in the global economy, are located in the international centres of power and seriously impact national policy.[10] It is not surprising, therefore, that the financial institutions of the Western world are the target of militants and terrorists.

MFIs are not sympathetic towards the problems faced by the less privileged in the poorer countries of the world. It is not part of their job. The fact that the International Monetary Fund (IMF) has been monitoring the performance of the Pakistani economy directly, through its own personnel, imposing taxes, albeit through the government of Pakistan, is an indication of the loss of sovereignty.[11] The emphasis on commercial transactions in a global marketplace, rather than development assistance, means there is no moral pressure to assist states in a weak economic position. In this marketplace Pakistan has borrowed at a mark up of 22 per cent in the past, while multilateral institutions delay the provision of concessional assistance. There is a need to seriously examine why countries like Pakistan find themselves in such a position, vulnerable to political and economic blackmail, after forty years of so-called concessionary development assistance.

The countries that more or less control the MFIs are now openly admitting that they have '...a growing stake in how other countries govern or misgovern...'[12] This stake makes the United States, among others, a constituency that national politicians must satisfy. Such influence translates into concrete interference in the affairs of weaker nations through the manipulation of social, political and economic systems and the provision of all kinds of support for internationationally acceptable political entities, regardless of their domestic agenda, which may or may not be acceptable to the constituency at home. Obviously this is a new phase in the creation of interdependent systems that are more likely, among other things, to toe the line on security issues and maintain international commitments such as the repayment of loans. This situation exists in all the weak economies including that of Russia and the newly Independent States. These strategies for securing control of state systems have been pushing broad swathes of the population towards conservative religious movements that are conveniently accessible to those with limited influence in society.

States that resolve to remain independent may be able to manoeuvre within the existing global system. Strategies need to be reviewed and nations need to assess the needs of their people at two levels: the basic needs of the population as a whole and the needs of different categories of people as producers. Self-sufficiency and import substitution remain the key to sovereignty. The skills to carry out such strategic exercises, devise a plan of action, implement and manage it through existing institutions, are either available within the permanent establishment, or, can be acquired within the country. Moral commitment and integrity may be more difficult to find.

A country's ability to invest in the social development of the population may be limited by what it can spend, but there is no price tag on strategic planning. Dependence on extra-national sources for policy planning has led to major debacles in the past. Pressure to open a weak economy to international economic forces appears to have been part of a series of well planned moves to curtail sovereignty and could have a fundamental impact not just on the economic health of a country but its security options. Social sector programs that exclude weaker sections of society automatically, by virtue of their design, create entire classes of people who will seek assistance through alternative support systems that may promote their own agenda. This is one reason why the economic and social pressures created by globalisation and issues of ethnicity are of profound importance for the successful containment of terrorism.

The concept of globalisation[13] of the world economy emerged well over three decades ago. Serious institutional change required for the globalisation of trade, finance and capital movement began to take place two decades ago with the communications revolution. International legislation to manage and facilitate globalisation came with the World Trade Organisation and reform of international laws governing trade, services as well as the movement of capital.[14] The scale and extent of facility created for the movement of international capital, which could enter and exit economies without notice, led to crises in several nation states. By 1995 the myth of globalisation as an instrument of progressive economic change had been exposed,[15] but by that time a number of newly industrialised countries had been devastated. The slowing down of the economy of Japan and the depressed economies of East Asia[16] highlight the problems that can occur as soon as competition for capital and markets crosses a given tolerance level in weaker economies. A major problem that can emerge as a result is communal tension and the political regrouping of populations along ethnic lines. As soon as the economy weakened in Indonesia, relatively indigenous groups attacked prosperous Chinese communities. Subsequently, Christian communities that had lived side by side with Muslims for generations were attacked by them.

Such fault lines appear in the economically weaker areas of industrialised countries as well. For instance, many countries in Western Europe admit there is resentment towards immigrants from Third World countries who may be displacing low paid, local workers. There is less resentment towards racially similar immigrants. In industrialised countries, such situations are often anticipated and official measures are promptly taken to diffuse tension and ease economic hardship: there were public protests against Mexican imports after the signing of NAFTA.[17] Trucks carrying goods were forcibly stopped at entry points on the Mexico-US border. Protests died down after the US Department of Commerce revealed that, subsequent to the signing of NAFTA, thousands of jobs had been created in areas where local employees had thought they would lose their jobs because Mexican imports would undercut local products.

The banana war between the United States and the countries of the European Union is a case in point. The EU was asked not to purchase cheaper bananas from poor countries in Africa and the Caribbean, as this would affect the business of US companies operating from third countries. By 5 March 1999,[18] the United States had slapped customs duties on EU products, effectively doubling their price in the US, without waiting for World Trade Organization (WTO) arbitration on the matter. In this case, not just the health of US companies, but also the economies of South America are more important than the principle of keeping a share in world markets for the poorest countries of the world.

Political relations between, and within, nation states are often determined by economic considerations. It is not surprising, therefore, that changes in political consciousness have followed the reorganisation of economic systems after war or decolonisation. At such times reorganisation of populations around a common ethnic identity can be demanded. The division of Czechoslovakia and Yugoslavia took place along more or less historic, administrative lines in case of the former, and along ethnic lines in the case of the latter. There can be little doubt that outstanding issues will be settled on the basis of ethno-economic considerations. The state will react to issues of autonomy raised by indigenous groups while capital/enterprise will react to possibilities of exclusion from markets that could be created once political issues are resolved.

National people's in the Soviet Union, those ethnic groups that had a distinct cultural identity, were regionally dominant but lost their autonomous status to the political movement that created the Soviet

Union.[19] Through administrative measures they were maintained as separate units. The centrally planned economy linked them to other units in the Soviet Union. While there was a marked difference in the nature and level of development of European USSR and Central Asian USSR, ethnic tension, inequalities and discrimination remained lower in Eastern Europe and the Soviet Union than in other parts of the world, including the industrialised countries. This was a direct result of programs designed to create opportunities and raise the status of smaller national groups.[20] There is no reason why the policy guidelines, planning and implementation of such programs should not provide guidance for those states facing similar problems and national integration issues in other parts of the world. It is not surprising that ethnic protest and rebellion were at an all time low in the USSR during the post-Second World War era but escalated during the 1980s as the Soviet economy began to break down following the initial phase of the war in Afghanistan.

An important question is whether the resentments and demands of ethnic groups are a direct consequence of deliberate state policies of deprivation and domination by a majority, or a stronger group or, whether they arise as a result of the desire to protect and preserve a distinct group identity. In Pakistan, as elsewhere, the oft-repeated assertion that the shared religion, Islam, wipes out all socio-cultural differences remains limited to the universal acceptance of the basic tenets of the faith in Muslim societies. Inevitably, ritual and tradition colour the practice of the faith and are derived from local culture. Similarly, it is recognised that there is a marked difference in the nature of the Hutus and Tutsis in Africa. The Hutus were generally considered aggressive and dominant. After suffering repeated attacks, Tutsis organised for retaliation.[21]

Where tolerance of differences in religious-cultural practice is high, there is less likelihood of demands for autonomy. In such high tolerance areas, demands of ethnic and national groups may be limited to specific economic benefits or political recognition within the state, or even the protection of social and cultural identity, rather than a desire to separate from the state. It is important that the root cause of such demands be examined and analysed. It would be a good idea for Pakistan to remember that in recent history the only ethno-nationalist group to achieve independence from an existing state were the Muslim East Pakistanis.

Unfulfilled nationalist aspirations are the driving force behind the struggles of the Kurds and the Palestinians for they are nations and have a history of nationhood.[22] In Turkey, the Kurds are not recognized as a nation and it is a cognisable offence to use the word—they may only call themselves 'the mountain people'. After several years of building institutions on the West Bank, Israel set out to destroy these symbols of Palestinian nationhood before re-occupying the West Bank. Such build and break policies and the systematic elimination of the leadership, and potential leadership, in these national groups, over several generations, have not been able to suppress Palestinian or Kurdish aspirations. What will keep them going, in their struggle for the revival of nationhood, is the lack of tolerance and insufficient political accommodation by dominant groups in the states in which they exist, in the case of the former, and the region in which they exist,[23] in the case of the latter.

Where there is no economic competition between national groups, and no apparent cultural or political link between individuals of different ethnic groups and nationalities, the origin of racially motivated aggression can be baffling. It could be due to fear or feelings of inferiority; it may be the reflex of a history of domination or, merely the expression of a desire to dominate through emotional manipulation. It is the equivalent of war without physical weaponry, that seeks to break the spirit. Manipulation can be most vicious at the highest levels in society. A Pakistani seeking information about treatment for a specific, non-serious condition, in the United Kingdom, was informed by the information desk at the Royal Society for Tropical Diseases that, '...We are sorry...only Dr. Raisin (meaning, a black physician...) can help you, we have no one who deals with this tropical condition on our roster...sorry...'[24] This was definitely an attempt at exclusion on the basis of race, a crude classification of illness and disease by race. The public, not just in the West but in less developed countries, needs to remain alert to such signals from society. An internationally acceptable code of conduct for inter-racial communication should be in place by now, but it is not. The absence of such a code as well as economic and political exclusion and discriminatory legislation create a fertile breeding ground for resentment and can become the basis for sub-national struggles.

REFERENCES

1. Drucker, Peter F., 'The Global Economy and The Nation State', *Foreign Affairs* Vol. 76, No. 5, September/October, 1997; World Bank Annual Report, Washington D.C., WB/IDA Publications, 1970; A Strategy for Plenty, (The Indicative World Plan for Agricultural Development), Rome: FAO, 1970.
2. Deliberations of the Trilateral Commission (United Nations), The Club of Rome.
3. Diamond, Larry, 'Is the Third Wave Over?', *Journal of Democracy*, Vol. 7, No. 3, July 1996.
4. Ibid., see 2 above; Mandelbaum, Michael, ed., 'Central Asia and the World', Council of Foreign Relations, New York, 1994.
5. Polack, Fred, 'Controlling Global Finance', *World Policy Journal*, Vol. 13, No. 3. Fall 1996, pp. 24-34.
6. Ibid., see 5 above; Londregan, John B. and Keith T. Pool, 'Does High Income Promote Democracy?', *World Politics*, Vol. 49, No. 1, October 1996, pp. 1-30.
7. Dorff, Robert H. 'Democratization and Failed States: The Challenge of Ungovernability'. *Parameters*, Vol. 26, No. 2. Summer 1996: pp. 17-31.
8. Ibid., see 7 above; 'Charter of the United Nations, 59 Stat 1031 T.S. No. 993', United Nations Human Rights Commission, Geneva 2002; General Assembly Resolution 217 A (III), 10 December 1958; U.N. Charter, Article 55 ©,*United Nations*, New York.
9. Ibid., see 7 above.
10. Ibid., see 5 above.
11. Ibid., see 5 above.
12. Talbot, Strobe, US Assistant Secretary of State, 1994.
13. Schwab, Klaus and Claude Smadja, 'Power and Policy', *Harvard Business Review*. November-December 1994.
14. Report, *The News* (Islamabad), AFP Paris; 6 March 1999.
15. Ibid., see 5 above.
16. Ibid., see 5 above.
17. Graham, Carol, Safety Nets, Politics and the Poor: Transitions to Market Economies, Washington D.C.: The Brookings Institution, 1994.
18. Report, *The News* (Islamabad), AFP Paris; 6 March 1999.
19. Starr, S. Frederick, 'Making Eurasia Stable'. *Foreign Affairs*, January-February 1996, p. 1; Desch, Michael C, 'War and Strong States, Peace and Weak States', *International Organization*, Vol. 50, No. 2. Spring 1996, pp. 240 and 250.
20. Ibid., see 19 above.
21. Calonego, Bernadette, 'Six Years After Rwanda' (The German Newspaper news service), *Khaleej Times*, 18 August 2000.
22. Jentleson and Paterson, eds. *Encyclopaedia of US Foreign Relations Vol. 4* (Turkey), 1977, Oxford University Press, New York 1997, pp. 224-225.
23. Report, *The Nation* (Islamabad); Reuters, 15 May 2002.
24. Author's telephone conversation with the Administration, Royal Society for the Prevention of Tropical Disease, London, 8 September 1979.

4

TERRORISM: STATES AND HUMAN RIGHTS

A number of recent events involving old actors on the world stage highlight the inability of states, communities, religious groups and individuals, to agree on enforceable and humane standards where human rights are concerned. Such unresolved issues create tensions within society that can lead to unforeseen reactions. Official spokesmen generally laugh at the concepts espoused by international human rights activists: it is convenient to say that in a world where universal human rights, such as the right to sufficient nutrition, basic education, shelter, security and opportunity are not guaranteed, freedom in its various forms is irrelevant to the human situation and concepts of oppression must be defined in the existing socio-political scenario. Since international organisations deal with states, their activities are generally restricted to those issues that are compatible with the exercise of sovereign power. This power is used to obtain and control resources and put them to the use of individual states and power groups within states.[1] Morality is seldom the issue.

Organized activity for the redress of public grievances can take various forms. In cases of extreme injustice and lack of avenues for the redress of injustice, acts of retaliatory violence can be called terrorism by state entities. During the past few decades, some progress has been made as a result of the decolonisation of enclaves previously controlled by Western governments in various parts of the world, including Africa. This, however, has not yielded peace and prosperity to all communities in the areas under discussion. Rival factions fighting for control of states and their resources are supported both by private parties, such as multinationals, and other, interested countries.[2] Representatives of influential industrialised countries are active in the UN and nominated to senior positions in international human rights organisations where they manipulate activities. Although they are expected to remain pragmatic, they generally pursue the interests of their country of origin. Concepts of human rights are circumscribed by internationally accepted norms of state jurisdiction over such rights.[3]

Pragmatism and potential nuisance value rules the choice of crises and areas that will receive international attention and economic assistance at any given point in time: for instance, the intransigence of Israel is as responsible for the pledging of economic assistance for the Palestinians amounting to US$3 billion, as anything else. However, it can never compensate for the encroachment of Israel on Palestinian territory. The construction of homes for Jewish settlers almost tripled the size of the West Bank enclave of Kochav Yaacov. Such moves are not conducive to harmony between the two communities that are expected to live together in the area. Moderate Israelis, seeking reconciliation with Palestinians, know this. In such areas, survival is the immediate problem, not human rights.

Individual states dealing with each other, such as Britain and China in the case of Hong Kong, have managed better. Although the former British governor of Hong Kong wept as his country's flag was lowered, the former British colony has passed relatively smoothly into the fold of the People's Republic of China (PRC), with the status of a special, administered autonomous area. There have been no major complaints of human rights violations or retrogressive economic change in Hong Kong, apart from the crackdown on the Fulangong movement.[4] China is not only keen to maintain Hong Kong's international links but to facilitate their extension to the Mainland.

The bias against indigenous freedom movements and their leaders is a matter of recorded history. Until they succeed, that is. For example, not so long ago, Mrs Thatcher, as Britain's Prime Minister, condemned Mr Nelson Mandela of South Africa as a terrorist. Under laws enacted during 1998 in Britain, ostensibly to counteract random acts of violence by elements of the Irish Republican Army (IRA), and in order to control political dissidents of various nationalities resident in Britain, Mr Mandela would have been prosecuted in that country. He has, however, survived to be called a statesman.

In order to understand human rights concepts at the national, rather than individual level and the impact of the abuse of human rights on the growth of terrorist activity, it is necessary to examine the true nature, the greed, the underlying ruthlessness of a nation (Britain) that cooperated in the perpetuation of apartheid on a territory several thousand miles from its shores. It is also necessary to review its civilisation and its history of human rights violations closer to home: the Scottish revolution took place against the English monarchy and those practises of the Crown that were designed to destroy the spirit of the Scottish nation (such as the practise of 'droit de seigneur' which was meant to create a nation of bastards in Scotland). This unChristian practise was not allowed to be documented until the turn of the twentieth century. These methods of subjugation are not very different in nature from the kind of atrocities committed against Bosnian women by the Serbs during the 1990s war in Bosnia Herzegovina, in order to break the spirit of the people. Knowledge of the historical use of such methods of subjugation makes it easier to understand why the international community tolerated such atrocities for years before the North Atlantic Treaty Organization (NATO) intervened in Bosnia-Herzegovina.[5] English overlords allowed an entire generation of Irish people to die miserably in the potato famine of Ireland and the people of that country still weep when they read and speak of those times. Atrocities committed are never forgotten but pass into the national psyche of the victims as well as the perpetrators. They influence attitudes not just for decades but over centuries.

Despite national legislation and ratification, with or without reservations, of international human rights conventions, individual nations guard their own rights over their citizens zealously—often at the expense of human rights. Today, the United States has a sincere and powerful lobby of concerned private individuals, who work to secure human rights within their own country and worldwide. They do not always succeed. Great progress has been made in securing civil rights for blacks in the United States since the 1950s. Nevertheless, pockets of bigotry and exploitation exist, particularly in low-income areas.

It was only in the late 1990s that the US government apologised to those low income black farm labourers, and their families, who were included in so-called 'medical experiments' in which treatment for venereal diseases was withheld from some, without their knowledge, in order to observe the progress of diseases. Other ethnic minorities and blacks, and some white soldiers, were the subject of mind bending experiments. In many such experiments psychotropic drugs were used without the knowledge of those in the control groups. Fortunately the press and the judicial system in the United States often helps secure relief for the victims of such atrocious experiments, once evidence comes to light.

It is the lack of implementation, or a selective implementation of the law and the yardstick by which human rights abuse is measured, which creates the kind of confusion caused by the arrest and possible extradition of former Chilean President Pinochet from Britain to Spain, at the request of the latter. Accused of terrorism, torture and genocide during his seventeen year regime, the General was placed under treatment for 'stress-related' disorders in Britain. Mrs Thatcher, an old friend, called his detention disgraceful and asked for his release. The government of Chile, on the other hand, considered it a question impinging on sovereignty, since the General had been made a Senator for life to forestall just such an eventuality. The US government sympathised with all those who had to deal with the matter, rather than taking a principled stand.

In the last week of November 1998, during the first state visit to Japan by a Chinese President after the Second World War, Mr Jiang Zemin made a very wise observation. He told Japanese legislators that history plays an important role in determining bilateral relations. Hoping to receive a written declaration, Mr Jiang Zemin only received a verbal apology for Japan's brutal invasion of China during the Second World War, when widespread massacres and biological experiments were conducted by the invading Japanese troops. In October 1998, a full apology was extended to South Korea for the 1910–1945 rule of Japan over the Korean Peninsula.[6] An entire generation of Koreans was subjected to similar brutalities at that time.

So much for the past.

History is being created today in the Middle East and Eastern and Central Europe, not to mention Kashmir and other territories where human rights violations are taking place. Fifty years after the 1948 declaration of Universal Human Rights by the United Nations, it is clear that relatively small groups of concerned individuals lead the struggle while states continue to dodge their duty at every level. Nation states need to review their record on human rights at this time and consider the reasons for large scale human rights abuse worldwide, whether such abuse takes place at the community level, within states or across national boundaries. Those charged with the task must persuade all members of the world community that it is in their long-term interest to do so.

Human rights, including civil, political as well as economic, social and cultural rights, are not the invention of the United Nations or any particular country. Human rights are not the invention of a single religion, civilisation, culture or era, including the present. Similarly, the abuse of human rights is not confined to a single country, religion, civilisation, culture or even point in time. In many cases, the systematic abuse of human rights is a by-product of statecraft that concentrates on the acquisition and exercise of power and exploitation of resources, rather than statesmanship that emphasises benevolent management and a judicious distribution of resources. It is questionable whether state authorities will ever agree on universal standards with regard to issues of human rights, for the patriot of one country may well be considered the enemy by another.

At a talk sponsored by the Society for International Development in Washington D.C. in December 1998, the United Nations High Commissioner for Human Rights was reported to have said that 'over the past twelve months there has been a great push to fulfil the mandate that the United Nations set for human rights through a "profound process of change". In that process, she stated, the UN looked at "how to improve the machinery of what we do"...' The fact is that fifty years after the Universal Declaration of Human Rights, it is still not clear what the UN thinks it does in this sector. Until it is clear on this account, the UN will continue to deliver platitudes where action is needed. After the events of 11 September 2001 and the worldwide hunt for suspected terrorists, this has become all the more necessary.

Most of the governments cooperating with the United States in its war on terrorism have amended existing laws to permit the indefinite detention of persons on mere suspicion of terrorist links, without charge or trial. Such prisoners are routinely held in sub-human conditions that harm their capacity to defend themselves. The governments in the so-called 'Coalition Against Terror' have, in fact, created a shadow justice system that is devoid of many crucial components and safeguards present in their regular criminal justice systems. These developments have encouraged repressive regimes across the globe to tighten their grip on political opponents who are now being hunted down as terrorists.[7]

The emphasis on universal, rather than community and individual, human rights is convenient for states that are routine abusers in the latter categories. It also tends to take the pressure off when assessments are made of how national laws inter-relate with international law on human rights as one of the criteria for being aid and trade-worthy. At one level this could require a determination on the justification for setting up Military Courts in the Sindh province of Pakistan where a civil judiciary is also supposedly functional. At another level it would require a statement on the status of the uprising in Jammu and Kashmir.

Under the circumstances, it is not surprising that states tend to accommodate each other by ignoring the violation of accepted international standards on human rights. In the United States, academics, activists and groups monitoring human rights in other parts of the world, have suggested making human rights issues integral in the development of foreign policy. In 1994, there was a broad ranging debate in the United States on the trade status of China in relation to its policy on human rights. Economists were of the view that to deny China Most Favoured Nation (MFN) status would hurt the United States more than it would hurt China in lost economic opportunities. When the United States demanded the China improve its human rights policy, China said the United States was interfering in its internal affairs. China retained its Most Favoured Nation trading status. During his 1998 visit to China, the US President was under pressure to speak on human rights issues. When he did speak, his hosts were understanding and said they knew he was doing so as a result of domestic political pressure.[8]

In a paper on 'The Use of Trade Sanctions as an Enforcement Mechanism for Basic Human Rights etc.' published in 1996 in the American University Journal of International Law and Policy, the author says '...Basing the sanctions for violations (of Human Rights) on international trade, an economic activity practised by virtually all nations, will allow swift, effective enforcement within an already existing trade regime...' and further observes '...sanctions against a nation whose trade practices injure the economy of another nation appear to have greater (international) support than do sanctions for other misdeeds such as violations of human rights...'[9] In the case of Iraq, trade sanctions became an internationally sanctioned violation of basic universal human rights due to the suffering caused to the weak, the elderly, to children and women. Recognising this, a number of human rights groups in the United States ferried food and medical supplies to that country, and urged a quick resolution of outstanding issues that would allow the lifting of sanctions.

The international human rights community has a great deal to answer for: a number of mechanisms established for monitoring violations and securing relief have been placed in the hands of non-governmental organisations that are not properly supervised by funding authorities. These funding authorities include international institutions, individual governments and foundations in both the industrialised world and less developed countries. NGOs are, more often than not, staffed by dilettantes and easily recognisable undercover, or retired, establishment personnel with contacts in government circles. For instance, on 12 December 1998, on its program *The World Today*, the British Broadcasting Corporation invited a former British employee of the defunct Bank of Commerce and Credit International's (BCCI) Third World Foundation, to speak on the subject, as the representative of a UK-based human rights organization. In 1978-1979 she had visited Pakistan and met General Ziaul Haq as part of an assignment for the British government. She advised the General not to allow certain individuals that the British government wished to eliminate, to achieve public prominence in Pakistan. This was done indirectly, during a meeting held at the State Guest House (formerly called 'Bachan Niwas') in Rawalpindi, where she met Pakistan's President Ziaul Haq in the presence of Mr Masoodur Rauf, Additional Secretary, Ministry of Information and Broadcasting, and three other persons, including myself.[10] The General and his coterie followed her advice.

Her activities at the time, and the subsequent harassment of a Pakistani visitor to London, who was not aware of the activity behind the scenes, proved that she exercised authority within the system:[11] she was, apparently, rewarded for getting a Pakistani lady dragged through the streets of London at night, with an arm lock around her neck. She openly flaunted expensive gifts she received for doing so, besides furthering the interests of various international elements with the British establishment.[12] The presence of such individuals within non-governmental organizations that are supposed to be working to safeguard human rights, should be enough to frighten off many victims of human rights abuse.

Information about the procedure for registration, processing and investigation of individual and joint complaints through non-governmental human rights organizations is not readily available. As a result, many believe that they must come with a personal introduction before their case will be considered. In any event, such organisations have a record of concentrating on high profile cases that will get them publicity. Such publicity can endanger complainants. But publicity tends to attract funds more easily than quiet work. Funding from government sources, national or otherwise, can lead to compromises. The United Nations itself has often shown poor judgement in selecting those it involves in human rights advocacy on its behalf. Over the years, a motley crowd has served as its goodwill ambassadors and ambassadors for UNICEF. Some choices are openly political, others could only be friends of friends. It is truly unfortunate that these flawed organisations and individuals become the only recourse of communities, sub-national groups and individuals suffering violations of basic human rights.

States, expected to guarantee the safety of their citizens, tend to look the other way when the rights of these citizens are violated by domestic or international civil, military or criminal forces and it is not convenient, or in the interest of governments or senior personnel to intervene. Although large scale internal abuse of human rights has been well documented in the United States and is a matter of history, that country considers it a question of national honour to protect its citizens abroad. It is interesting that its foreign policy routinely puts its own citizens at risk all over the world. For instance, the United States government would be doing its citizens a service if it made an effort to determine and then to publicly explain why a man like Aimal Kansi, who knew them and had worked with them, found it necessary to travel to Washington D.C. to kill former American colleagues. Although he gave a general statement about his motives in an interview with the BBC/Urdu Service before he was executed, no one knows precisely what provoked him.[13]

The activities of a new generation of international crooks and ultra smart public servants, who are generally urbane, sophisticated, cosmopolitan and well educated, have captured public interest. Their country of birth could be the United States, France, Italy, Brazil or Pakistan, the Philippines or Thailand. It is their understanding of financial systems, their ability to handle politicians and lawmen and the possession of the wherewithal with which to do so, that makes them so similar in their activities around the globe. Their ability to establish a credible front through government and public or political service furthers their business activities. Nevertheless, the commodities in which they deal on a transnational scale are political influence, assassination, traditional and new drugs, arms, slave labour, and organized prostitution, among other things. These activities use the weakest sections of society for their raw material, and lead to large scale human rights violations across national boundaries, that are practically impossible to prosecute.[14]

There was a rise in the number of territorial and ethnic disputes during the 1990s. A number of disputes arose after political change on the European and African continents. Populations suffered as a result of clashes over territorial jurisdiction and control of resources. The setting up of an International Criminal Court (ICC) was not only expected to provide justice for victims of crimes that had occurred under such conditions, its decisions were also expected to serve as a deterrent to future violations of human rights. The United States government has been criticised by activists, at home and abroad, for withholding ratification of the ICC Charter for several years, finally, refusing to sign the treaty and seeking bilateral arrangements with other states instead. The United States has said it fears US soldiers and other personnel may be called to face politically motivated charges before such a tribunal and wants the option of vetoing the prosecution of any American citizen before it will sign. This is not a practical proviso as events in Iraq are showing the world. It is not acceptable to the world community. Meanwhile, misgivings have been expressed about the clarity of definitions of delegation of authority and the extent of individual responsibility when actions are taken under orders of superiors.[15] Many such definitions, arrived at as far back as the Nuremberg trials, are being debated and questioned now.

Given the enormous numbers that are being displaced, internally and across international boundaries as a result of the new waves of conflict that have hit the world, the protection of populations, including refugees, is as important today as it was after the Second World War. Important lessons remain to be learnt from that earlier experience: women and children are most easily displaced and exploited in war situations and as refugees. Refugee camps across the globe continue to be the hunting and recruiting ground of criminal and other anti-social elements, just as they were fifty years ago. This is where many terror networks have found rootless recruits. In our times, the refugees of economic upheaval are as vulnerable as the victims of war.

Concern for victims of political oppression was on the rise at the height of the Cold War. Publicity about human rights abuse was useful for the containment of communism. With the dissolution of the Soviet Union, there has been a marked loss of interest in human rights issues and an incremental rise in militant activity by populations that are oppressed by state authorities. International organisations as well as

NGOs are now concentrating on violations of human rights as a result of economic and social inequality, deprivation and discrimination. These organisations need to consider the impact of this kind of vacillation, from interest in human rights to interest in universal human rights, on their credibility. They need to urge states to act with the long-term welfare of world populations in mind and they need to do so themselves. Work in the field of human rights should not be subject to fashion, it should be the result of a commitment to civilisation. Such committment will yield peace dividends.

REFERENCES

1. Human Rights Watch, World Report 1995, (New York: Human Rights Watch, 1996); Freedom House, Freedom in the World 1994-1995, pp. 5-7; Larry Diamond, Is the Third Wave Over? *Journal of Democracy*, Vol. 7, No. 3, July 1996.
2. 'Angola's Diamond Deal: Luanda', *The Economist*, London (13 July 1996); 'Shell Appeal Over Nigeria Executions Rejected', Financial Times Online, London, 23 March 2001.
3. Report, *The News* (Reuter), 20 September 1993 and 4 January 1994; Report, *U.S. News*, 4 July 1994, p. 49.
4. Report, *The Economist*, London, 12 July 1997, pp. 81-82.
5. Report, *The News* (Reuter), 10 February 1994; Report, *The News* (Reuter). 24 March 1994.
6. Ji'ang Zemin, President of the People's Republic of China, speech in Tokyo, Japan, 1998 November.
7. 'Special Report: Are The Geneva Conventions Redundant', *The News on Sunday*, 9 December 2001; 'Due Process and Terrorism'. Swiss Press Review and *News Report* (Geneva), Vol. 34, No. 13, 5 July 1993.
8. 'Special Report', *The New York Times*, 15 July 1998.
9. Stirling, Patricia. 'The Use of Trade Sanctions as an Enforcement Mechanism for Basic Human Rights: A Proposal for Addition to the World Trade Organization', *American University Journal of International Law and Policy*, Vol. 11, No. 1 (1996); pp. 1-46; Boudreau, Donald G. 'Economic Sanctions and Military Force in the Twenty-First Century', *European Security*, Vol. 6, No. 2, Summer 1997, pp. 28-46.
10. Meeting with President Ziaul Haq at the State Guest House (Bachan Niwas) in Rawalpindi, February 1979, Records of the Government of Pakistan, Ministry of Information and Broadcasting, Ministry of Foreign Affairs, Ministry of Interior. Islamabad, Pakistan.
11. Events of Wednesday, 11 September 1989, London: Annual Conference of the International Institute of Communications, 1979.
12. Ibid., see 10 and 11 above.
13. Report, *The Nation* (Islamabad), 15 November 2002; Report in Sairbeen (magazine programme). BBC Urdu Service Online, 13 November 2002; 'List of official

personnel, 1990-1994', Record of the USAID/Pakistan and Afghanistan Office, USAID Executive Office, Islamabad.

14. Kiltgaard, Robert, 'Subverting Corruption' *Finance and Development*, Vol. 37, No. 2, June 2000, pp. 10-23; Ayres, Ed, 'The Expanding Shadow Economy', *World Watch* Vol. 9, No. 4; July/Aug 1996, pp. 10-23.

15. Roth, Kenneth and Ruth Wedgwood, 'Is America's Withdrawal From The International Criminal Court Justified?', *WorldLink*, Vol. 15, No. 4, July/August 2002.

5

MIND WARS

The development of a category of weaponry generally known as 'non-lethal', originally designed for use within a military context but increasingly applied to the control of civilians is a cause for concern. The alliance between mercenaries, irregulars and the military of some of the most powerful countries in the world has led to the proliferation of the technology of non-lethal weapons and increased the risk of the unauthorized use and misuse of such weaponry in peacetime by militants and terrorists. The development of such weapons has been justified on the grounds that the nature of threats to powerful industrialised countries has changed. A 'Task Force on the Military Options and Implications of Non-Lethal Technologies' sponsored by the United States Council on Foreign Relations (1995)[1] does not do justice to the potential for the misuse, or indiscriminate use, of such technologies to control civilians and non-combatants although it did attempt to discuss whether such technologies should be shared with traditional allies of the United States.

It is obvious from a study of available information and public reports on the subject that scattered bits of knowledge about non-lethal weapons are in the public domain. Information about the spectrum of non-lethal weaponry in use at this time is available with the establishments of the major powers. Biological and chemical as well as information technology research institutes associated with weapons development are working together on second and third generation products. This has created a problem of proliferation of first generation products, some of which are now available commercially. At the same time, as a result of efforts to expand available arsenals and develop exclusive categories, many types of non-lethal or 'less than lethal' as the French call them, weapon development programs are underway. The most sophisticated technology continues to be highly classified.

In 1986, Gorbachev (President of Russia) stated that 'new non-nuclear weapons (such as)...radio wave, infrasonic...which in terms of their destructive potential, could be no less dangerous than already existing weapons of mass destruction...(BBC, 1986: Amnesty International).[2] Stefan Possony of the Hoover Institute wrote about 'messaging directly into a target mind with low frequency waves' in 1983, four decades after the technology was actually developed. Between 1975 and 1998, the UN Committee on Disarmament discussed a Russian proposal to ban so-called new types of weapons of mass destruction, one category of which was described by the Russians as 'infrasonic acoustic radiation weapons' that would utilize the harmful effects of infrasonic oscillations on biocurrents of the brain and nervous system. Psychotronic is the Russian name for electromagnetic mind control weapons. In 1985 the Pentagon said that radio frequency weapons are too sensitive to discuss but there was no doubt that transfer of technology had taken place during the Afghan War of the decade of the 1980s. This transfer of technology created a dangerous situation for political, and other targets, of the establishment in countries like Pakistan.

For nearly three decades now, such institutions in Pakistan have been actively involved in the creation of political elites and the neutralisation of those perceived to be a threat to existing power structures. For this purpose non-lethal weapons are used. In Pakistan, such information has been publicly ridiculed. For instance, at a meeting of a government think tank senior officials, including the Chairman of the National Assembly's Standing Committee on Defence (Colonel Cheema), openly ridiculed the term 'telepathy' as he called it. Apart from the paranormal manifestation in certain genetically inclined individuals, something called 'synthetic telepathy', the use of ultra high frequency sound and radio waves is probably the oldest method of thought manipulation and control ('Synthetic Telepathy', *International Defence Review*, Vol. 26, No. 3, p. 247).[3] This technology was introduced into the subcontinent by the British after the Second World War.

In less developed countries the justification given for the use of such weaponry is that fragile economic and political systems can suffer due to the activities of what are generally referred to as 'de-stabilising elements' in society, therefore any and all means to suppress them are justified. The development and use of such methodologies and weaponry should be within the jurisdiction of international agencies concerned with arms control. However, international organisations deal with states, therefore, their activities are generally restricted to those concerns that are raised by nation states and considered compatible with the exercise of sovereign power. This power is used to obtain and control resources and put them to the use of individual states and power groups within states. Theoretically, morality is an important issue but it rarely dictates the conduct of international, regional and bilateral relations, unless a lack of morality in such conduct threatens to destabilise the status quo.

Since these non-lethal weapons technologies of political control are being freely used now, there is a need to raise public awareness of the existence of these tools of war: unwary civilians may be the target of domestic or extra-national forces even though a war-like situation does not exist in the vicinity and they are non-combatants in any case. These weapons have been used in Somalia and Iraq by US forces and in Bosnia by NATO peacekeeping forces[4] despite unresolved questions about their long-term effects on human physiology and the environment.[5] In many cases the term 'non-lethal' is misleading in describing such weapons because death can be caused by their use. Permanent physical damage continues to be a possibility.

Use and dissemination of non-lethal weapons technology has primarily been through the United States Department of Defense and its agencies. There is no doubt that US allies and those countries with which the United States has defence cooperation, and military training arrangements, have been provided access to this technology. While United States law restricts the use of such technology against civilians and non-combatants, US allies have been using a number of dangerous categories of these weapons against civilian non-combatants, particularly high profile intellectuals and dissidents, within their own countries as well as on foreign soil. The development of doctrine covering operational criteria has not been a priority for the use of non-lethal weapons. The use of radio technology to brainwash susceptible individuals was a technique developed during the first half of the twentieth century and is extensively used against political prisoners and others in third world countries, including Pakistan, and in Turkey and Israel. Unfortunately, the use of a number of categories of these weapons is not covered by international arms control commitments and international legal restraints. Military applications have been under scrutiny, however, the use of blinding lasers against fighter pilots was prohibited by a UN convention adopted in 1995.

Fortunately, the United States government is bound to reveal certain categories of information under its Freedom of Information Act and this includes information about non lethal weapons. This points to the need for similar legislation, in the public interest, by other governments. In 1995 the CORONA meeting (US Air Force) reviewed one thousand potential projects, one of which was called 'Put the Enemy to Sleep/Keep the Enemy Sleeping.' The meeting called for exploration of acoustics, microwaves and brain-wave manipulation to alter sleep patterns, and approved three projects. Such projects are not peculiar to the United States establishment but are being conducted by many other governments. *The British Medical Journal* (7/12/97) published an article titled 'Non-Lethal Weapons:Precipitating a New Arms Race' by Robin M. Coupland[6] in which the author examines the terminology used and maintains that a 'weapon' is something designed to cause bodily harm whereas the term 'non-lethal' implies zero fatalities which is unrealistic. In the process of disabling individuals, many questions arise regarding the use of non-lethal weapons, including the period for which the person must be disabled to fulfil a political or strategic objective and whether the various energy forms that are used to target the central nervous system will leave the victim with permanent neuro-physiological effects. Civilian doctors to whom the majority of casualties of non-lethal weapons are bound to be referred do not know the precise effects of these weapons. The subject has been discussed by special committees established by the European Union and in a symposium held by the International Committee of the Red Cross in 1996 on 'The Medical Profession and the Effects of Weapons.'[7]

Some non-lethal weapons are basic and well known, having been developed for domestic law enforcement. They were subsequently adapted for use by the military. Non-lethal weapons in this category include non-penetrating and semi-penetrating projectiles, or bullets, that are related to ballistic weapons. The former are used to stun, inflict temporary pain; the latter penetrate the skin, causing surface wounds or broken bones without causing internal organ damage. Tasers and electric stun weapons generate low amperage electric shocks stunning targeted individuals and causing loss of muscle control. Aqueous foam mixed with pepper spray creates a soapy barrier that affects those who attempt to penetrate the barrier. The use of these, as well as ballistically delivered entanglement nets to incapacitate people and vehicles, require proximity to the target.

There are a number of infinitely more dangerous, so-called non-lethal weapons that are being used to incapacitate perceived hostile elements. Low energy lasers and other optical systems such as pulsed light can temporarily blind people and make them dizzy and disoriented. These as well as radio waves that mimic and alter human brain waves can be used unobtrusively in relatively crowded areas and from a greater distance than that needed to fire a rubber bullet. Towards the end of the Second World War and during the mid-1940s, acoustic and German vortex technology were being used: US Army and Navy projects to refine these are still underway. Another, even more dangerous system, is now more easily used as a result of the spread of computer technology and fibre optics, which have made satellite telephone links much less expensive and common: acoustic systems using infrasound or ultrasound and ultra high frequency radio waves can cause a loss of muscle control, nausea and even lead to unconsciousness. Directed energy microwaves can, and do, cause progressive incapacitation—this begins with a rise in body temperature (up to 105-107 degrees Fahrenheit), unexplained biological changes occur, and ultimately, death. Electrical activity in the brain can be influenced, sleep and other behaviour, can be induced through low frequency electromagnetic radiation. This is done by remote devices as well as instruments fixed to act on contact by scrambling signals from the cortex of the brain. A number of these non-lethal technologies are now available through military as well as private sector sources to individuals, states as well as other groups.

Non-lethal weapon technology is classified as top secret by the United States establishment. However, it is known that biological and chemical forms, as well as laser, acoustic, electromagnetic radiation, directed energy or high power microwave (HPM) weapons can be used where knowledge is available of the target as well as the environment (buildings, existing walls etc.), in which the target is located. Ultrasound, ultra high frequency sound, vortex and combinations of these technologies make it difficult to pin point the source of attack without proper equipment. It may also be difficult to identify whether the establishment employing the technology is national or extra-national. Symptoms can be confused with those produced by ordinary mental aberrations and illness. For example, a US News and World Report (7 December 1997) story[8] explained how, by using very low frequency electromagnetic radiation, the brain could be induced to release behaviour-regulating chemicals and how magnetic fields were used to cause certain brain cells to release histamine causing instant flu-like symptoms and nausea. The fields created are weak, therefore undetectable, and establishments have used them to disable people temporarily. The use of such equipment to control and disable as well as discreetly eliminate political or other elements that are considered destabilising, is considered preferable to outright elimination that may result in a public outcry.

What constitutes the misuse of non-lethal weaponry? The definition of 'misuse' in a given scenario is with reference to the nature of weaponry and its ability to destroy. The civilised world seeks a ban on chemical and biological weapons that destroy combatants and non-combatants alike. For over fifty-four years, (since the Second World War) when they were being refined, non-lethal weapons have been tested and used on groups of special children, often without the knowledge of their guardians, to control and then observe behavioural changes. In many reported cases, orphans and wards of the state have been the subject of such experiments without a thought being given to the psychological and physiological consequences of such brutality. Non-lethal weapons have been deployed in commercial aircraft to target specific individuals but their impact is felt by all those on board. This should shed new light on cases of 'air rage' that have been reported in recent years. There is no longer room for doubt that auto accidents in which drivers report 'going blank' or blacking out, can be a result of interference with brain waves through radio frequency manipulation. This can happen accidentally when so-called listening posts are located in crowded residential areas, markets or near highways, but it is often the result of experimentation to perfect weaponry.

There are many cases in which such technologies were used unnecessarily, when there were simpler, more humane methods of testing, or controlling the behaviour of individuals in unusual situations. In order to measure stress tolerance in a UNICEF employee[9] travelling abroad for the agency for the first time, high intensity radio waves near human brain wave frequency were used in a commercial aircraft when passengers were asked to fill out a disembarkation card. The radio waves affected the nervous system and caused dizziness, disorientation and nausea, causing the subject to write in a disjointed, crazy script. This was done to give the impression that the new employee was nervous and disoriented by travel that was to be a part of employee's routine work. Many passengers in the same aircraft knew what was happening and refused to fill out the disembarkation cards on board. (20 May 1973, Lufthansa, Islamabad-Bangkok).

There is a conspiracy of silence about non-lethal weapons as a result of cooperation between the establishments of nation states which have a vested interest in developing covert methods of controlling populations and individuals. In establishment terminology, their own employees are said to have been 'put on ice' when they are withdrawn from active duty with their knowledge. But when those who are not employees, including non-combatant civilians and ordinary citizens with special abilities including intellectuals and scientists, who are protected under the Geneva Convention, are to be rendered inactive, they are disabled through the use of non-lethal weapons. A conspiracy of silence prevents public access to information about mind, behaviour and health, manipulating technologies that are being used now and still newer technologies incorporating advances in medical and biological science with support from communication technology which are being developed.

As with the use and deployment of weapons of mass destruction, important questions arise: Who authorises the use of non-lethal weaponry? And who determines the type of weapon that will be used on a particular target for a given length of time? A close relative of such weapons are low frequency surveillance devices such as those used to keep track of the United States President and to which Mr Clinton obliquely referred during the 1998 impeachment proceedings by saying, 'I was never alone with Miss Lewinsky. I am never alone'. A code of conduct apparently governs the use of information gained through such surveillance in the United States. This does not permit the use of information gained through such means to be used for purposes other than the safety of the person being monitored. In other parts of the world this is often not the case.

In a paper titled 'Non-lethal Weapons, A Global Issue' (C. Welsh), the author writes about[10] 'possible remedies from the international community concerning the illegal use and experimentation with electromagnetic and mind control technology'. It is unlikely that establishments that have been actively involved in the development and use of this technology for over sixty years will voluntarily provide remedies. Most sections of the official establishment in less developed countries had no knowledge of these technologies until reports began to appear in the western press during the decade of the 1990s. Those who happened to acquire knowledge without official consent were eliminated one way or another. During the first half of the twentieth century, the Parsee community was considered ideal for the transfer and control of this technology in the subcontinent because their priesthood already had a highly refined mind control program for training children who were destined to become priests. Control groups were set up and monitored and experiments were conducted. Targets of different categories of non-lethal weaponry exist at a number of different levels within society and establishments may request authorization from their controllers for general disabling, making targets ineffective, without specifying the method to be used. As a result, a fair amount of responsibility is shifted to the operational level. A variety of methods may be used in conjunction: for instance, water cannons may be used, followed by chemicals, such as pepper spray; tear gas may be used to create an invisible barrier between rioters and enforcers; stun batons may be used in close combat when they penetrate that barrier; pulse weapons that disorient and blind may be used on the leaders of groups that are to be controlled. In many cases, the effectiveness of such weapons is enhanced by the lack of information that the public has about them. Continued effectiveness may depend on maintaining the confidential nature of the anti-material and anti-personnel impact of such weapons.

No doubt, in the democratic countries of the West, heads of state and government authorise the disabling rather than the outright elimination, of what are considered potentially dangerous or destabilising elements both at home and abroad. Their decisions are based on analysis of intelligence reports of the danger posed by such individuals to their, so called, vital interests. They have no way of verifying these intelligence reports. The information that the political, non-technical administrative leadership is likely to have about the use of non-lethal weapons is limited, unless they have been exposed to such weapons themselves or, they have a military cum information technology background and have been exposed to signals/communication activity.

Those who authorise disabling through the use of non-lethal weapons are not likely to specify which type of non-lethal weaponry, or combination of weaponry, and social as well as economic sanctions, will be employed against subject 'x' or subject 'y'. This limits their responsibility in the operation and gives the establishment enormous discretion over the life of vulnerable individuals. Obviously, since non-lethal weapons seek to covertly incapacitate, menially and physically debilitate targeted individuals, such individuals are not protected by establishments and are vulnerable. It is an unfair war.

An environment in which the misuse of non-lethal weaponry is certain is created by a combination of poor moral and ethical arguments and personal considerations. The political leadership in many countries has been known to base decisions to pursue opponents and dissidents on spurious charges. Non-lethal weapons provide a convenient and covert alternative to direct physical methods of dealing with opposition. In such an environment, the proliferation of such weaponry is bound to occur. Since this undercover activity is designed to escape public detection when it is authorised by the state, its use is not easy to prove. It is practically impossible to obtain relief through a court of law. In Third World countries the question of doing so does not arise. The legal implications of this need to be discussed at the international level. The use of these technologies for military purposes, their significance in the strategic landscape and as tools of political manipulation, as well as issues of global regulation and control, need to be discussed.

In order to prevent the indiscriminate use of such technologies for political suppression and social control, it has become necessary to ensure that a doctrine is developed regarding their use in all the states that have been provided access to this technology by the five major powers. This is one of the matters discussed in an occasional paper titled 'Non-Lethal Technologies: Implications for Military Strategy',[11] written by Col. Joseph Siniscalchi, USAF, March 1998, for the Center for Strategy and Technology, Air War College, Air University, Maxwell Air Force Base, Alabama, USA. This, as well as other research papers and documents, skim over the use of, and experiments with, such weapons on civilians, non-combatants and weak sections of society, without their knowledge, by the establishment and other extra-establishment elements. It is wrong to assume that all those in control of such technologies are responsible, sensible people who will not use these technologies to achieve personal objectives, or can be controlled by the establishment. In one case, documented prior to the partition of the subcontinent, and now within the knowledge of the United Nations, local operatives attached to the Viceroy's staff used non-lethal technology, including German vortex and acoustic technology acquired during the Second World War, as well as progressively severe electric shocks, to measure biological and physiological reactions in an attempt to induce aberrant behavior. A child was used in the experiments because it was thought the child would forget what had been done.[12] One of the pair of operatives involved was removed when the matter became public knowledge.

In cases documented by the State Department of the United States, radio frequency and microwave based anti-personnel weapons were used against its staff at its Embassy in Moscow by the KGB of the former Soviet Union. During the 1960s, at least three secretaries to various US Ambassadors to the Soviet Union had to be evacuated from Moscow after they showed unexplained signs of ill health and two former US Ambassadors to Moscow died of leukaemia believed to have been the result of microwave induced physiological damage. The establishments of the USSR and a number of East European countries as well as former Yugoslavia and Turkey not only used, but could also detect the use of similar weaponry. An international treaty to cover the use of such weapons does not exist. The creation of such a treaty is likely to be resisted by intelligence establishments worldwide. What makes this task all the more urgent are moves to refine anti-material and anti-personnel applications with a view to controlling future conflicts, the nature and scope of which are acknowledged to have changed. In the future, mind wars are likely to be as important as military campaigns.

REFERENCES

1. Report of the Task Force on the Military Options and Implications of Non-Lethal Technologies, United States Council on Foreign Relations (1995).
2. Possony, Stefan, 'Scientific Advances Hold Dramatic Prospects for Psy-Strategy' *Defense and Foreign Affairs*, July 1983.
3. Report, *International Defense Review*, Vol. 26, No. 3, p. 247.
4. Coupland, Robin M. 'Non-Lethal' Weapons: Precipitating a New Arms Race', *The British Medical Journal*, 12 July 1997.
5. International Committee of the Red Cross, Geneva, *The Medical Profession and the Effects of Weapons*, 1996.
6. Ibid., see 4 above.
7. Ibid., see 5 above.
8. Report, *U.S. News and World Report*, 12 July 1997.
9. Ibid., see 4 above, p. 1-2; Coupland, Robin M., 'The effect of weapons: defining superfluous injury and unnecessary suffering', *Med. Global Survival* 1996, 3: A1.
10. Welsh, Cheryl, 'Nonlethal Weapons, A Global Issue', 5 October 1999, C.A.H.R.A. http://www.morethanconquerors.simplenet.com/MCF/welsh598.htm.

11. Siniscalchi, Col. Joseph (USAF), 'Non-Lethal Technologies: Implications
    Military Strategy', *The Center for Strategy and Technology*, Air War College, Ai
    University, Maxwell Air Force Base, Alabama, USA, March 1998.
12. Horsley, Sir Peter, Chapter 2, Reference 4 of this book: and Department of
    Commerce: Government of India. 'Letter in connection with recruitment, No. 71.
    20 (T)nb, 30 December 1946.

6

ES FIGHT TERRORISM?

In view of the rising tide of terrorist activity across the globe, questions have been raised about the ability of states and societies to fight terrorism through traditional strategies at the national and international level. Such strategies are more suited to fighting crime than they are to fighting new wave terrorism. The origin of, and rationale for terrorism as an instrument of political change is quite different from the rationale for criminal activity. This, of course, precludes discussion of mercenaries who commit terrorist acts on behalf of others for cash. Before an effective new strategy to combat terrorism can be formulated, it is necessary to admit that there are many sources of terrorist activity and the state is just as capable of terrorism as political organisations and individuals are. The reference here is not just to foreign interference that may seek to destabilise unfriendly regimes in other countries, but also to the activities of national agencies within parent countries where the rule of law is not the norm and extra-judicial acts often go unpunished. Terror does not always come out of the barrel of a gun or in the shape of a bomb or grenade. Intimidation, harassment, threat of violence or the creation of an environment of imminent violence can be enough to paralyse civil life and kill enterprise and creativity. Such tactics can also lead to violent retaliation by those oppressed.[1]

Terrorism comes from a number of sources and an equally broad range of initiatives have to be taken to combat it. If the state has to be vigilant against terrorism of domestic and international origin, citizens must also review the stresses in the environment in which they live: they are not only at risk from random acts of violence but from specific situations created to mould their thoughts and actions. Non-compliance may attract retaliation not just from extreme elements in society, but also from the establishment itself. It is easy to become a scapegoat in such an environment: there are a number of classic cases that are

Solve Problem

Answer

frequently cited. In August 1978, over four hundred people were killed in a fire in a cinema in Iran. The fire was said to be the work of Islamic revolutionaries and a man by the name of Takbalizadeh was arrested.[2] It is believed that the arson was committed by the establishment and used as an excuse to begin a crackdown on religious elements and create hatred against them. Discrediting political movements by engineering terrorist incidents is standard practise.

To understand the nature of terrorist activity in a specific region or country it is necessary to examine the kind of behaviour, or act, that attracts retaliation of a specific type from a specific source, if identifiable. Are terrorist acts aimed at punishing a specific organisation or instrument of government, are they random acts carried out to spread panic and disorder, or do these acts merely serve to divert the attention of a dissatisfied public from their grievances? Do random terrorist acts generally seek to embarrass government by revealing weaknesses in administration? In such cases, it becomes necessary to assess how politically damaging they really are and how such embarrassment affects the standing of the government. Terrorist acts, in which the general public loses life and property, are important to those in power only if the government really does derive its power from the people and is dependent for its existence on the goodwill of the populace. This is true in democracies such as the United States where the government will be accountable forever for the loss of even a single life through a terrorist act that the public perceives to have been preventable. In countries like Pakistan they are of less consequence to government.

The fate of government may not hinge on the loss of life through terrorism in countries like Pakistan. The destruction of civil works and strategic installations may be a more serious matter for the government. As a result, when acts of terrorism are perpetrated against innocent civilians, there is a question as to whether they are really motivated by disruptionist forces within, or outside, national borders or merely seek to subdue the public through fear. On the other hand, when the Dry Port in Lahore (Pakistan) burns for the second time in six months, different questions arise.[3] It could be terrorist activity aimed at undermining confidence in national security institutions, or, it could just as easily be an attempt to cover up pilferage and theft. On the other hand, it could be an accident.

There are policies and methodologies that determined governments can adopt in order to minimise the possibility of terrorism on their territory. The resolution of festering political issues is an obvious method. The British government was not able to control terrorist activity in the United Kingdom during the conflict with the Irish and has negotiated a settlement with the Irish Republican Army itself. The exact nature and source of terrorism in Karachi continues to be shrouded in accusations and counter accusations and is now believed to have been suppressed through draconian measures.[4] A more constructive way of dealing with the entire issue is emerging through political activity initiated by the political opposition in Pakistan: MQM representatives have been seen and heard at political rallies throughout the country. Since they are no longer marginalized and confined to one area of one province, there is a distinct possibility that they will enter mainstream national politics and find it more profitable for their constituency to do so. Confrontation with extreme elements is an exercise in futility. This is true at the national and the international level. Neutralisation of hostility and resolution of underlying problems is the only solution.

At the international level, it may be necessary to opt out of other people's wars if it is in the national interest. It is always a good idea to remember they will opt out of yours at the drop of a hat. For instance, during the height of the Palestinian guerrilla struggle against Israel, Pakistan befriended the Palestinian people quietly. Thousands of young Palestinians studied in Pakistani universities and graduated to work in different parts of the world.[5] During periods of student agitation against an authoritarian government in power in Pakistan (1969-1970), they withdrew to their hostels and closed the doors. There were no Palestinian partisans in the domestic affairs of Pakistan. There was, on the other hand, an unwritten agreement that no terrorist act against governments considered unfriendly by the Palestinians would take place in Pakistan. Similarly, the Palestinians were safe from harassment by unfriendly governments on Pakistani soil. The world was not safe but Pakistan was safe. It was a clean-cut, deliberate government policy that kept it safe. New struggles have surfaced in recent decades, and a principled stand in support of freedom struggles is the need of the hour.

In 1995, as a result of US pressure, the Pakistan government said it was declaring war on right wing elements and fundamentalist 'mullahs'. These pronouncements were preceded by a number of dramatic extraditions of alleged terrorists of nondescript nationality to the United States and elsewhere. Such dramatic activities appear to have been calculated to create goodwill in the West for Pakistan: they were yet another exercise in futility. The protection from terrorism that Pakistan enjoyed as neutral territory during the 1960s, 1970s and much of the 1980s was lifted. Acts of violence that had not been seen before began to take place. The forerunner of these acts of violence was the blast at the Egyptian Embassy in Islamabad that everyone would like to forget, but should not.[6]

In an effort to modernise society there is no need to declare war on anyone: the government merely needs to enforce existing laws regarding freedom of expression and association, and to protect citizens going about their business in their own way. Just as people have a right to a liberal attitude, others have a right to follow a more orthodox way of life as long as they do not coerce others along the same path. There is definitely a need to keep an eye on political and social groups receiving monetary assistance from foreign countries with a view to promoting specific ideologies. It may be a good idea to remember that in Pakistan, modernist elements are receiving as much assistance from their patrons in the West as conservative elements are receiving from their supporters in other parts of the world. No one group should be allowed to become a tool in the hands of foreign powers. Neither group should be marginalized. The strength and practicality of their messages will ultimately determine the extent of their influence within the country. Since the *modus operandi* of those promoting such opposing ideals is different, there is a need to monitor the tools each group uses. For instance, there is a need to monitor the flow of arms, money and propaganda material into the country. There is also a need to see that officially supported and sanctioned cultural expression through various media is a true but enhanced reflection of ordinary life in the country. Modernisation will come from the grassroots if it is considered profitable by the general public. The extent of modernity that people will accept will be decided by them. As the evolving political and cultural experiments in Iran, Algeria and Turkey have shown the world, government coercion and official decrees cannot bring about in-depth modernisation. The perception of modernity differs not just from country to country and society to society, but also from time to time.[7]

The primary ingredient in any solution to the problem has to be identification of what triggers terrorism. Social, economic, political and demographic changes have upset power equations within societies. When terrorist activity is an offshoot of suppressed political opposition, it takes on entities that are larger, better organised and more powerful. These may include the state and its institutions as well as the government. The price terrorists are willing to pay in order to achieve their objectives is higher than the price that governments or states can pay. Terrorism is generally the last resort of those political elements that can find no other method of entering the system in order to change it. Examined close up, terrorism has little to do with pluralist roots and ethnicity until exploitation, as well as political, social and economic deprivation of sub-groups in society become the catalyst, the agent of change. Exploitation can occur within one ethnic group but is more likely to occur between different ethnic groups. The state usually has prior knowledge of such exploitation and of possible responses to that exploitation. Such responses may include terrorist activity and crime. They are usually aware of the kind of impact various levels of terrorist activity will have on the polity. An honest assessment of who is likely to benefit as a consequence of that impact is necessary before terrorist activity can be tackled. Just as elements within societies must not be allowed to commit acts of terror to achieve their objectives, states must not be allowed to terrorise the people. An informed public is in a better position to act in its own interest and compel government to do the same.

Many regimes tend to blur the line between terrorism and crime. This does not help combat either. At a United Nations conference on the prevention of crime held in Cairo, April-May 1995,[8] speakers declared that international crime 'threatens to undermine the foundations of all states', and '...terrorism has become one of the most dangerous forms of international crime...' No one is likely to quibble over the definition of a criminal act since it is one that breaches the law, but there is no single definition of terrorism that holds true in all circumstances around the world. One man's struggle for freedom can be considered terrorism by another. There are many sources of terrorist activity: state terrorism was practically institutionalised in South American states during the late 1960s and 1970s when military juntas sought to suppress political movements in the region. South Africa's apartheid regime also institutionalised terror tactics to control the indigenous population.[9]

Uruguay had the world's highest per capita population of political prisoners during the 1960s and 1970s. According to statistics collected by America Watch, one out of every fifty Uruguayans was detained and one out of every five hundred was jailed; most were routinely tortured. Extra-judicial killings were the norm.[10] In Argentina, President Alfonsin Pinochet (1989), the first civilian to complete his term in office since 1928, was blamed for excusing all but top officers from prosecution for similar crimes. He even promoted accused torturers. In Egypt, the government is reported to be concerned about the potential of the Muslim Brotherhood for emerging as a legitimate political force, just as the FIS did in Algeria in 1991. Key figures in the Muslim Brotherhood, respected and well liked professionals with money, were detained and presented in court in iron cages prior to the elections in 1995 because reports and forecasts had predicted they would do better than the government wished them to, in the national elections.

State terrorism can, and does, flow across national boundaries. Organisations that are sponsored by foreign governments tend to have a momentum of their own and can slip out of control of the original organisers: this is what happened with the Liberation Tigers of Tamil Elam (LTTE) separatists of Sri Lanka, who were originally trained and equipped by Indian agencies. It was one of their suicide bombers who assassinated Rajiv Gandhi, Prime Minister of India. The LTTE now operates on its own and has a publicity and propaganda wing, business enterprises, a fundraising wing and a well-organised arms procurement organisation. There are many similar militant groups around the world that are now out of control of their original organisers.

Many tactics employed by political organisations may be used by the state itself to run so-called covert operations. The irresponsible retired head of a sensitive agency in Pakistan once declared before a gathering of intellectuals and diplomats that '...I can activate 14 separatist organisations in "x country" within 24 hours...' In Panama, it turned out that the notorious President Noriega had been a CIA agent. The last time something about him appeared in the American press, he was being prosecuted in the United States on charges of drug smuggling, among other things. The Golden Triangle states of the Far East are well known for the easygoing relationship between their law enforcement agencies and the semi-political warlords who smuggle drugs to finance their activities.

It is alleged that the practise of recruiting prisoners serving life terms to carry out political assassinations continues to be widespread in Pakistan. During 1972, Dr Nazir, a JI (Jama'at-i-Islami) activist was killed in his clinic, and Khwaja Rafiq, a labour leader was shot dead in a street in Lahore. It was widely rumoured that the assassins of Dr Nazir and Khwaja Rafiq, both vociferous opponents of the Pakistan Peoples Party (PPP) regime, were killed in this way. As soon as the deed is done, such assassins are safely back in prison and there is no chance they will talk. As a result, the perpetrators of such criminal acts and other acts of terrorism are never found. Whenever there is an incident and 'no clue' is found, thoughts turn towards such standard operating procedures used by state agencies.

Private individuals and political organisations can be responsible for terrorism that either seeks the destruction of a specific target, or, merely to cause chaos and random violence thereby undermining the writ of the government. The objective is to bring about change. Serious organisations with long-term political objectives never permit the general public to become the direct target of their violent acts. They choose to attack specific persons or groups that represent what the organisation wishes to replace. Peaceful means for the replacement of such individuals or groups, or for bringing about social and political change may be denied by the state, or other forces within the country, hence recourse to violence. For example, attacks by Islamic militants against foreign tourists in Egypt undermined the tourism industry there. Islamists consider the tourism industry representative of the prostitution of culture and values for the pleasure of Westerners.[11]

Politically motivated acts of terrorism have a purpose. When the process of negotiation between government and those who seek to bring about change is not an option, militant organisations seek to make it clear that no one, neither the leadership nor the general public that elects or supports such a leadership, will live in peace until there is a settlement of some sort. On one occasion, the LTTE in Sri Lanka wanted to make it clear to the international community that the Sri Lankan government's claims, subsequent to the recapture of Jaffna by it, about the restoration of peace in the country, were not correct. LTTE guerrillas blew up the Central Bank in Colombo, the docks, and then, a commuter train, to make their presence felt. The LTTE does not seek the support of the general Sinhalese public, which was badly affected by these acts. Its constituency is the Tamils of the world and it is, therefore, unconcerned about the loss of life in such cases.

An illustration of a difference in perception of what may be considered terrorism is found in Screbrenica. In July 1995, General

Mladic, a war criminal sought by the War Crimes Tribunal set up by the International Court of Justice in The Hague, said that his army's onslaught against the enclave was undertaken to 'neutralise' what he called 'terrorists' there. He was referring to 'Gen.' Oric, a man who was regarded by the Bosnian Muslims as a kind of Robin Hood who kept the enclave fed and defended when the United Nations Protection Force (UNProfor) and the world community held back and delayed helping them.[12]

There is a great difference between the origin and purpose of violent, terrorist attacks that were perpetrated by militant groups in the late 1960s and 1970s in Europe, the terror that was seen in Latin America and the present waves of terrorism that are sweeping across the world today. Revelations made during the 1990s by responsible personnel, now retired, of intelligence agencies of many countries and institutions, indicate that leftist university groups in Europe and the United States were penetrated by their operatives and actually trained members of such groups to achieve the objectives of certain states through acts of terrorism. The purpose of such groups was to seek a reaction, destabilise the establishment of various states. The objective of government operatives who penetrated these organisations was to use the groups as a cover to eliminate political elements that were considered a threat to European security by NATO. New information which has emerged about the Baader Meinhoff gang and the Red Brigade confirms this.[13]

There are shadowy links between many semi-political extremist organisations and government institutions in various countries. Many such organisations may originally have been sponsored by agencies in the countries in which they exist, as well as by neighbouring, or third countries. An interesting episode was the kidnapping of a USIS officer by some Palestinians, when the PLO and other extremist groups were apparently abhorred by the US. US officials went crazy looking for him. The officer's wife finally managed to get word to Mr George Habash, with whom her husband had studied at the American University in Beirut. In fact, some renegades in the movement had lifted him and he was being held in a garage a few doors away from his home. When Habash intervened he was released and allowed to walk over to his home.[14]

There has always been differentiation between freedom movements and terrorist activity in discussions at the United Nations. However, US acceptance of a dialogue with the Palestine Liberation Organisation (PLO) was a watershed in relations between militant organisations and governments. This acceptance also meant that extreme elements in both camps, the US government and the PLO, who were unwilling to compromise on certain issues would have to intensify their activities. Two categories emerged: organisations that governments might negotiate with and those that governments were unwilling to acknowledge.[15] The activities of the latter have become increasingly sophisticated during the past two decades. Their business activities span the legitimate and the illegal, including investment in business enterprises as well as the smuggling of arms and drugs across international boundaries. This is done with the cooperation of governments in industrialised countries that tend to look the other way when their own people are making a fast buck and are promoting their foreign policy agenda, one way or another.

The focus of terrorist activity is believed to have shifted in both geographic, political and ideological terms. Isolated instances, such as the bombing of the Federal Building in the United States suggest that inequities within capitalist societies have created the potential for terrorism by those who have been marginalized. As a result of this understanding, the crash of a TWA flight from New York to Paris was not immediately laid at the door of a Muslim organisation or country. However, for some reason, that incident led to further severity in economic sanctions against Iran by the United States. Extreme frustration with political and social systems that appear impervious to change are leading to an escalation in violence within societies and against the symbols of inequity. Instead of beating up someone, marginalized elements are likely to torture, and instead of just killing someone, they are likely to mutilate as well.

The proliferation of militant political organisations and sub-national groups in the post Cold War era is seen as an opportunity by the arms industry and mercenaries not just in the industrialised countries but in the Third World as well. An Australian arms dealer and Israel are believed to have supplied the Tamil Tigers in the past. Dealers in Hong Kong and Singapore supply dual-purpose equipment such as computers, electronic equipment and the like, to them. The Croat National Guard is believed to have been supplied by Hungary, Rumania, South Africa and Singapore. The Afghan theatre has been an important source of arms for many such groups. According to one press report, the civil authorities in Pakistan once planned to purchase armoured vehicles for use in Sindh from the Afghans. India increased exports of light weapons from US$28.9 million in 1991-1992 to US$156 million in 1994-1995[16] by selling to sub-national groups.

The incremental increase in expenditure by governments seeking to combat terrorism can be of added benefit to arms dealers and their ilk. For instance, in order to combat insurgency, Sri Lanka had to increase military expenditure from US$25 million in 1982 to US$583 million by 1988. The budget was reduced to US$450 million in 1991. There were incremental increases thereafter, until early 2002, when a new President negotiated an effective ceasefire with the LTTE. In Pakistan, the allocation for law and order was doubled from Rs 5.093 billion in 1994-1995 to Rs 11 billion in 1995-1996. However, by April 1995, Rs 13 billion had already been spent. There has been an exponential increase in expenditure on law and order during each subsequent year, but there has been little improvement in the situation on the ground in Pakistan. Terrorists continue to act whenever and wherever they wish; although the number of incidents had decreased by 2002, their intensity, the parts of the country affected and the destruction caused when such incidents did occur, increased.

The first G-7 meeting to discuss the prevention of terrorism concluded on 30 July 1996. A dual track policy that was expected to encompass twenty-five measures ranging from bilateral, multilateral and international cooperation between institutions, security services and the judiciary was approved. An expert committee prepared a new international convention on terrorism involving explosives. Nevertheless, most states agreed that the dimensions of the problem had changed[17] and the relationship between terrorism and political, social and economic change had to be reviewed. These new dimensions of terrorism need to be carefully examined before effective lines of action can be determined. Action against individual states, such as the imposition of economic sanctions during the 1990s by the United States, is not the answer. Similarly, pinning terrorist acts on individuals or groups, was not considered the long-term answer to terrorism or violence. Pressures within socio-political systems create entire classes of people who may begin to feel that peaceful change is not possible. Many political groups with militant wings have large numbers of adherents. It is fortunate for society that only a few have the will and the means to perpetuate terrorist acts.

REFERENCES

1. Susser, Ezra S. et al., 'Combating the Terror of Terrorism', *Scientific American*, Vol. 287, No. 2, August 2002: pp. 72-77.

2. APA Report, *The Pakistan Times* (Rawalpindi), 30 August 1978.

3. APP Report, *The News* (Islamabad), 24 May 1998.

4. Anwar Ahmad, 'MQM: Failure of Strategy', *The News* (Islamabad), 30 July 1994.

5. Registrar. 'Record of Foreign Students enrolled 1965-1972', Punjab University.

6. APP Report, *The Muslim* (Islamabad), 29 July 1994.

7. Ahmad, Professor Khurshid, 'Islam and the New World Order', *The News* (Islamabad), 4 December 1993.

8. Office of the Secretary General, Proceedings of the UN Conference on the Prevention of Crime May 1995, UN Headquarters, New York.

9. 'Salute to South Africa,' *Swiss Press Review and News Report*, Vol. 35, No. 9, 25 April 1995; Eigen, Peter. 'Corruption in a Globalized World,' *SAIS Review*, Vol. 22, No. 1, Winter/Spring 2002, pp. 45-59.

10. *Freedom in the World: The Annual Survey of Political Rights and Civil Liberties 1989-1990*, Freedom House, 1991, New York; and *Freedom in the World: The Annual Survey of Political Rights and Civil Liberties 1994-1995*, Freedom House 1995, New York; *America Watch*, 'Report on Latin America', *1985-1986*, *America Watch*, 1996, New York, Bosco, David, 'Dictators in the Dock', *American Prospect*, Vol. 11, No. 18, 14 August 2000, pp. 26-29.

11. Reuters, *The News*, 2 March 1994.

12. Reuters, *The News*, 1 January 1994.

13. 'NATO during the Cold War', *BBC World*, October 1994.

14. Stewart, Virginia, as recounted to the author, 1988; and see Appendix.

15. Talbot, Strobe, 'Self-Determination in an Interdependent World,' *Foreign Policy*, No. 118, Spring 2000, pp. 152-162.

16. Annual Report, *SIPRI*, 1998.

17. Joint Statement on the conclusion of the G-7 Meeting on Combating Terrorism, G-7 Secretariat, 30 July 1996; and see Appendix. The G-7 include the United States, Britain, France, Germany, Japan, Canada and Russia.

7

TERRORISM: ANOTHER DIMENSION

A basic objective of security systems at both the national and international level is the preservation of order and stability. At the national level, this task is performed in the interest of civil society and at the international level, it is performed in the interest of member states. At some levels, the nature of threats to both national and international security has changed. Mechanisms to contain, control and deal with these new threats have yet to be evolved. Effective mechanisms can be created only after the nature and origin of such threats is understood. For instance, a number of threats to international security today are radically different from those of the Cold War period in which the enemy was known and control mechanisms to avoid open conflict had been installed. At the national level, economic and social change have created new counter forces that work on the fringe of society and national institutions[1].

The emergence of states, such as Iran and Iraq, with the political will and the means to conduct an independent foreign policy and thereby establish new centres of (strategic) power, has been viewed as a threat to the management of the world by the major powers. It has been dealt with as such. The emergence of independent thinkers in client states, people with the will and ability to create public opinion and evolve policy in the national interest, is also seen as a threat to the management of the world by major powers. The emergence of reformist movements in states (such as Algeria, Sudan and Egypt) where governments have not been able to satisfy the needs of their people is considered a threat to international stability. It is a paradox that officially sponsored and assisted reform through non-governmental activity is not viewed with the same suspicion that reformist movements are.[2]

It is now understood that aggression against a nation state may come from a number of entities, not just other states or sub-national groups. Economic security and civil order are critical to national security and vulnerable to external forces: the opening up of weak economic systems to multiple global forces of financial manipulation and control have exposed weaknesses in civil society and given a new meaning to the term national security. The impact of certain categories of ideas and concepts that are introduced through transnational satellite communication and information technology is profound—particularly where such ideas and concepts reinforce existing tendencies and biases. Terrorism as a tool of destabilisation, between social and economic groups, both within and between states, has emerged as a concern that needs to be addressed. There is a need to determine the extent to which such activity is a consequence of official or institutional policy and the extent to which it is the work of individuals and groups.

Between 1987 and 1995, there was a manifold increase in terrorist activity in Sindh (Pakistan). The need to finance militant politics led to an increase in crime. Efforts to control the situation included the deployment of paramilitary forces that work under rules that differ from those of civil security agencies. There were allegations of extra-judicial killings. The majority of reported incidents took place in urban areas. They were attributed to infighting between rival factions of the Mohajir, later Muttahida, Qaumi Movement (MQM), which is widely believed to be yet another political brainchild of the establishment.[3] Some incidents were attributed to external forces seeking to create civil disturbance[4] with a view to discouraging foreign investment in Pakistan, a government priority.

In October 1994,[5] over 24 persons were killed in one week and the Federal Interior Ministry was asked to take steps to control the situation. Legislators admitted that the spate of violence was worse than anything seen before. Certain groups suggested that the army be called in once again. The stage seemed to be set for a reversion to the earlier position when the Federal government had taken charge of the maintenance of law and order in urban Sindh. The breakdown of law and order, as well as a number of high profile killings, led to the removal of the government.

In 1997, the government of Pakistan was again faced with a renewal of terrorist activity. In July it was '...reported to be considering amendments to existing laws pertaining to the maintenance of civil order and in support of good government...' Such moves were being considered in response to the deteriorating law and order situation. The debate on reform in existing laws and the legal system was followed closely by sections of the public, opinion leaders and institutions. Certain opinions appeared to have been formed in the light of past experience. These opinions reflected the concerns and interests of politicians as well as a number of special interest groups that might be affected by changes in the law. There was a consensus that legislation and the creation of institutions parallel to existing ones would not improve the situation on the ground. There was also a consensus that such moves would have a profound impact on democratic practice and the human rights situation in the country.

Nevertheless, a comprehensive eight page ordinance called 'The Sectarian and Political Violence Ordinance 1997'[6] was prepared and promulgated. The Ordinance provided for stringent punishment of sectarian and political terrorists, as well as encroachers. It redefined the term 'terrorist' and broadened the definition of terrorism to include a 'disruption of production of commodities, services, means of communication essential to the community, endangering of property or the making of threats which, having regard to the circumstances, is likely or is intended to put the public or any of its section in fear or terror; adversely affect the harmony between different religions, political, ethnic or regional groups or communities; or coerce or overawe the government established under law...facilitate or enable the carrying out of illegal construction of multi-storeyed buildings...endanger the sovereignty and integrity of Pakistan...' By this time terrorist activity and alleged extra-judicial killings were common in the Punjab. Sectarian violence had claimed many lives in all four provinces.

The legislation allowed for arrest without a warrant, entry and search without a warrant and no recourse to any court of law (including the High Court and Supreme Court) for bail or a stay or prohibiting order in relation to any action taken, or intended to be taken. The law also provided for the declaration of a virtual state of emergency in a violence affected area and the stationing of the armed forces and security forces in any such area by order of the federal or provincial government. These were the provisions under which the chief minister of Sindh was later removed. These are the provisions under which former Prime Minister (Nawaz Sharif, Pakistan Muslim League-Nawaz Group) and his associates were tried for alleged hijacking.

Another related development was the establishment of special anti-terrorist courts to provide 'speedy justice'. The then Chief Justice of the Supreme Court discussed the matter with the Prime Minister and called a meeting of the Law Commission observing that '...the country's judicial system, despite some weaknesses, is the only system to have survived when all other institutions of the state failed...' Allegations that the incumbent Chief Justice was politically motivated in his activism, was widely reported in the national press and his views did not carry weight with the establishment.[7] However, it is true that a body of law, covering all eventualities, does exist and by establishing precedents through their judgments, the judiciary can adapt existing laws to modern needs. This does not always happen. One of the more extreme results of the failure of the executive, followed by the failure of the legal system, was the growing number of extra judicial killings in Sindh and Punjab. The Ordinance had limited impact on crime and random acts of terrorism.

In some cases, instead of preventing terrorist activity, official elements in intelligence webs thrown out to collect information have been known to cooperate with terrorists and help cover their tracks. There are shadowy links between many semi-political extremist organisations and governments, many of which are believed to have been created by intelligence agencies. Revelations made during the 1990s by responsible personnel, now retired, of intelligence agencies of many countries and institutions indicate that leftist university groups in the West were penetrated by their operatives and actually trained students and others in terrorism to achieve the objectives of interested states.[8] This was often done to trigger public reaction against the existing administration in countries in which the terrorist act was to take place and to shake the status quo. Another objective was to use such organisations as a cover to eliminate those political elements that were considered a threat to European security (in this case). By its very definition 'government', the rule of law, is the anti-thesis of anarchy, a state of lawlessness. Nevertheless, the underworld of government employs many tools to maintain the authority of the state in different situations. These can include the institutionalised use of fear and systematic intimidation to enforce and maintain authority. The terrorizing of civilians and non-combatants should not be considered necessary.

For several weeks in March and April 1998, civilian security forces in Pakistan were on red alert. According to newspaper reports, some agencies had intercepted information that led them to believe terrorists would target key installations in the country.[9] It was stated at the time that US interests worldwide were also under threat. Thereafter, analysts rejected the official reason given for the security alert and decided there were probably 'other reasons' for it. As the means for perpetrating terrorist acts become widely available, it is becoming increasingly difficult to differentiate between acts of international terrorism, the terrorist activity of criminal elements and that of domestic political malcontents.

Developments that are taking place in strategic cooperation at the regional level in South and West Asia hold special significance for national security in the concerned states, including Pakistan. The United States' Coalition against terror has brought the USA, Israel and India together. Combined with the Pakistan establishment-USA axis, this creates a unique, previously undocumented, strategic equation from a cultural and historical point of view. This equation has had an impact on the situation in the Middle East and will have an impact on proposed US military action in the Gulf region. As a result, Pakistan, the main Muslim actor within the Coalition, is bound to face civil unrest. On other occasions, the Pakistan establishment may have worked under the table on similar lines, but there is little record of such activity and the public has never been asked to approve or collaborate in such enterprises.

Regional cooperation in the field of defence remains abysmally inadequate in the South Asia region as a result of historical factors.[10] In South-east Asia military cooperation between ASEAN forces has contributed to peace and stability, eliminating the need for outside intervention. This has been a boon for national and domestic security management. In Malaysia, for instance, the General Border Agreement (GBA) with Indonesia and Thailand has enabled the containment of the activities of the Communist Party of Malaysia (CPM), which is considered undesirable by the state and is believed to have the potential for creating instability within the country.[11] In South Asia, on the other hand, the fight for regional ascendancy between states and the support of rival political groups by external forces, continues to destabilise those borders areas of Iran and Pakistan that are contiguous with Afghanistan. Armed action against the Taliban has not been decisive and additional pockets of militancy are being created as a result of resentment due to collateral damage in the area,[12] among other things.

Many groups, in the tribal belt that extends from the north of Pakistan to the coast, have legitimate grievances against state authority and these grievances need to be addressed. These grievances have already been brought to the attention of the government. However, a number of power struggles have crossed borders not as a result of activities of political militants but of renegades and criminals, who are capable of using the proceeds of smuggling to control entire sub-divisions, in the border provinces of Balochistan and NWFP, with the connivance of local law enforcement personnel. This drains the strategic potential of the area. Without the full support of the local population, the area will continue to be undesirable for development activity and this has strategic implications. Towards the north, the border provinces of China with Pakistan and of Afghanistan with Tajikistan, not to mention the Kashmir Valley, have the potential for becoming full-fledged war zones from time to time. It would be unrealistic to expect a change in the situation unless core issues are settled and the struggle for ascendancy of groups sponsored by one country or other is resolved through negotiation.[13]

The settlement of core issues between Europe, Russia and the United States has facilitated regional cooperation in military matters on an unprecedented scale, enabling the industrialised countries to phase down military establishments that were constituted to deal with possible hostilities between the East and the West. As a result, the nature of military deployment changed and there were substantial reductions in procurement as well. US military spending constituted 58.7 per cent of total NATO (North Atlantic Treaty Organisation) spending but was down by 6.2 per cent in 1995 from levels in 1994. Britain's military spending fell by 5.9 per cent over the previous year while France and Germany's spending fell by 4.4 per cent and 5 per cent respectively. The same downward trend was seen in Italy, Spain and the Netherlands. In Russia, military spending declined, but not as a percentage of the Gross Domestic Product (GDP). Turkey, on the other hand, increased spending on defence procurement due to civil strife within its borders and interest in the newly independent states of Central Asia where it wants to make its presence felt. Decrease in procurement by some has, however, meant more aggressive marketing of defence equipment abroad by the industrialised countries. This has had a profound impact on strategic alliances that are now emerging at the regional level, particularly in South and West Asia. Only a few

European countries have successfully phased down defence production by diversifying[14] into other types of production activity.

Of thirty-six major armed conflicts in twenty five locations around the world, three were thought to have the potential for escalating into full scale wars in 1995. Now, the Sri Lankan government has negotiated an effective ceasefire with the insurgent Tamil Tigers. The government of Turkey continues to battle with the Kurdish Worker's Party (PKK) but the prospect of integration into the European Union has become a moderating factor in its policy towards the Kurds.[15] The war in Afghanistan continues to take its toll on the civilian population. Its intensity increased after the Taliban regrouped in early 2003. The situation in Indian Held Kashmir (IHK) is as bad as ever. The Palestinians and Israel are back to square one now that the institutions set up under the Multilateral Peace Agreement have been destroyed by Israel. During the 1990s, most major conflicts took place within nations, rather than between them. This implies, as in the case of the on-going struggle between the Egyptian government and the Islamist opposition, in Algeria and in Pakistan, that the polarisation of political forces within countries is on the rise and accommodation and dialogue have been set aside as a means of resolving differences. In fact, this continues to be the position although the number of incidents of extreme violence may have decreased in some areas. The use of the military option to deal with political differences has failed to change the psyche of populations, but is nevertheless used.

Activities undertaken within the country in the name of security, strategic interests, and national defence have a profound impact on civil society. They lead to the introduction of political regimes that try to justify the suppression of freedom of speech and association because the political status quo is projected as being essential to the national security. Alliances between unpopular political movements, regimes or individuals, and the armed forces are unfortunate. They have the potential for creating a violent backlash in due course. The armed forces are constituted to manage external threats and preserve territorial integrity. Their intervention within the country is generally sought in order to attain, or maintain, power and privilege for specific elite groups. Such situations are not productive for broad cross-sections of society that are denied their share of national resources, and therefore, such situations cannot endure. It is wrong to assume that support for national security as perceived by the political and military elite exists as a matter of course, and unconditionally. That such unconditional support is expected to exist is a separate matter altogether. The implications of such situations for national security are obvious and should not be ignored. It goes without saying that the threshold of violence in any organized resistance against a military regime will be high.

REFERENCES

1. Fuller, Graham F. and John Arquilla, 'The Intractable Problem of Regional Powers', *Orbis,* Fall 1996, p. 609.
2. Ibid., p. 612.
3. M/o Information and Broadcasting Government of Pakistan, 1977-1979.
4. APP Report, *The Muslim* (Islamabad), 15 February 1994.
5. APP Report, *The News* (Islamabad), 23 October 1994; and APP Report, *The News* (Islamabad), 29 July 1995; APP Report, *The News* (Islamabad), 16 February 1996.
6. 'The Sectarian and Political Violence Ordinance 1997', Ministry of Law and Parliamentary Affairs, Government of Pakistan.
7. The Supreme Court of Pakistan, Proceedings of the Contempt of Court case against Prime Minister Mr Nawaz Sharif, Islamabad, 1997.
8. APP Report, *The News* (Islamabad), 16 February 1996; and BBC World, Documentaries on NATO during the Cold War, October 1994.
9. APP Report, *The News* (Islamabad), 15 April 1998; and APP Report, *The Nation* (Islamabad), 28 April 1998.
10. 'Resolving Bilateral Conflicts Through Regional Cooperation,' seminar organized by FES, CASAC, SAMA, 22-23 April 1995, Rawalpindi (Pakistan); and Report on the Fifth ASEAN Summit,' *The Economist* (London), 14-15 December 1995.
11. Ibid.
12. AFP Report, *The News* (Islamabad), 1 June 1997; and AFP Report, *The Nation* (Islamabad), 26 July 1997; APA Report, *The Nation* (Islamabad), 10 November 2002.
13. Rashid, Ahmad, 'China and Central Asia III-Stability in Xinjiang,' *The Nation* (Islamabad), 18 February 1998.
14. SIPRI, *Annual Report 1995*; and AFP Report, *The Nation* (Islamabad), 25 August 1995; Rudney, Robert and Stanley Willis, 'Debating Proposals for Strategic Nuclear Forces: A Critical Analysis', *Comparative Strategy*, Vol. 19, No. 1, July/March 2000, pp. 1-34.
15. 'Kurds in Turkey and Regional Strategy,' *Swiss Press Review and News Report*, Vol. 34, No. 25, 6 December 1993.

8

TERRORISM AND THE STATE

Major armed conflicts are defined as 'a contested incompatibility that concerns government and/or territory over which the use of armed force between the military forces of two parties, of which at least one is the government of a state, has resulted in at least 1000 battle-related deaths in a single year.' According to this definition, there were twenty-four major armed conflicts in the world during 2001. Two-thirds took place in Asia and Africa. The Stockholm International Peace Research Institute (SIPRI), which monitors conflicts worldwide, has observed that the total number[1] of major armed conflicts around the world in 2001 was slightly lower than in 2000.

The only new conflict registered in the world during 2001 was that between the United States and the so-called Al-Qaeda network that has been held responsible for the 11 September 2001 attacks on US territory. The attacks claimed more than three thousand lives in a matter of hours and changed the foreign policy of the United States, the world's major military power in the space of a day.[2] As a result of the formation of a Coalition to fight terrorism, the priorities of a number of states changed overnight. These included the United States and a number of western democracies. Democratic norms such as civil rights and the rule of law, values touted by the American government as a defense against retrogressive forces, were set aside in pursuit of the new enemy. There has been grave concern about changes in investigation and related procedures that now transgress accepted judicial norms.

Fifteen of the world's most vicious conflicts have lasted for eight years or more. These conflicts have not been resolved because neither side has been able to prevail over the other by force. In some cases this has led to compromise followed by a stalemate and relative calm. An example is the peace negotiated by the new government (2002) in Sri Lanka with the Tamil Tigers. This has led to the re-opening of civilian traffic between the Jaffna peninsula and the rest of the country. In the vast majority of cases, guerrilla military strategy against state forces has been supplemented by terrorist activity that undermines the writ of the government outside the main area of conflict. This not only makes it difficult for nation states to use their full military strength against smaller, more mobile opponents, but also ensures that even apparent military victory does not secure peace. This is what has happened in Afghanistan where US forces have been battling an elusive enemy. Bombed out of existence in one area, the enemy appears in another area.[3] This is what is happening in Iraq.

Before an effective strategy to combat terrorism can be formulated, it is necessary to admit that there are many sources of terrorist activity, and the state is just as capable of terrorism as any political organisation or individual. The reference here is not just to external sponsorship of terrorist activity that seeks to destabilise unfriendly regimes in other countries, but also to the activities of national agencies within parent countries where the rule of law is not the norm and extra-judicial acts often go unpunished. In Pakistan, there is a question about the terrorist activity witnessed in the province of Sindh during the tenure of civilian governments—such activity destabilised democratically elected governments and was seen as the failure of the civilian administration.[4] The activity ceased immediately after the installation of a military regime, which implies that elements in the establishment were pulling the strings.

As mentioned in Chapter 5 (Mind Wars) and in Chapter 6 (Can States Fight Terrorism), terror does not always come out of the barrel of a gun or in the shape of an explosive device or hand grenade.[5] Intimidation, harassment and threat of violence are tactics known to be part of a design to limit the capacity of individuals to function normally and influence community and society. Such tactics are frequently used by Israelis to intimidate Palestinians; militant groups in Pakistan also use such tactics against other groups within the nation. Both countries consider themselves to be at war with parts of their own population. Throughout the world, the kind of harassment civilians face under military regimes ranges from the use of non-lethal biological weapons as simple as influenza, anthrax and other germs to cause repeated debilitating attacks of illness as well as the use of simple chemicals such as teargas sprayed in vehicles to induce temporary blindness in drivers in order to cause physical symptoms leading to accidents. Also common is the use of radio surveillance frequencies that induce pain, dizziness, nausea, muscular spasms, and disturbance in brain waves causing confusion, disorientation and the inability to perform even simple tasks.

The British, French and American governments used these methods freely, or watched their allies do so, as part of a strategy to incapacitate potential leadership in Third World countries during the Cold War, and thereafter, for prolonged periods of time. At the same time, civil rights campaigners in their countries protested the use of similar methods in the USSR during the 1960s and 1970s in the controlled environment of mental asylums, where many political dissidents and intellectuals were confined. During the 1980s, information about non-lethal weapons began to appear in journals in the West. Now these and other, more advanced versions are freely used in countries like Pakistan, Turkey, Israel and Afghanistan, among others, and their use by multinational intelligence teams is being justified on various grounds in the states that belong to the international coalition against terrorism. Instead of contributing to containing terrorist activity, such methods have failed spectacularly.[6]

The power to use such methods can be a double-edged sword. It creates resistance as well as the capacity and determination to tolerate increasingly intense levels of non-lethal torture. Misuse of authority in such operations is common at many levels and also contributes to failure. In June 2002, with investigations into the financial resources of terrorist organizations in full swing worldwide, the FBI of the United States found that a group of its own agents, deputed to watch international financial transactions thought to be made by terrorist organisations, had perpetrated financial scams, using information collected while on duty. In many cases, those targeted were victims of personal vendettas and hostility rather than carefully investigated suspects. Victimisation tends to lead to violent retaliation by those oppressed.[7]

To understand the nature of terrorist activity in a specific region or country it is necessary to examine the kind of behaviour or act that attracts retaliation of a specific type from a specific source[8], if identifiable. Are terrorist acts aimed at punishing a specific organisation or instrument of government? Or, are they random acts, merely serving to divert the attention of a dissatisfied public from their grievances? Do random terrorist acts generally seek to embarrass government by revealing weaknesses in administration? In such cases, it becomes necessary to assess how politically damaging they really are and how such embarrassment affects the standing of a government at the national level and in the community of nations.

Hopes for world peace were raised as a result of the success of alliances, security arrangements and mechanisms that controlled conflict during the Cold War. It was thought that the experience gained would provide guidelines for keeping order in other parts of the world. After the end of the Cold War, the United States, along with the Russian Federation its new ally, traditional North Atlantic Treaty Organization allies and states of the European Union, began to review the future of strategic alliances.[9] In many areas, trends had already been set through discreet cooperation, often in non-military fields, but these efforts did not take into account the response that would be required after the rise of new types of threats to global security and the unique nature of the environment in which such threats were emerging.

Earlier, political and military alliances, economic arrangements and political support groups had worked to contain communist influence, counter communist military presence and match communist nuclear capability. Political stability and control was maintained through the support of friendly elements in various countries and the dispersal of military resources at strategic locations around the world to facilitate deployment when necessary. An important function of naval activity was to secure freedom of the seas to ensure the ability of the West to trade with other countries and create wealth. The freedom of the skies was strictly regulated to secure the same objective. This is just one of the reasons why the use of civil aircraft to destroy the twin towers in the United States on 11 September 2001 was so effective as a method of terror. The subsequent fall in all kinds of air traffic led to the bankruptcy of major airlines and the tourism industry. It also changed the very psyche of Western industrialized nations and not just their military doctrine.

Security mechanisms and arrangements to ensure the fulfillment of the objectives mentioned above, at the international and regional level, had been reinforced through special bilateral and multilateral arrangements covering the political, economic, socio-cultural, as well as military spheres. The arrangements were mutually supportive, if not interactive in every case. The basic objective of such arrangements and alliances, the preservation of international stability and security in the interest of member states, has not changed although the *raison d'etre* of alliances that were conceived soon after the Second World War, but which matured over a period of fifty years, has changed with the demise of communism. New forces and potential threats to international security and stability have emerged and the dynamics of the strategic environment in which foreign policy operates has changed. Events have shown us that the nature and extent of change was not fully appreciated at the time, just as the nature and substance of potential threats was not properly evaluated. In order to prepare for the future it is time to consider various aspects of the response to such changes.[10]

Serious threats to international security today are radically different from those faced by the world over the previous half-century or so. During that period, the enemy was a known quantity and control mechanisms to avoid open conflict had been installed. The return of an era in which there is a similar type of dialogue between relatively equal opponents is a remote possibility. Tension and rhetoric between India and Pakistan, both nuclear capable states, after the December 2001 attack[11] on the Indian Parliament building, cannot be considered in the same category because the precise nature of the nuclear arsenal of each is not known. Meanwhile, a broad range of short-term threats to global security can be identified. These include a number of festering regional and ethnic conflicts of varying intensity in almost all continents. The emergence of states with an indigenous doctrine, the means and the will to conduct an independent foreign policy and establish new centres of strategic power is also seen as a threat to the management of the world by the major powers. The emergence of reformist movements in those states that were unable to satisfy the needs of their people has been considered a somewhat less important threat to international security. This view needs to be re-evaluated. The availability of nuclear technology, nuclear weapons as well as other weapons of mass destruction, and the means to deliver them are a serious threat to global peace—out of the thirty countries that have ballistic missiles at this time, half are located in the Middle East, North Africa and Asia.

Needless to say, terrorism as a tool of destabilization, both within and between states, has emerged as a concern that has not been properly addressed. The economic integration of the global economy with dependence on the free movement of private capital and the use of information technology has created a new area of vulnerability for state entities. Militant and sub-national groups have established substantial assets in legitimate enterprises worldwide during the last three decades (1970-2000). The opening up of weak economic systems to multiple global forces of financial manipulation and control have exposed states and given a new dimension to the meaning of national security. All this did not happen overnight and points to a major lapse in security planning. Obviously, security organizations did not understand the full range of threats to global security.

Security mechanisms and their component, strategic alliances, may be considered from a number of different perspectives depending on their scope of action as instruments for the maintenance of peace and stability in international security systems within which states co-exist. Within traditional security systems, sub-national entities and other groups fall in the jurisdiction of national governments and must be tackled by them. International strategic alliances seek to achieve various levels of integration into national security systems at the analysis, policy, planning and implementation level in response to threats, or, in order to achieve objectives and goals that are perceived to be common to all parties involved. The integration of such objectives into national security systems is critical to their effectiveness.

National security is traditionally considered in terms of response to external threats of a military nature. The existence of such threats may lead to the establishment of any number of arrangements including bilateral security dialogues and arrangements with individual states and the development of regional security institutions or groups. The states of a region may be involved in efforts to maintain a forward presence, face a common threat or counter the influence of other powers. Combinations of such arrangement may also be made. In order to make decisions regarding available strategic choices and options, governments depend upon management information, intelligence and analyses from a variety of sources. As a result, the control of such sources of information, intelligence and analyses is critical to national security. A global network of individuals, institutions and organizations supported and operated by the resource rich major global powers and entities, both private and official, ruthlessly manipulates intelligence information and intelligentsia worldwide in order to retain control of strategic planning. Often this is done with the connivance of incompetent national leadership. This particular strategic alliance controls all others.

Governments generally depend on consultation and advice from several levels within national systems in order to arrive at decisions on matters of strategic importance. An important source of counsel for national governments, as well as the international community, is members of the intelligentsia working within and outside structured advisory arrangements with governments. In order to test the thesis that a number of independent thinkers were blacklisted by a range of research publications at the international level and that a number of so-called independent publications on strategic affairs only consider material arriving (unofficially) through official channels and by introduction, we sent an article that had already been published in it, to one such prestigious United States university publication, this time as the work of a blacklisted author. It was sent for a first review to a minor scholar working on Asia who advised that it be rejected on the grounds that the theory was 'unusual' and two line items had no references!

On another occasion, a few years before Kosovo and Rwanda/ Burundi, a research fellow based at a prestigious research institution in Oxford, England and reporting to the State Department in Washington D.C. on intellectual activity in Pakistan, was asked to look at an article titled 'The Rise of Ethnicity'.[12] To my utter disbelief, after reading it in my presence, he exclaimed, 'I will not allow that to be published! I have written two books...it goes against everything I have written, and said. It may be correct...but I cannot allow it', or words to that effect.[13] The story was repeated in Pakistan when a speech[14] delivered by a scholar at a premier national institution, unwittingly revealed the enormous, self-serving holes in theories and plans for securing the strategic interests of the next and future government of Pakistan, and not those of Pakistan. The plans had been prepared by a group of forty well paid, feted and lavishly maintained government and forces officials over a period of six months. The entire group was subsequently absorbed in key positions by the military regime that took control of the country through military action on 12 October 1999, and continues to live high off the hog. There is no doubt at all that the intellectual dishonesty and the complacency of many key research organizations and institutions, as well as individuals that advise governments in the industrialized West helped to underplay and disguise the true nature of political developments taking place in the Middle East, West and South Asia as well as East Asia. This helped create the environment in which events such as those of 11 September 2001, among others, were bound to take place. A similar environment exists in South Asia today, for much the same reason.

REFERENCES

1. Annual Report. *SIPRI (Stockholm International Peace Research Institute)*, 2001.
2. Mann, Charles C., 'Homeland Insecurity', *Atlantic Monthly*, Vol. 390, No. 2, September 2002, pp. 81-102.
3. *CNN*, News Report, 11 October 2001.
4. *The News,* APP, 9 July 1995; *The News,* APP, 29 July 1995.
5. Hoffman, Bruce, Rand Corporation, 'Terrorism C.3. Chemicals and Biological Weapons', *Terrorism MSN@Encarta,*. 15 November 2002.
6. Welsh, Cheryl, 'Nonlethal Weapons: A Global Issue', www.cahra.com, 20 April 1999.
7. Kelly, Jack A. and Joseph Conway, 'Nonlethal Weapons: Emerging Requirements for Security Strategy' *Institute for Political Analysis* 1996, May; Barbara Opall, 'US-Russia Hope to Safeguard Mind Control Techniques' *Defense News No. 4*, 11-17 January 1993; Rupert Pengelley, 'Wanted: A Watch on Nonlethal Weapons', *International Defense Review*, 1 April 1994.
8. Report, *CNN Online*, 4 July 2002.
9. Cumbala, Stephen J., 'NATO Enlargement and Russia', *Security Review*, Vol. 24, No. 2, Spring 1996.
10. Mansfield, Edward D. and Jack Snyder, 'Democratic Transitions, Institutional Strength and War', *International Organization*, Spring 2002 Vol. 56 No. 2, pp. 297-337.
11. Report, *The News (Islamabad)*, 24 December 2001.
12. Dr Gowher Rizvi conversations with the author, September-October 1991; US Department of State, 'The Role of Think Tanks in U.S. Foreign Policy,' *US Foreign Policy Agenda*, Vol. 7, No. 3, November 2002: the journal provides insight into the reason why US Think Tanks have failed to provide useful options and alternatives for American policy makers.
13. Ibid.
14. Address by the author, National Defence College, (Islamabad/Pakistan) 23 February 1998.

9

TERRORISM
AND ARMS CONTROL

A worldwide struggle between obscurantist religious groups and progressive modernism entered a third phase after the declaration of the United States' so-called war on terror and the setting up of a coalition of states to fight it. During the second phase there had been riots between religious communities in Indonesia and attacks on the Christian minority in India. At the time, parallels were drawn between the mentality that led to the organized destruction of the Babri mosque in Ayodhya and the genocide of Kosovar Muslims by Serb forces. However, NATO intervention in Kosovo undercut accusations of religious bias that had surfaced in Europe after the Bosnian conflict.[1] The withdrawal of Israeli forces from Lebanon and the interest of the Clinton administration in furthering the Middle East peace process went a long way towards reducing tension in many parts of the world for information media systems have created communities that transcend international borders. The significance of this, and a number of other developments, was not fully understood and given the consideration it deserved in future strategic planning by the major powers and multilateral institutions. The root causes of terrorism were not addressed. Analysis reveals that as a result of various measures taken by the United States, and its allies, in reaction to attacks on US territory in September 2001, violence was not contained. After an initial lull, there was an escalation in the intensity of violence (such as suicide bombings) and the frequency of violence in the struggle between communities with different interests. This increase in intensity occurred in a shorter time span than expected.[2] Commercial interest fuelled conflict: it is a good idea to remember that each time a gun is fired or a missile launched, someone makes money. War is big business.

The first two casualties of the so-called global war on terror were multi-culturism and the rule of law. The third casualty has been democratic practice. A series of extra-legal actions were undertaken by the United States at the national and international level in response to attacks on its territory. In member states of the international coalition formed to fight terrorism, the natural allies of anti-terror forces were the armed forces and police personnel. In a number of cases, retrograde elements in law enforcement agencies saw this as a chance to garner international support in order to strengthen their hold on state institutions and government machinery.[5] Many instances have been cited in which such elements have reportedly created sectarian trouble and encouraged communal violence to discredit political as well as religious organizations and promote authoritarian rule. The situation in Indonesia and Pakistan, among other countries, is disturbing. There is no doubt that as social awareness grows and economic effectiveness increases, depressed communities tend to re-organize and explore political possibilities.[6]

The emergence of conservative Islam as a political force, with power gained through due political process, is not a new development in Muslim countries. In Algeria, Jordan, Kuwait and Sudan, elections have been won by such groups through the electoral process. Conservatives continue to surface in Bosnia and Chechnya, among other countries. In such cases, it may not be wise to indefinitely block the transfer of authority to groups that have won power through the electoral process simply because of their theological bias nor is it a good idea to rig the electoral process to benefit secular elements that are considered desirable incumbents in office by the international community.[7] It may be a better idea to understand and work around the socio-political deprivations that create the constituency of conservative groups.

Four years ago, an analysis of trends revealed that sometime in the not too distant future, fundamentalists of many religions, including Islam, could be left waging war between themselves for political supremacy, against those belonging to other sects of their religion and against those whom they consider less committed to their cause. A quick look at so-called fundamentalist movements around the world confirms that for the most part Muslim activists are embroiled in a war with those who are more liberal in their interpretation of Islam easy-going in the observance of the rituals and less conformist in observing outward manifestations that some consider an essential part of the faith.[8] This is a manifestation of caste within religion, and it is as rigid as any caste system that ever existed.[9] In such a volatile environment the possibility that sophisticated weaponry, including that which had been pilfered from the stockpiles of the former Soviet Union, might find its way into the arsenals of sub-national groups, has been a cause for serious concern.

During the 1980s arms control within the five nuclear powers and the United States and Soviet Union in particular, centered around five initiatives. A major task was the physical reduction of nuclear arsenals. This task was tackled through negotiation on neutral territory. Another major task was to minimise the danger of inadvertent nuclear conflict. Mechanisms that were automatically activated during times of crisis were installed. In order to minimise chances of conflict as a result of misperceptions about the relative strength of adversaries, efforts were made to stop the proliferation of weapons of mass destruction and limits were placed on the stockpiling of conventional weapons. For this purpose transparency in military affairs was encouraged and confidence-building regimes were put in place. Such arms control initiatives have been used as models and control regimes in other parts of the world, including South Asia, have been derived from combinations thereof.

As part of their non-proliferation work, the US and the other four nuclear powers are involved in intense monitoring and surveillance of nuclear facilities worldwide. They are also involved in regulating scientific training, transfer of technology and sale of fissile material. The possibility exists that these countries may undertake pre-emptive strikes, with the help of regional allies, against the installations and infrastructure of countries suspected of developing nuclear technology for the purpose of making weapons. In order to prevent conflict, de-escalate tension and encourage a realistic assessment of the power of adversaries, international security control strategies encourage transparency of military programmes and activities. This is done through on-site inspection, verification, data exchanges, confidence building measures as well as advance notification of exercises and joint operations with other states and other measures. However, on-site inspection is often considered an intrusion eroding national sovereignty and advance notification agreements are often ignored. Verification by national technical means (NTM) or reconnaissance satellites and remote sensors is more common.

The international debate on the merits of curtailing national defence expenditure and developing effective global arms control mechanisms appears to have been derailed by the rising number of armed conflicts that had taken place in the recent past; these now include organized militant activity and terrorism against national and international targets. Discussions about downsizing defence establishments were triggered by changes that had taken place in the global security environment during the 1990s. Twenty-seven significant armed conflicts took place at twenty-six locations in 1998. In 1989, at the end of the Cold War there were thirty-six armed conflicts at thirty-two locations. During the 1980s and 1990s, three civil wars claimed the highest number of casualties: in Algeria, between 40,000 and 100,000 dead since 1992, in Sudan, between 37,000 and 40,000 dead since 1983, and in Afghanistan, about 20,000 dead since 1992. Some other major conflicts during this period were internecine, or ethnic. However, third country, multilateral or international intervention was, and continues to be, required for their resolution. As a result two categories of buyers have been active in the armament markets—nations and sub-national groups.[10]

This has led to changes in the nature of trade in defence equipment and the transfer of technology with military end-use: this area of world trade, previously shared by the Western industrialised countries in their own spheres of influence, has been challenged by new suppliers who want a share of the market and buyers aggressively looking for bargains. A number of countries with regional security concerns must provide for defence while dealing with the twin problems of resource constraint and discrimination in the transfer of technology, particularly dual use technology, from the top five suppliers in the world. These top conventional weapons exporters continue to be the United States, France, Russia, Germany and Britain. During 1998, the United States exported equipment worth $12,342 million, France exported $3815 million worth, Russia $1276 million worth, Germany $1064 million worth and Britain $673 million worth. A 10 per cent increase in the value of sales is expected each year.

In industrialised countries, the market for conventional arms has shrunk, while that for refined, interactive high-tech systems, requiring investment in research and development, has increased. At present world arms expenditure stands at about $745 billion. This is a third of what was being spent ten years ago. The decline has been sharpest in East and Central Europe as the onus for security has shifted to the transatlantic alliance and the fulfilment of 'Partnership for Peace' defence restructuring requirements. Arms expenditure has not declined significantly in Asia and the Middle East where attempts are being made to upgrade systems.

Spending in Asia has increased now that the responsibility for regional security has become a bilateral concern. There is less interest in the region since the dissolution of the USSR. Interest was revived as a result of nuclear testing in the subcontinent but intervention by world powers is unlikely as long as conflicts, as in the case of India and Pakistan, remain localised and conventional arms are used. In the Middle East, spending has been static since the Gulf War despite a number of collective regional security proposals from the West that would have led to higher levels of expenditure on defence. Africa has reduced military spending by 25 per cent on the average although ethnic conflict and civil wars have increased the burden for keeping order on the continent on a number of national defence forces. In South America, there has been a 30 per cent decrease in defence spending as a result of reduced US military allocations for the region. It is estimated that China is spending an average of 1.9 per cent of its Gross National Product on defence. Russian military expenditure is down by about 55 per cent—the average annual rate of decline has been 30 per cent since 1992. The 1998 economic crisis has had an impact on military reform which was geared towards creating a reduced but efficient, mobile force capable of dealing swiftly with localised conflicts in the near abroad and the Russian republics. Lack of resources has also hindered the inspection, proper storage and destruction of chemical and biological weapon stockpiles in Russia, creating fears of accidents and proliferation,[11] for which the world is not prepared.

Commenting on a process called the Quadrennial Defence Review from which future policy emerges, in 1997, the US Deputy Secretary of Defence indicated that the United States will need to reduce about 100,000 civilian and military personnel in its defense establishment in order to divert resources to the development and testing of new technologies and concepts. The importance of the defense industrial base for the economies of major suppliers in the world, and the need to sustain it, has led to emphasis on export as well as internationalisation and collaboration in the processes of research, development and the manufacture of defense equipment. This has been NATO policy for some time. In future, along with privatisation, emphasis on high tech defense equipment will be an important component of European Union security policy where the revitalisation of the defence industry will be part of a Common European Security Policy. The export of equipment is important to the large defense industrial complexes in major supplier countries while avowed foreign policy objectives require the regulation of arms flows. The situation is tailor-made for discrimination in the supply of arms to some and restrictions on supply to others.

Policy regarding the export of dual use technologies from the industrialised countries is best illustrated by transactions between the United States defense industry, the US government and client countries between 1950 and 1976.[12] Such transactions laid the foundations of defense production in many parts of the world. Economic considerations often compel the US government to protect its defense industry at the expense of avowed national foreign policy goals. In June 1996, the United States President approved a waiver for the ban on defence technology exports to the People's Republic of China (PRC) to allow the sale of US made telecommunications satellites for a satellite based mobile phone system, to Asia Pacific Telecommunications Satellite (APMT). APMT was formed by partners from the PRC and Singapore. Services are being provided in the PRC, Singapore and Thailand. Other waivers have been granted since the 1989 ban on technology transfer which followed the Tiennenmen Square crackdown by the authorities.

The controls imposed by the US Arms Export Control Act, the Munitions List and the multilateral export control regime COCOM have become meaningless in the global marketplace.[13] In fact, COCOM, set up by NATO countries in 1949 to prevent the transfer of advanced military and related technology to the Soviet Union, China and their allies, was dissolved on 31 March 1994. This was done in order to allow twenty-eight countries, blacklisted during the Cold War, to acquire the technology they needed to build market economies. Now there is no official blacklist but a number of countries including China, Iran, Iraq, North Korea and Libya continue to face restrictions on the transfer of technology. Such restrictions have been particularly pronounced in the transfer of dual use technology. This refers to technologies that are intended for commercial civilian use but are known to have significant military applications and include seismic technology, computer and telecommunications equipment, fibre optics etc.

Countries that are taking advantage of opportunities for technology transfer from new sources, and have the resources to do so, will now gain an edge over those that have traditionally been in the forefront of technological development. South Korea, Taiwan and other East Asian countries have signed up entire Russian science institutes to conduct research for them. The services of individual scientists have also been acquired by these countries at nominal wages for work on specific commercial and military projects. A widely advertised feature of the latest model of video heads for VCRs made in 2000 by Samsung of South Korea was developed by the space technology think tank, Kurchatov Institute based in Moscow and bought for just US$30,000. The current situation presents an ideal opportunity to formulate policies and action plans that will lead to the transfer of critical technology and enhance national security in less developed countries. Before this can be done on a large scale, an interdisciplinary review is needed to consider the possibilities of such transfer of technology, despite resistance from those with a vested interest in preventing it, and despite political, economic and commercial implications at the national and multilateral level.

A US State Department review of technology transfer policy admitted that the Soviet Union matched the United States in technological fields with '…critical implications for military balance and international security…' It had established a research oriented Academy of Sciences with about 200,000 research workers and 970,000 personnel based in Moscow alone. The enormous science and research establishment that Russia inherited from the Soviet Union was not able to sustain itself or contribute to the creation of prosperity for the Russian people. Other components necessary for the successful management of this enormous resource were lacking. As the Russian science establishment crumbled due to a lack of direction, funds and opportunities for application, about 700 scientists moved to South Korea and Taiwan. The PRC has paid Russia for transfer of technology. It paid a lump sum of about US$2 billion for the licence to produce Su-27 fighter planes in China.[14] Technology is moving into countries where there are ample funds to sustain research and development and where plans for the creation and management of products exist and there is a realisation that modern technology is just one of the components of national power. Many sub-national groups and militant organizations are competing for power with state authorities in different parts of the world. Such sub-national groups and rebel forces in

Colombia, Afghanistan and elsewhere also appear to have easy access to arms, and thereby, to an element of national power.[15] Efforts are being made to regulate trade in arms and dual use technology with sub-national groups and other entities, or, at least, to document such trade. There is a great deal of money to be made in gun running, however, and most governments tend to look the other way when their own nationals are doing business.

REFERENCES

1. Rubin, James P. 'A Very Personal War.' *FT Weekend* September 30-October 1 and 7-8 October 2000.
2. Fisk, Robert. Report in *The Independent*, reproduced in *The News* by arrangement, 16 November 1993.
3. *The Nation* (APP). 28 July 2002; *The Nation* (APP). 28 May 2002.
4. Tyler, Christian. 'Justice not Vengeance: an interview of Simon Wiesenthal.' *FT Weekend* 3-4, July 1999.
5. Ibid., See 4 above: Wallerstein, Mitchel B. 'Wither the Role of Private Foundations in Support of International Security, Politics.' *Nonproliferation Review* Vol. 9, No. 1, Spring 2002: pp. 83-91.
6. *The Nation*, APA/AFP, 29 June 2002.
7. Braibanti, Ralph. 'Strategic Significance of Pakistan.' *Journal of South Asia and Middle East Studies*, Vol. 20, No. 1, Fall 1996: p. 1.
8. Braibanti, Ralph. 'The Nature and Structure of the Islamic World.' *International Politics and Strategy Institute*, Chicago: 1995: pp. 29-33.
9. Ishtiaq Hussain Qureshi. 'Islamic Elements of Political Thought in Pakistan.' contributed to *Traditions, Values and Socio-Economic Development* ed. Ralph Braibanti and Joseph J. Spengler. Duke University Press, Durham, N.C. 1961: pp. 21-26.
10. *UNHCR*. Annual Report.1997.
11. *SIPRI*. Annual Report. 1999.
12. Ibid.
13. MacIntyre, John R. and Richard Cupitt. *Multilateral Strategic Trade Controls within the Western Alliance-a Report on the U.S. and Alliance Export Control Policies*. Department of State 1973: *The Battle Act Reports*. Department of State 1950-1973.
14. *The News* (AFP Report) 24 July 1996.
15. *The News* (APA Report) 21 March 1999.

10

THE CHALLENGE FOR LEADERSHIP

A combination of economic and political developments during the 1990s led to changes in the distribution of power within economic, political and security systems across the globe. This placed unique responsibilities on national and international leadership in various spheres of human endeavour. Adjustment became necessary in traditional approaches to dealing with crises in changing times. Such adjustments can only be made if reliable information for decision-making is available. In order to review developments and specify the direction of future change, it is necessary to consider the objectives of the major power groups that have emerged worldwide in the past two decades.[1]

Apart from nations and regional groups, these power groups now include multilateral financial institutions and transnational corporations. Their manipulation of national economic policies through the provision, or alternatively, withholding of credit and support, has led to political change in the countries in which they are active. Between 1994–1997 monetary crises in the Far East shook the strong, growing economies of Malaysia, South Korea as well as Indonesia.[2] The creation of a multilateral fund to manage such monetary crisis brought the economies of these countries, which were on the verge of joining the more prosperous countries of the world, under the guidance of multilateral financial institutions in the manner of developing and underdeveloped countries. The timing of these crises and the proposed solutions provide food for thought, for economic crises led to political instability.

According to reliable surveys,[3] there were two divergent trends during the 1990s: continued growth of electoral democracy and the stagnation of liberal democracy, an indication of a decline in freedom.

The number of formal or electoral democracies in the world grew from 76 in 1990 to 117 in 1995 but the percentage of liberal democracies declined from 85 to 65 per cent of the total during the same period. This has remained a fluctuating percentage but the trend has been consistent. Exactly the same situation prevails today. A factor that has had an adverse impact on democratic institutions and democratic institution building is the war of the United States and its allies on global terrorism: breaches of democratic norms that were considered a case for the imposition of sanctions are now tolerated, as in the case of Pakistan, where the military regime became acceptable once it became a key ally in the November 2001 war against Afghanistan.

In a number of countries, the electoral process continues to be nothing more than a charade to obtain international legitimacy and economic rewards. Of interest to observers is the fact that such charades are more easily tolerated by the international community now, than ever before, since all other concerns have been set aside in the pursuit of terrorists. This approach is likely to be counterproductive in the long run for it leads to the suppression of tensions within society and creates grounds for change through militant activity. Local populations, under pressure due to economic restructuring, express a desire for security, economic and political stability and civil order. Power elites tend to use this as an opportunity to return to paternalistic patterns of governance. In Pakistan, Poland, Venezuela, Brazil, Peru and Turkey among others, the quality of democracy is questionable by traditional standards. The military continues to intervene, in one manner or other, to regulate and oversee political institutions.

When authoritarian systems break down and a restructuring of political systems takes place, a certain level of external investment may be required to avoid chaos. This investment may include financial assistance, technical expertise and help with institution building in order to make a go of democracy, and build sustainable economic systems while reinforcing supportive regional institutions. At a secondary stage, adjustments to suit peculiar national circumstances can be expected. The international community was aware that the rise of sub-nationalism and revival of old territorial conflicts was likely under the semi-anarchic conditions that emerged in a number of states of the former Soviet Union after its disintegration.[4]

The extent of economic and social dislocation caused by the political and systemic changes promoted by the West through so-called democratic reforms and the introduction of a free market economy, has been horrific. Organised crime, corruption and the destitution of entire populations deprived of state protection is evident. Regardless of the promises made, it became clear soon after the disintegration of the Soviet Union that the leadership in the industrialised West would not invest at required levels in the states of the former Soviet Union and had begun to concentrate on domestic priorities. These domestic priorities included revival of their own recession stricken economies and controlling political upheaval at home.[5]

Today, national leaders need to determine whether western industrialized countries were ever serious in promoting democracy, economic equality and peace in developing countries. They also need to consider whether internationally sponsored efforts to ease the condition of the common man were of any use. There is no doubt that the failure of governments to provide relief increased the hostility of the general public towards those national leaders who enjoyed international support. This hostility contributed to an increase in terrorism at the national and international level. An assessment of the nature of the alternative agenda of the leadership in Western industrialised countries is called for, as well as an assessment of how this has failed to achieve their objectives. In order to determine the nature of their real agenda, a review is needed of the measures that were, and were not, taken by nations, by the international community and by regional and multilateral institutions in order to bring about change in the political, economic and security environment of the post Cold War era.[6] The weaker nations of the world are less able than ever before to influence international events. With a clear worldview they can, however, adjust their own policies to safeguard national interest.

Countries that control MFIs openly admit that they have '...a growing stake in how other countries govern or misgovern...'.[7] Chief among these is the United States. This stake makes the United States, among others, a constituency that national politicians must satisfy. Such influence is given concrete shape in the affairs of weaker nations through the manipulation of political and economic systems and the provision of all kinds of support for internationally acceptable political entities, regardless of their domestic agenda, which may or may not be acceptable to the constituency at home. Obviously this is a new phase in the creation of interdependent systems run by a leadership that is more likely, among other things, to toe the line on security issues and maintain international commitments such as the repayment of loans. However, the capacity to manipulate national systems has limitations.

Perhaps, more than anything else, it is this control of present and future leadership, the systematic elimination of indigenous nationalist leadership potential and the degradation of the functions of leadership, that is responsible for the sorry state of less developed countries. This realisation and increased political awareness amongst the general public has created new dynamics within political systems. The growing realisation that political leadership is created through a combination of national and extra-national vested interests working together is leading to the establishment of sub-groups that seek alternative sources of power to achieve objectives.

A leadership which draws strength from extra-national entities that grip the economic and security lifelines of a country and small, but powerful, vested interest groups at home, which may include intelligence agencies, will have a superficial grip on the national psyche. This has been observed. Madame Ciller was given US citizenship under special arrangement in 1973, in New York,[8] and was introduced into the politics of her country at a high level almost twenty years later. She used to deny the fact. The majority of Pakistan's new generation of politicians were carefully nurtured and trained in Britain and the United States and feted by France or Germany, or both. They were also educated in the methodology of corrupt practice and enriched by all these countries, one way or another. Their undisguised avarice, and a global movement against corruption revealed how ruthlessly and systematically many of these politicians and their associates stripped the economy of Pakistan. According to those who are in the know, there are numerous others in positions of authority in government, the administration and the forces, who would fall in the same category on investigation. Such people cannot be expected to rise to the challenges of the future. These challenges will include dealing with a highly politicised and aggressive population.

About five decades after they were established, a number of international and multilateral organisations began examining their own viability in a changing world. New organisations to supplement their activities in various parts of the world were also being created. Such new organisations and the plans of action that emerged from appraisals of existing ones can be expected to set the trend of bilateral, regional and multilateral activity in a number of fields for the next fifty years to come. This has encouraged the public to take an interest in deliberations on the future of such organisations.

The membership of international and multilateral organizations expanded rapidly during the 1990s as newly independent states of the former Soviet Union and countries that had stayed away in a bipolar world found it advantageous, even necessary, to join up in a unipolar world. A number of countries that had avoided such organizations in the past were keen to join them at this point in history and sought the most favourable terms for doing so through established economic, political as well as military alliances, such as NATO. Changes in NATO's mandate led to the formalisation of its political initiatives which, in the final analysis, seek to keep the communists out of power in Russia and the states of the former USSR and promote the creation of a market based economy there.[9]

While Europeans continue to delegate the task of the defence of Europe to NATO, citing their contribution to the organisation as one reason for doing so, the Western European Union (WEU) has been activated to take up the task of creating a common defense policy for the states in the European Union. A number of steps have been taken, but direct control of WEU forces by the EU will be resisted by a number of states within the European Union. The initiatives of the fifty-five member Organisation for Security and Cooperation in Europe (OSCE), which works on the basis of consensus, have been well received. The organisation expects to work in the field of crisis prevention and crisis resolution.[10]

A number of international and multilateral organizations faced criticism of past performance at every level of operation during the 1990s. Two of the most powerful multilateral financial organizations involved in providing assistance to the weaker economies of the world, the International Monetary Fund (IMF) and the World Bank, have faced criticism on account of the results of past performance. They are confronted by a worldwide economic transformation that has left many of the poor countries they have been guiding on the brink of bankruptcy and domestic political leadership facing a hostile, demanding public.[11] These institutions are also being criticised for poor internal management and well-heeled bureaucracies that have no knowledge of grass root realities in the poorer parts of the world. Such bureaucracies have overestimated the capacity of leadership in the less developed countries to control political and social unrest when economic policies create pressure on the weaker sections of society.[12] A movement against their activities has been gaining ground in the countries in which they have been active.

The capacity of the leadership of regional, international and multilateral alliances and institutions to cope with, and respond to change in the political and economic environment of the world is critical for the preservation of global security. It is also vital for the stability of nation states that are members of such alliances and clients of such regional, international and multilateral institutions.

A test case of new parameters in security management and alliance building was the induction of troops of various nationalities to provide protection to the administration installed in Kabul after the ouster of the Taliban by US forces. Within a year, several concerned governments were calling for the replacement of coalition forces by a NATO force with a mandate from the alliance and a timetable for eventual withdrawal from Afghanistan. An advance team was sent to Kabul to prepare for the 11 August 2003 takeover of ISAF (International Security Assistance Force)[13] by NATO forces. On 13 July 2003, the team was joined by a squad of NATO troops. ISAF had been operating under a United Nations mandate and was comprised of 4600 personnel from 28 countries of which only 14 were members of NATO. The replacement of ISAF by NATO forces was a significant indicator of change in the politics of global security management.

Despite the setbacks faced by the ISAF in Afghanistan, in May 2003 the United States began to lobby friendly countries for manpower for a similar coalition of armed forces to help it control occupied Iraq. Since the United States has adopted a new military doctrine that includes the option of unilateral, pre-emptive military strikes against nation states that it perceives to be a threat to the United States, this pattern of military action, followed by occupation and reconstruction, can now be repeated anywhere in the world. Resistance to such patterns of intervention is creating new cadres of militants who, strictly speaking, cannot be classified as terrorists.

REFERENCES

1. *Politics in Developing Countries: Comparing Experiences and Democracy* (Boulder Co: Lynne Rienner. 1995): p. 7: *The News* (Islamabad). AFP. 25 September 1995.
2. Ibid., see 1 above.

3. Kararnycky, Adrian. 'The Comparative Survey of Freedom 1994: Democracies on the Rise, Democracies at Risk' *Freedom Review, 26(1)* 1995: p. 15: *Freedom in the World : The Annual Survey of Political Rights and Civil Liberties 1994-1995* (New York, 1995): pp. 3, 12, 15.

4. M.M. Ali. 'Soviet Empire's Disintegration Alters the Face of Asia and the Middle East' *Washington Report on Middle Eastern Affairs*. March 1992: p. 49.

5. Kiltgaard, Robert. 'Political Corruption: Strategies for Reform' *Journal of Democracy*, Vol. 2, No. 4. Fall 1991.

6. Mehrotra, O.M. 'Russian Political Portents' *Strategic Analysis*. April 1996.

7. Talbot, Strobe. *Foreign Affairs*. Nov/Dec, 1996

8. See Appendix.

9. Kaiser, Karl. 'Reforming NATO' *Foreign Policy*, *No. 103* Summer 1996: pp. 129, 131, 132-134.

10. See Ref. 8 above.

11. Remmer, Karen L. 'Democracy and Economic Crisis: the Latin American Experience' *World Politics, Vol. 42, No. 3* April 1990: pp. 315-335.

12. Franck, Thomas. 'The Emerging Right to Democratic Governance' *The American Journal of International Law*, Vol. 86, No. 46 1992: pp. 50-51: *The News (Islamabad)* AFP. 14 November 2002.

13. 'NATO Troops Arrive in Kabul'. *The Nation (Islamabad)*. Page 11, 14 July 2003.

11

THE INFORMATION WAR

There has been an increase in public awareness that various kinds of communications media activity can encourage specific behavior and consumption patterns. Besides influencing the social and business culture in a country, media activity can also contribute to the creation of a political environment. The creation of a specific type of political environment is likely to be undertaken because it serves the strategic, political and economic agendas of alliances of national, regional and international power brokers, institutions and coalitions organized to perform specific tasks. The creation of such an environment can also serve the purpose of other types of vested interest groups. Awareness of these facts has grown during the past three decades.[1] During this period, the results of research and official discussion on the subject have been made public by social scientists in the industrialized countries. Political activists have also commented on the human rights implications of such activity. Some information has also filtered down to the populations of less developed countries. These populations need such information in order to see the truth, the reality behind media hype, in order to make well-considered political choices. A small dose of background information is usually enough to trigger further investigation. Communities automatically begin to sift through the mass of material being provided to them through various media of communication.

The idea that media activity, by itself, can change public opinion is a misconception. Lack of information and disinformation can, however, distort public perceptions of a situation. Public opinion is created through the interaction of information with a number of things including traditional and socio-religious values, hopes and fears, perceptions of reality, needs, etc. Facts and analyses presented through media reflect images of reality to which the public reacts. For instance, anti-war demonstrators in Europe, Britain and the United States came out by the thousand to protest against civilian casualties in the United

States' war in Afghanistan—obviously what they were seeing on television was not their idea of a war on terrorism.

Such protest demonstrations served one other purpose: a show of popular disapproval of civilian casualties in a severely impoverished part of the world was one way of deflecting the hostility of extreme elements and Muslim populations from ordinary citizens in the states of the coalition fighting in Afghanistan. Similar protests in Pakistan, on the other hand, have highlighted the enormous, and growing, gulf between the government's policy and public opinion. A peaceful rally by moderate middle class elements, including workers, in the city of Rawalpindi, in December 2001,[2] was the breaking point for officialdom. It was thought to herald a larger political movement and led to the swift incarceration of a large number of political activists. Since this was perceived to have been instigated by the American presence in Pakistan, as were the negotiations for a rapprochement with many discredited political elements, there was a swelling wave of anger and dislike for the Coalition at war in Afghanistan.

Research shows that the public gravitates towards those media, specific information channels, newspapers and magazines that reinforce the views they already hold, or, are inclined towards.[3] Nevertheless, media faces pressure to toe the official line at every level. There is international pressure to promote global values regardless of the lack of relevance in local conditions: for example, you must want a refrigerator even if you do not have electricity. National broadcasting systems and local networks aspire to shift attention to the micro level and address national and community concerns. The manner in which media are handled and communications systems are organized in a country, or community, reflect a political decision based on a prevalent value system. Such decisions may be taken by leaders on the basis of their perception of public needs. If this perception differs from the actual needs of the population it soon becomes apparent through the rejection of messages conveyed.

Shifts in official value systems may take place due to any number of reasons. Whenever major shifts in value are observed in public policy regarding information provision, these are of interest to the international community as a whole and at the bilateral level as well. Management and censorship are expected to exist in less developed regions: there are reports that during the war on Afghanistan in 2001, the Bush administration requested Qatar to 'contain' the

Al-Jazeera television channel, which has a potential audience of 35 million Arabic speakers. The channel was the only one reporting directly from within Afghanistan. The request was denied with the comment that press freedom is fundamental to parliamentary democracy which Qatar expects to introduce within the next two years. Meanwhile, the Bush administration virtually censored the use of Al-Jazeera clips reporting the situation in Afghanistan with graphic coverage of civilian casualties and destruction of infrastructure.

There was a marked decrease in the use of footage from Al-Jazeera by major Western networks within two weeks of the war on Afghanistan. Once US and British personnel entered the country and established communication networks, information gleaned from Al-Jazeera footage was no longer necessary for military purposes. On the other hand, its persistent coverage of civilian losses inflamed public opinion and made it a nuisance. The charge that US bombers targeted the Kabul office of Al-Jazeera satellite television channel on Monday, 12 November 2001,[4] therefore, needs to be taken seriously. The US government had been given the location of the channel's office in Kabul. During hostilities, third country non-combatants may even signal their presence to bombers by breaking the blackout and flashing lights. BBC and Al-Jazeera were reportedly on the air when the latter's office was bombed. The channel was allowed to operate from Afghanistan while the information it was providing was needed by the US military. Then it was punished. These are not the rules by which the game is played on US territory. Such incidents are a reminder that the rules of the game are different on foreign soil.

Throughout the Western world there are regular, institutionalized discussions to assess the moral and socio-political impact of national and transnational communications media activity. Such discussions are based on the feedback from carefully chosen target groups in society and are expected to contribute to the evolution of guidelines for public policy with regard to media regulation. Such guidelines are expected to safeguard public interest. What they often do is nudge media into promoting the official line. The BBC, for instance, has an independent board of governors but it is a public corporation dependent on government funds and money from license fees, which it is authorized to collect by the state.[5] In those countries where major media conglomerates are privately owned and less dependent on official patronage, the opinions of the political leadership and media owners and managers may differ, not only with regard to the relative importance of various issues, but with regard to the stance that needs to be taken. A strong business community that is a source of revenue through advertising will create its own media presence. Similarly, if various organs of the state are a source of revenue and support, their presence will become visible. Media provides groups working for social and political change with a voice and diffuses tension in social systems.

In Pakistan, the interest of the military in civil affairs and politics grew by leaps and bounds after the early years of independence. To satisfy the lust for political power that could not be satisfied at the very outset, by an abortive coup in 1951, military competence has been a carefully cultivated myth protected by sweeping national security laws—probably the only laws that are actually enforced in Pakistan. It is debatable whether political instability in Pakistan led to military intervention in civil affairs or vice versa. Many methods were used to increase the stature of the armed forces in Pakistan, although they had suffered a number of reverses over the years. Although they did not win it, the war of 1965 led to a patriotic upsurge. At that time an elitist concept of military supremacy replaced the institutional separation of the civil and military functions of state authority.

A popular media campaign was designed to establish this elitist vision of the military and its superiority over civilian culture in all aspects. National songs eulogized not specific feats or battles but the military breed or 'race', in Pakistan. A Punjabi song of this genre says, in effect, that the mothers of soldiers are a breed apart from ordinary womenfolk in the country. It is significant that this song remains an anthem that is replayed every year on Defense Day. The men who helped create these myths and those who grew up with them and sheltered under them are now finding it hard to share power with another phenomenon they helped create: the religious militias that were to wage jihad and conquer the world for them. The speed with which the military government of Pakistan abandoned its erstwhile allies in Afghanistan speaks volumes about truth and fiction in national policy and the substance of spiritual values that is said to underlie military enterprise in Islam, the official religion of the country.

Surveys show that recession and a cut in travel and tourism has led to a boom in home entertainment devices and related services in the industrialized countries.[6] Similarly, low cost devices and services continue to be priority items for low-income families in some of the poorest countries of the world. This is a revolutionizing factor in socio-cultural development that has become difficult to manage (officially) after the introduction of transnational and cable networks. In crisis situations, highly politicized audiences react sharply to situations such as that prevailing in Konduz after Northern Alliance forces entered the city during the US war in Afghanistan. Journalists were not allowed to send visuals of the bloodbath that ensued but the very fact that there was an information blackout was revealing and inflammatory. Highly stylized coverage of the invasion of southern Afghanistan by US troops appeared to be an effort to minimize hostility in Muslim populations by avoiding the screening of visuals of combat between Muslim and Christian troops.

Some applications of information technology serve to politicize and educate populations while other applications of information technology can serve to enhance productivity and effectiveness. However, in order to use technology, it is necessary to have basic education, technical skill, knowledge of the possibilities of technology and an appropriate environment in which to use this knowledge. Remarkable new social and political alliances are emerging between those who share a common scientific and technical culture in at least two areas of activity: business and security. The more sophisticated applications of computer mediated information technology have led to the creation of a new class of information rich individuals within societies and within nations in the international community. Where information is not accompanied by opportunity and economic wherewithal, new tensions are created in society: there are those who are wealthy enough to afford such technologies and derive benefit from their use and those who are not in a position to do so.

The rhetoric about the globalization of business opportunity in the early 1990s helped create a culture in which information technology played a central role. This culture developed relatively quickly in the United States where employment patterns were changing in response to the rising social cost of conventional business. It was, however, accessible to a relatively small group of individuals and entities outside the United States who were generally people of high net worth. This restricted the growth of e-business and public interest in it. In retrospect, the response of financial groups and e-business service providers in Europe to inquiries from other parts of the world appears both smug and self-defeating: '... yes, we will let you see how well we are doing but, of course, you may not join us and of course, you may not partake of our success...' This was the point at which some tiers within the multitude of United Nations agencies for development and industrial growth should have intervened to discuss and remove legal and other concerns regarding international e-business and e-commerce, but they did not. It is American business with its global outreach, and forward-looking strategies for expanding business, that has been most helpful in combating cyber crime and harassment in other parts of the world.

Meanwhile, cyber crime and harassment through hacking and the release of viruses etc., both custom-made and global versions, have undermined the effectiveness of information technology and related activities, besides posing a serious threat to users all over the world.[7] Mischievous software programs and nuisance toys that are being produced under patents, on a commercial scale, are often distributed through mail order services in the United States. They can be lethal in certain hands. For instance, an ultra high frequency noise delivered during an ordinary telephone call made to a journalist in Pakistan caused a stroke, leading to temporary blindness, dizziness and loss of hearing. A respectable US financial journal (Smart Money, April 2001) advertised a similar device in a feature on its editorial pages in the following words, '...Sonic Nausea ($59.95). Hide it in your enemy's office, flip the switch and this small device generates ultra high frequency sound waves said to cause headaches, dizziness or even vomiting. Ah, the wonders of technology.' It is not difficult to imagine others refining this device further.

The need to combat cyber crime led to the development of many categories of expertise in the private and public sector. Allied developments provided both sectors with an unprecedented opportunity to gather information and intelligence for various purposes. This eventually led to public discussion of the social, political and security implications of the intrusive worldwide communications web run jointly by the United States, Britain, Canada and Australia with other states chipping in from time to time. The social, political and security implications of providing training to, and conducting joint exercises in cyber intelligence, with allies in less developed countries like Afghanistan and Pakistan, were not considered: in both countries, citizens still do not have recourse to an effective legal system when confronted by harassment and state terrorism.[8] This situation is similar to that of a number of South American countries during the 1970s and 1980s.

The development of security systems utilizing advanced information technology has added a new dimension to the formulation of defense strategies. In a column published in June 1996, it was stated that, '... Based on analyses of recent history the United States (and its allies) is evolving new systems on the assumption that in the future the primary function of its establishment is likely to be intervention to protect and defend allies. Within this scenario it is believed that information technology can facilitate such intervention and minimize impediments to conventional military assistance to allies. The idea is that the provision of strategic information can be an on-going process that is not easily detected, or as costly, as shipments of conventional arms. Superiority in this field is more easily achieved where the political will to provide it exists...Information critical to the integration, maintenance and indigenous upgrading of existing systems that allies possess can be of immense importance...'[9] The Nuclear Missile Defense (NMD) system that is being developed by the United States in close cooperation with a few regional allies, such as Britain, Germany, Canada, Australia, Japan, Israel and Turkey will use existing information technology resources available to these states besides introducing new applications. States that are not in the loop may find it safer to shut their information corridors and look to internal resources in order to survive.

In every major undertaking in the name of the international community, there are bound to be several information components designed to achieve a set of objectives. One important objective in any such undertaking is to gain public confidence, sympathy and support for international initiatives. Information is gathered, analyzed and subsequently used by the authorities to design public information programs that will help in the achievement of coalition objectives. There are bound to be short, medium term and long-term objectives. Public information is designed to garner support at various levels, within domestic and international populations, to facilitate the achievement of all categories of objectives. For instance, the international coalition that has been formed to support the efforts of the United States to fight terrorism has a number of short term, medium and long term objectives. In order to achieve these objectives, the authors of the coalition first solicited the cooperation and support of a number of governments, including the government of Pakistan, as well as international and multilateral organizations, including the United Nations and NATO. The interests of the countries cooperating with the United

States were known to be diverse and divergent. In fact, the interests of the United Nations, which represents the world community, and those of NATO, a regional security organization, should differ if they are to do their duty towards the world community, with honesty[10].

In order to form the coalition against terrorism, the United States had to enlist the cooperation of governments, many of whom were beholden to it, or enjoyed historical links with it.[11] Soliciting the support of the populations of the countries enlisted was a secondary, less important objective. In many cases this was expected to be the task of national governments within the coalition. In democracies, public support for government policies is important. Elsewhere it is not. In Pakistan, a country with a military government and an increasingly militarized bureaucracy, public support for the government's decision to join the war in Afghanistan was considered unimportant to achieving the objectives of the coalition. Propping up the military government was considered of prime importance.

The United States has a history of wheeling and dealing with military governments in South America and Asia, and aiding the perpetuation of military rule to the detriment of local populations. The variety of methods used have been well documented in the case of Ms Harbury, an American lawyer, who went looking for her Guatemalan husband, a political dissident. When Pakistan joined the United States in its war in Afghanistan, peaceful public demonstrations became an almost daily event in the major cities of the country. They were attended by moderate as well as conservative elements. It was clear that not all those participating had a vested interest in the Taliban rule in Afghanistan and many had been against some of the extreme policies of the Taliban authorities. Nevertheless, a body of opinion against Pakistan's involvement in an unequal war against a Muslim population, for uncertain objectives, existed and continues to exist in the country.[12] In response to daily demonstrations backed by the growing pressure of public opinion, the government arrested large numbers of demonstrators as well as the organizers and leaders of demonstrations. Thereafter, it claimed it was in control of the situation. Clearly the massive public information and public relations efforts mounted by the international coalition active in Afghanistan, and supported by Pakistan, had failed to win the hearts and minds of the population.[13] If the public relations and public information efforts of a powerful and resourceful coalition, that includes NATO, have failed then it is time to consider what is wrong with the objectives of its mission and the execution of plans in the sphere of public information.

One perception that has created intense resentment in countries like Pakistan is that in order to shift the responsibility for carnage in Afghanistan, and establish documentary evidence of internecine atrocities that can create permanent schisms in society, thereby creating permanent allies for itself, the United States has arranged for Afghans to kill Afghans, commit atrocities and be photographed in the act. In fact, this has been standard practice in the region for decades. In recent photographs, published during the US Coalition's Afghan campaign, Northern Alliance Afghans are shown castrating a Taliban while a photographer records the act.[14] A Northern Alliance Afghan pokes the mouth of a Taliban for a gold tooth while a photographer records the act. A Northern Alliance Afghan with a rifle is told to pose with his booted foot on the face of a dead Taliban soldier, in the foreground of the carnage at Killa-i-Jangi prison near Mazar-i-Sharif and a photographer records the moment: the uncomfortable Afghan is posing suspiciously like an English, big game hunter and one wonders who put him up to it. Muslims all over the world need to ask themselves who these Northern Alliance Afghans are and what they are fighting for.

They also need to ask themselves who the architects of the public information campaign about Afghanistan were. The campaign did not create goodwill for the so-called US war on terrorism or the Northern Alliance that is generally considered a body of disparate mercenary groups, whose takeover was facilitated through the most intense bombing of a country since the Second World War. Anti-war demonstrations in many parts of the Western world tell us that images of atrocities in Afghanistan do not comfort populations that were traumatized by the attacks on US territory on 11 September 2001.[15] And the US response does not seem to terrify committed militants in other parts of the world. Obviously, a different approach is called for.

This thesis is borne out by the formal declaration of another offshoot of the US war on terrorism in another part of the world. After his visit to Washington was disrupted by the news of violence in a number of Israeli cities, Mr Ariel Sharon returned to Israel to declare his own war on 'terrorism' in the Middle East. Mr Sharon has actually been at war in the Middle East for a long time. Under Mr Sharon, Israel has undermined the painstakingly conducted multilateral peace process that was initiated during the 1980s. Moderate Israelis who supported efforts to make the peace process a success, have been firmly pushed aside. The easiest route to a dramatic decrease in violence would have been the acceptance of international observers under United Nations, OSCE or EU auspices, but the proposal was rejected. For almost a year, Israel has been bombing territories under the control of the Palestinian Authority. It has been shelling cities and refugee camps that are no more than shanty towns, causing civilian casualties. It has been mining streets and paths believed to be used by militants but definitely used by civilians, including children.[16] Now a wall has been built to section off Palestinian and Israeli territory on the West Bank. This confines Palestinians to ghetto-like camps and makes movement from one Palestinian area to the other, difficult. As a result of their own experience of racial and communal discrimination, the Israelis should know better than to do this.

The latest round of hostilities between Israel and the Palestinians has serious implications for the region. Building a wall to fence off Palestinian areas in the West Bank is another example of Israeli disregard for the basic principles of peaceful co-existence. Israel has targeted the leadership and infrastructure of the Palestinian Authority as well as its security personnel. This round of Israeli military action is believed to have the tacit support of the United States and is designed to engineer the removal of the present administration of the Palestinian Authority, marking the beginning of a wider war in the region, a mop-up operation before the new global security system, Nuclear Missile Defense, with Israel as the regional hub, is installed in the Middle East. This is not too different from the medium to long-term goals of the United States in South, West and Central Asia. These goals are expected to include a number of initiatives to monitor the region and control social, political and strategic developments, thereby re-establishing US influence in the area. Keeping this in mind, it would be appropriate to consider what the war on terrorism has been able to achieve so far by way of winning over the populations of the areas the United States seeks to influence. Only limited public support may be bought with cash and favours for those nominated leadership cadres that enjoy official patronage. It has proved well nigh impossible to eliminate committed political opposition to such nominees through strong-arm tactics. Strong messages that have the power to displace existing beliefs are needed to capture the hearts and minds of populations. This is what the international coalition working in Afghanistan, with enormous resources at its disposal, has not been able to do. It appears to have little to sell.

REFERENCES

1. Katz, Elihu. 'Television is a Horseless Carriage' *Communication Technology and Social Policy: Understanding the New Cultural Revolution* ed. George Gerbner, Larry P. Gross and William H. Melody, Publishers: John Wiley and Sons, 1973, New York: p. 389.
2. *The News* (Islamabad) APP. 14 December 2001.
3. Gabor, Dennis. 'Social Control Through Communications' *Communication Technology and Social Policy: Understanding the New Cultural Revolution* ed. by George Gerbner, Larry P. Gross and William H. Melody: John Wiley and Sons, 1973: New York: pp. 83-99.
4. Report. The Nation/ Al-Jazeera Television/ BBC World/ AFP. 13 November 2001.
5. 'Rules of Business.' *BBC Board of Governors*, 2000.
6. 'Business Today.' *BBC World,* 15 June 2002.
7. 'Findings of the Computer Crimes and Security Survey,' *Backgrounder.* FBI (US Federal Bureau of Investigation), Embassy of the United States, Office of Public Affairs, Backgrounder dated 14 March 2001.
8. Ibid., 7, p. 3: also refer to *http://www.nipc.gov/infragard.htm.*
9. Molander, Roger C. Andrew S. Riddile and Peter Wilson. 'Strategic Information Warfare,: A New Face Of War' *Parameters*, Vol. 26, No. 3, Autumn 1996: pp. 81-92, (see Fig. 1, p. 84).
10. 'Fact Sheet: Coalition Contributions to the War on Terrorism,' *Backgrounder.* Embassy of the United States, Office of Public Affairs. 11 June 2002.
11. Ibid., see 10 above: 'Report' *The News/ APP/ NNI/ PPI.* 21 December 2001.
12. The Muttahida Majlis Amal, a coalition of Pakistan's religious political parties won about a third of the seats in general elections to the National Assembly that were held in the October 2002. It also won a majority in two Provinces, the North West Frontier Province and Balochistan/ Blanton, Thomas. 'The World's Right to Know' *Foreign Policy* July/August 2002: pp. 50-58.
13. Ibid., see 12 above.
14. 'Reportage of the War in Afghanistan' *APA, Reuters and AFP* November 2001 to March 2002.
15. 'Public Reaction to Reports about the War in Afghanistan/Comments of Families of Victims.' *CNN News Report*: 20 February 2002.
16. *The Nation (Islamabad)* Reuters/APA: 25 July 2002.

PART II

SOCIAL, ECONOMIC AND CULTURAL FACTORS INFLUENCING THE RISING TIDE OF TERRORIST ACTIVITY

12

ECONOMIC WARS

In the future, conflicts between nations will not be wars over territory alone, there will be economic wars: wars that are motivated by economic interests and concerns and a desire to seize control of the resources of the world. There will be skirmishes to test the strength of tariff structures, territorial conflicts to seize markets and regional alliances to protect economic interests. These wars will take place between the major industrial powers of the world. Less-developed countries will have to fight each other and the industrialised countries for a place in the world economy. As large areas of the world become industrialised and productive, the fight for copyrights and the protection of intellectual property have assumed importance. The fight for exclusive control over certain types of technology, productive activity and commodities will also intensify. This has already begun to happen. Some are winning, some are losing.

An indication of the serious nature of future conflicts on economic issues is the reordering of security priorities in the post cold war era. According to press reports, the CIA has been asked to protect the economic interests of the US through economic counter-intelligence activities mainly directed against its own allies, which include Britain, France, Germany and Japan, in space technology, aeronautics, chemistry, biotechnology and the arms industry.[1]

There is a great deal of heartburning over the fact that US aerospace firms sold over US$14.5 billion worth of products in Europe in 1995 while the Europeans sold a mere US$8.8 billion worth in the US. With a five-year time lag on delivery, these contracts are due to close shortly, putting the pressure on national governments to lobby and secure new ones. The British Prime Minister made several trips to India in 2002 to help secure contracts for the supply of British helicopters and aircraft to India. A new contract was signed between Britain and India in August 2003. The British PM also spoke to India about the Kashmir dispute during his visits. Shortly thereafter, India signed a contract with Israel, for the critical defence equipment. The US government has set up a programme, almost a marketing subsidy, to help firms seeking to enter the European market. The industrialised countries will seize manufacturing opportunities wherever they can, limit the transfer of technology between themselves and to the less-developed countries in an attempt to secure as many jobs as they can, both within and outside their borders, for their own people.

Evidence of these developments in the global economy is all around us. In February 1997, the Russian government announced a new aggressive marketing policy to penetrate markets in Asia, the Far East, South America and the Arab countries. The sale of Russian technology to commercial enterprises in East Asia accelerated the production of goods that have an edge over those from the industrialised countries—they are as good if not better and much cheaper. The introduction of relatively inexpensive, and sophisticated, Russian technology into the global marketplace indicated a change in the balance of technological power in the world. Countries with the capacity and know-how to adjust this technology for indigenous production will be liberated from dependence on limited doses of Western technology.

Regions that were the traditional markets of the United States are drifting away. During the early 1990s, the European Union emerged as an important alternative for states keen on economic cooperation but under pressure from the United States. Anti-Cuba and anti-Iran legislation that sought to penalize firms contracting business (over a certain financial limit) with Iran, invoked national security as the reason for lawsuits in US courts against those European companies, and executives of companies, that trade with Cuba.[2] This legislation was not well received on the whole. The World Trade Organisation set up a panel to decide whether the invocation of national security is justified. A number of countries, as well as the Vatican, are concerned about the human suffering that economic embargoes can cause.

Morality aside, the business and trading communities can effectively exert pressure on the government to change policy in order to protect their own interests: in March 1997, the US administration announced an exception to a forty-seven-year old embargo on trade with North Korea for a grain export deal between Cargill, an American food conglomerate and North Korea.[3]

The Far East including South Korea, Taiwan and Japan are emerging as major competitors of the United States and the EU in the global economy. New styles of economic interchange are on offer and under negotiation. The most significant aspects of cooperation and competition relate to national and international regulation of market access. This is highlighted by a 1997 dispute between the United States and Japan over film and paper imports. According to the United States, the Japanese government has created a '...web of policies and practises conceived and deliberately undertaken by the Japanese government for the express purpose of limiting imports in this sector...' The US is seeking redress through the World Trade Organisation and observes that this is '...classic protectionism accomplished through novel means...' So far such disputes have not spilled over into the area of foreign policy where the US needs the cooperation of Japan in order to manage the Asia-Pacific region.

The Gulf Cooperation Council (GCC) states plan to forge new relationships with Japan, the European Union as well as other regional economic groups. For several years now, these countries have been locked in a struggle to acquire technology essential for building an industrial base in order to reduce their dependence on oil earnings, which are so easily manipulated in the world markets. Re-export trade is not a long-term solution. So far, industrialised countries have been reluctant to transfer technology to the Gulf, arguing that the region is too small to absorb large industrial projects and that its industry must be limited to light and medium products: no one is keen to let another competitor into the global marketplace.[4] As the Western industrial countries compete with each other, it is more than likely that one or the other will break away from the group to supply the GCC with the technology it has been seeking. There is likely to be a showdown soon because the GCC also wants the EU to lift customs barriers for GCC petrochemicals, aluminium and other non-oil exports on the grounds that the EU has free access to Gulf markets, the biggest consumers in the Middle East.

Oil-producing states are notorious for scheming to breach production quotas in their own interest[5] and in order to raise prices in the international market: the rationale for Iraq's attack on Kuwait is, therefore, difficult to understand. The attack was bound to lead to a stoppage of oil production in Iraq, and the imposition of economic and political sanctions because the Kuwaitis had the wherewithal to mobilise the international community. The attack did lead to a broad range of economic and other sanctions that punished the Iraqi people for retaining Saddam Hussein as President. As if they had a choice.

Political change was not an option for the Iraqi people at the time. After occupation by US forces, the situation of the majority continues to be perilous.

From a historical point of view, Iraq's attack on Kuwait must be seen for what it actually was: a bid to change the status quo in the region. In fact, it marked a watershed in the Middle East, requiring swift action from the West because it challenged boundaries put in place around the world after the Second World War. If one boundary could be challenged and breached, so could others. The implications were there. If a relatively low level of development compared to the West, and economic prosperity based on the sale of a single commodity could embolden a country to the extent that it felt it was in a position to change the status quo in the region and attack a national entity, the potential for future progress and prosperity in the region would have to be controlled, in order to contain the likelihood of future aggression, by other ambitious states.

The imposition of a no-fly zone, the United Nation's crippling economic sanctions which caused great hardship to the weakest sections of society, as well as incursions by Turkey into Iraqi Kurdistan, apparently in pursuit of Kurd guerillas, undermined and limited the sovereignty of Iraq. The decrease in Iraqi oil sales benefited other oil producing countries. United Nations officials reported that even after the Security Council doubled 'oil for food' sale levels to US$ 2 billion every six months, Iraq did not benefit because production capacity had been degraded and Iraq was unable to produce enough to earn the sanctioned amount. Machinery and spare parts for the oil industry were badly damaged during the Gulf War. Thereafter replacements were denied as having dual purpose potential. All this was within the knowledge of the international community. It was also within the knowledge of the US and British intelligence communities when both countries decided to wage war and occupy Iraq in 2003, thereby seizing control of its vast oil reserves.

As the industrialised countries adjust into a competitive mode, increasing numbers of developing countries are seeking trade concessions and access to various kinds of technology, hitherto denied to them. It is necessary for those countries that have been denied trade concessions and technology transfer for decades to realise that the economic climate of the world has changed. The industrialised countries need their customers and markets just as much as the poorer countries need technological goods and services. It is time to shop for the best deal even if it comes from an unfamiliar source. Traditional economic partnerships are not sacrosanct and must not be allowed to work to the disadvantage of national populations.[6] Europe reacted sharply to protectionist policies adopted by the United States after the events of 11 September 2001, which have devastated its economy, by imposing tariffs and fines on United States goods entering European Union states. The EU made no excuses for doing so.

National economic policies can be a reliable indicator of the bias of government for or against sections of the population. As a result, a profile that is either supportive or discriminatory towards weaker sections of society develops. This has an impact on relations between various sections of society and the government. A number of trends in economic policy observed in Pakistan since the beginning of the decade of the 1990s have far-reaching political implications. These include unrealistic revenue collection targets and the subordination of all economic and social goals to revenue collection to fulfil the demands of debt servicing, defence and government's non-development expenditure. Another politically motivated policy has been to mask efforts to protect agricultural income from tax by imposing unrealistic levies on land, not income. Farmers agitate for the removal of such levies and the government ultimately obliges. It still does not impose taxes on agricultural income that are comparable to taxes imposed on urban income.[7] Devaluation has come to be used as a tool of management rather than fiscal management. The result is that successive governments have established policy lines that led to the erosion of 70 per cent of the value of the Pakistan rupee during the 1990s.

The primary reason given for the devaluation of the rupee over the years has been the need to make exports competitive in the international market. In 1997, the incumbent Finance Minister and his advisors gave the same reason for 8.71 per cent devaluation of the Pakistan rupee against the US dollar. As usual, the immediate benefit of the devaluation was limited to a small group of exporters who, presumably, had an exportable surplus and market access. Previous attempts to boost exports through devaluation had not succeeded. Only the book value of exports, not the volume, increased. In the past, devaluation was revealed to be an attempt to procure cash to meet local obligations and justify the excessive amount of currency in circulation in relation to reserves. Subsequently, the value of the Rupee against the US dollar fell by another 25 per cent (2002—Rs. 59.60: US$1.00).

The negative impact of the 8.71 per cent devaluation in 1997 was evident across the board, on the weakest economic groups as well as the middle classes and salaried workers, in real, measurable terms. The prices of essential commodities rose by 10-15 per cent. Nutrition and the ability to procure health services were directly affected, as the prices of essential commodities rose but wages did not. With the downsizing of government and the public sector, and the anticipated return of about 70,000 people from Saudi Arabia and the Gulf, unemployment rose by 30 per cent by the beginning of 1998. Attempts to divert dislocated employees to other types of employment, by boosting small enterprise, did not succeed since the purchasing power of broad cross sections of society had been drastically reduced and demand in the domestic market for the products and services of small enterprises declined.

Private enterprise is supposed to be the key to progress now. If private sector activity were taking place on the scale projected by government it would show up in the GDP. The gross domestic product has shown a consistently low rate of growth in recent years (2-2.4 per cent between 1998 and 2002). The GDP growth rate remained below 5 per cent in 1992-1993 and 1993-1994. In 1995 it was 5 per cent and in 1996 3.1 per cent. The real rate of growth, however, is much lower since the annual rate of inflation and population growth should be subtracted from the GDP in order to get an accurate picture. The rate of growth of the population is estimated to be 3.1 per cent. According to unofficial estimates, inflation is as high as 20 per cent for the majority that spends half their income on food, clothing and housing and the other half on utilities, where available.[8] Such hardship cannot be eased through promises of future prosperity and some practical measures need to be taken to provide relief.

An area where immediate relief can be provided to the weakest economic groups is the provision of essential goods. Policies affecting food supply and distribution reflect the biases and priorities of government. These biases could be in favour of the rural population, the urban population and revenue boosting exports or the ideal of a market economy. Where government priorities do not coincide with those of the masses there could be political repercussions. In Pakistan, political considerations have been preventing a genuine crackdown on the smuggling of essential goods and commodities to neighbouring countries such as Afghanistan, causing hardship to the citizenry. If considerations other than that of ensuring a supply of foodstuff at affordable rates to low income consumers prevail in agriculture and food policy, vulnerable groups in the economy are likely to be affected first.[9] As crisis follows crisis in the provision of essential commodities to the population, there is obviously a need to review the mechanics of food security.

The objectives of devising agriculture price policies need to be examined and viewed in the perspective of existing economic realities as well as the anticipated social and political consequences of decisions taken. Attempts to favour one group of producers or one group of consumers without considering the impact on the system can and usually will, lead to disaster. The government needs to be clear about its long-term objectives. It must be clear whether the policies being devised are in order to secure increases in the production of exportable crops and their sale at advantageous rates, or to achieve self sufficiency in major agricultural commodities consumed within the country and to maintain stability in prices at the wholesale and retail level. Resource and credit allocations must be tailored accordingly. The endeavour should be to create a balance between enhanced revenues from an increase in the volume of commodity exports and to achieve stability in domestic prices of stocks of essentials. To create stability, these stocks should be replenished through timely and economical imports, where necessary.[10] This will only happen if the administration is not just well informed and well intentioned, but competent as well.

Government procurement policies and systems have been twisted and misused for personal gain at all levels in the food administration system with the connivance of unscrupulous political elements. As reported in the press, a number of deals in which the government lost in both the sale and purchase of commodities created food crises. Import/export policies that bar the sale of certain commodities and the purchase of others, are often designed to benefit special groups and individuals, rather than consumers. The supply of wheat, sugar and rice has been affected. Wheat is in short supply, there is a glut in sugar while the rice situation has just stabilised, this is a state of perpetual crisis for it could also work the other way. Cotton and other major crops also face the same fate.

If the prices of essentials rise while wages and income do not, the government must consider alternative methods of fulfilling the basic needs of the population. Subsidised foodstuff and a simple rationing system, covering the most vulnerable groups in society, should be instituted. Before this can happen, the government needs to admit that a large number of people do need assistance. This may divert government attention and resources from sectors that are potentially more productive and prestigious, but it is the job of a responsible government to consider and guard the interest of the weakest in the system. This is what separates a government from a business enterprise.[11]

There is no doubt that there is a great deal of general interest in economic policy at this time. Devaluation, inflation, industrial and trade policies, food policies and issues of employment are under scrutiny of not just economists, concerned businessmen and agriculturists, but the general public as well.[12] As a result, there is intense discussion on what should be, what is, and what used to be, in the market. The discussion is not engineered by politically motivated individuals or vested interest groups. It is initiated by those going about procuring essentials for their day to day needs. Interest has increased manifold in government policy, administration of public policy, activity or inactivity, and its effect on the standard of living of those keen to secure better living conditions. It is not surprising therefore, that inflation, rising prices of foodstuff, housing, health products and services, and the depreciation of the value of currency are the stuff of today's headlines and street talk. These are some of the issues which are the determinants of the political climate in the country. These are the issues over which political battles will be fought. Economic pressure and the unequal distribution of wealth and opportunity have contributed to the tensions that are encouraging a militant response to the need for political and social change.

REFERENCES

1. Scott, Bruce R. 'The Great Divide in the Global Village.' *Foreign Affairs* January/ February 2001: pp. 163-170: Kritz, Neil J. 'The CSCE in he New Era.' *Journal of Democracy*, Vol. 4, No. 3, July 1993: p. 128.
2. Tostemsen, Arene, and Beate Bull. 'Are Smart Sanctions Feasible.' *World Politics* Vol. 54, No. 3, April 2002: pp. 373-403: pp. 378-401.
3. *The Financial Times* (Reuters report) 15 March 1997.
4. Callaghy, Thomas A. 'Vision and Politics in the Transformation of the Global Economy.' *Global Transformation and the Third World* edited by Slater, Schutz, Dort: Boulder, CO: Lynne Riennet Publishers 1992: pp. 566-567.

5. *The Nation*, APP, June 1997.
6. *Annual Report on the State of the Economy*, Karachi. Public Relations Department SBP. September/October 1997.
7. *The Nation*. APP. 28 March 1996.
8. Political Economy Section. *The News*. 5 May 1994.
9. Editorial. *The Nation*. 13 November 2002.
10. Prahalad, C.K. and Allen Hammond. 'Serving the World's Poor Profitably.' *Harvard Business Review*. September 2002: pp. 48-57.
11. Ibid., see 10 above.
12. Business Section. *The Nation*. 7 November 2002.

13

THE SHADOW ECONOMY

What is euphemistically called the 'informal economy' is technically the unregulated and unofficial exchange of goods and services in barter trade or for monetary compensation within national boundaries where such exchange is subject to legislation. Now that the informal economy of the world is being examined for links with terrorist activity, it is a good idea to examine the nature and characteristics of the shadow economy, its links with the formal economy and its capacity to distort that formal economy. The meaning of an 'informal' or 'unofficial economy' can be taken in a totally different context in the industrialised countries and the Third World. It is understood that in developed countries the term could refer to economic activity such as domestic work where money does not change hands but service is nevertheless rendered, or a community barter trade system that does not fall within the purview of recognised economic activity. In the less developed countries, the term generally refers to illegal business, trade and production of prohibited substances. The very existence of such economies, or markets, is not acknowledged by governments and they exist parallel to the official, legitimate economy hence the origin of the term 'parallel economy'. However, such business activity cannot exist without the connivance of government functionaries and would not be profitable, or even necessary, if government policies were formulated to promote indigenous production and fulfil national needs.

The nature of a large part of activity in the shadow economy of the developed world differs from such activity in developing countries like Pakistan. In the industrialised countries, government regulates and taxes all economic activity with the exception of domestic barter trade. According to recent reports, the surge in the growth of the shadow economy in industrialised countries is a result of attempts to avoid compliance with broad ranging regulations governing economic activity and taxing them. For instance, the hiring of labour is subject to stringent welfare provisions, which make it an expensive proposition. If such hiring is done on an informal basis, the activity is not under scrutiny of the authorities and there is no question of paying minimum wages, keeping regular hours or paying mandatory social welfare allowances. According to recent reports, efforts to evade such regulations and taxes have led to the growth of the shadow economy in the industrialised world rather than the growth of hard-core criminal activity.[1] The share of criminal activity funds in the shadow economy has remained constant. Nevertheless, the growth of the shadow economy is estimated to have been three times as fast as the growth of the official gross development product (GDP) in the past thirty years and now averages 15 per cent of the official GDP in the industrialised world. This average is no indication of the situation on the ground: for example, Switzerland's black economy represents a mere 6 per cent of the GDP while France and Germany have a black economy representing 15 per cent of the GDP. The implication of such studies is that purely criminal activity is only a part of the shadow economy in the industrialised countries. There is a clear pattern: lack of implementation of regulations leads to exploitation of economies by both domestic and foreign interests. The most reliable information on the subject is with a number of special agencies of the United Nations.

In a number of developing countries including Pakistan, as well as some countries in Central and Eastern Europe and Russia, where the economy is managed to a greater or lesser extent, the nature of the black economy appears to be somewhat different. Deliberate misuse of regulatory powers by the authorities in order to enrich some and impoverish other sections of the public, the business community, traders and others, in return for a consideration, has been reported, in Pakistan, among other countries. Regulations in force (and those that are evaded) in industrialised countries seek to protect the legitimate economy, social systems and labour. On the other hand, those imposed in countries like Pakistan are often specifically designed to protect vested interests within the establishment: between 1996-1997 Parliament passed a number of regulations and tax laws that seemed to be custom made to protect the interests of parliamentarians in agriculture and commerce. Regulations were, and continue to be, used as a tool of political manipulation, to get errant politicians to toe the government line.[2] Knowledge of such practices creates enormous resentment in those sections of the population that are adversely affected as a result.

Circumventing official accounting regulations appears to have become an art, throughout the world, during the economic boom of the 1990s, as revelations about Enron, WorldCom and other giant corporations in the United States have shown. The fact that employees are now coming forward to disclose that almost every employee was in on the secret of the scams, has eroded confidence in US business on an unprecedented scale.[3] Since these corporations and multinationals were involved in operations in many parts of the world, an entire layer of business wheelers and dealers across the globe is being investigated. It is noteworthy that Enron sought and obtained energy contracts in India during the early 1990s. Within a year the company was under investigation there and Enron operations in India were closed down.

The systematic and institutionalised misuse of control of the regulatory processes is a recent phenomenon. On the other hand, the misuse of power over resources has carried over from the period immediately after the partition of the subcontinent in 1947: a substantial number of those in politics, and most of the government servants who opted for Pakistan, left no assets behind in India. Nevertheless, they scrambled to install relatives and friends in evacuee properties and filed fraudulent claims, which were regularised later through official channels, one way or another. It is in the same tradition that succeeding generations have milked concessionary development assistance given to the government of Pakistan even though it was possible to make money through legitimate business activity. When this source began to dry up, the same elements moved in to take advantage of large numbers of well endowed non-governmental organisations[4] that had been put in place a decade earlier 'to reach the people directly' according to a new Western strategy. During the late 1980s and 1990s, foreign direct investment has been milked in much the same way.[5]

Proceeds of illegal transactions and criminal activity must be used. In order to be used openly, such proceeds must be channelled into the legitimate economy. According to estimates provided by international financial institutions, about US$500 billion in proceeds from criminal activity find their way into legitimate businesses around the world annually. This provides criminals with the wherewithal to maintain luxurious lifestyles in the most exclusive surroundings. The business of money laundering is growing at the healthy rate of ten per cent each year and is set to become the single largest economic activity in the world within the next decade or so.

Many small, resource poor countries are havens for money launderers: there is nothing secret about the manner in which such transactions take place.[6] Most of the international editions of financial newspapers and journals, such as the *International Herald Tribune* and *The Economist*, carry advertisements[7] offering to facilitate the transfer of funds to countries that are tax havens, where second passports are also available for a consideration. Anonymity is guaranteed to all those transferring large sums in hard currency to local banks. After 9/11, international auditors began to review financial transactions between, and in, the major business capitals of the world with a view to tracing the financiers of those elements that could be linked to militant groups and terrorist organizations.

There are a number of locations near the United Kingdom and many obscure ones in the Caribbean that are tax havens. All the states, islands and principalities involved are members of the United Nations. The Bahamas began to accept funds from 'dubious' sources on their way to other destinations during the 1980s. It was reported that shady politicians, organised crime, renegades and criminals including drug traffickers, began to use the island as a base, corrupting local administration and financial institutions and driving away legitimate business and tourists. Cyprus became the first port of call for the funds of the Russian mafia. From banks in Cyprus, Russian money from criminal activity went on to destinations in the United States and Europe, including Switzerland. Now the government of the Seychelles has suggested that legislation should be enacted to provide immunity from prosecution and seizure of assets to those investing US$10 million or more, unless they are responsible for acts of violence or traffic in drugs in the Seychelles itself.

Now that concessionary development assistance that was channelled through official sources has become scarce, and the emphasis is on development through trade and private investment, many resource poor developing countries are competing with each other to attract foreign investment. Some, like the Seychelles, are willing to go to great lengths in order to do so. Offshore companies on many islands and principalities can be purchased, or established and registered for a few hundred dollars.[8] Money may then be deposited in the name of that company and later moved on its account to any part of the world. Property may also be acquired by the company in other parts of the world. These processes are now familiar to those in Pakistan who have been following the Ehtasaab (Accountability) Cell's activities. The deposit of a fixed amount with the government, or in a domestic bank for investment in some local enterprise buys immunity from local prosecution. The more established hideouts that have acquired some sort of government, a police force and the necessary infrastructure of statehood, now advertise for aspiring citizens, who can deposit hundreds of thousands in hard currency in their banks.

It is likely that instead of helping the economy of developing countries, the investment of funds of dubious origin will only expose them to criminal activity that they are not equipped to deal with. It will also weaken their economy in the long run: criminals are not likely to make a commitment to further the economic interests of any particular country or people. Funds acquired through criminal activity may leave an economy for greener pastures as suddenly as they arrive, damaging the country's financial stability and the reputation of its financial institutions. During the 1970s and 1980s, the government of Pakistan introduced many financial instruments[9] that could be purchased without revealing the source of funds. At the time, it was said that this was a one-time attempt to draw out hidden wealth regardless of how it had been acquired.

National Investment Trust (NIT) units, Prize Bonds and unregistered Special Saving Certificates as well as bonds issued by financial institutions and corporations such as WAPDA, were not taxable and the source of funds did not have to be revealed. An indication of the growth of officially sanctioned money laundering in Pakistan is the fact that the average rate of saving through bank deposits has gone down but the investment in government financial instruments has increased significantly. The amount invested in Prize Bonds increased from Rs. 24.8 billion in 1990 to Rs. 44.70 billion in 1995. The amount invested in Special Saving Certificates increased from Rs. 7 billion in 1990 to Rs. 76.90 billion in 1995. This was in excess of savings, at current rates, from the official GDP.

As long as proceeds from criminal activity can be legitimised and eventually used in the regular economy, it is difficult to prevent a web of complicity from developing in civil society in order to protect criminal activity, corruption and organised crime. The nature of such activity, and the severity of transgressions, may vary from society to society and economy to economy. The bulk of earnings from criminal activity continue to come from the drug trade,[10] manipulation of regulations, illegitimately acquired bank loans and advances, commissions on government deals and public works. In Pakistan, there was a sudden drying up of easy money in July 1996, when the incumbent government began to look shaky.[11] Purveyors of luxury goods and services reported poor sales and said that their clients had left the country. However, the drug trade, the second largest generator of wealth in the world, was not affected.

In the United States alone, the proceeds from annual sales of illegal hard drugs are in the range of 80 to 120 billion dollars. Hard drugs began to be sold openly in Pakistan during the 1980s. Money from the drug trade is known to have financed large enterprises and successful political campaigns that have put legislators sympathetic to the trade in positions of power. Recent reports confirm that entire areas and specific routes are protected by influentials well known to law enforcement agencies. Many fortunes were made during the 1980s, distorting moral and social values and the cultural mores of stable, traditional society. This has led to a severe backlash in the form of Islamic conservatism in the middle classes who reject exhibitionism and conspicuous consumption. There is a need to examine the background, the systematic rise to power, the emotional forces, the lack of a sense of intrinsic selfworth, that has resulted in pathological greed in those who became the ruling cadres in many developing countries, including Pakistan, after de-colonisation, and destroyed their economies.

The informal parallel economy gives rise to a number of problems. These problems must be recognised as off shoots of the informal economy before they can be appropriately dealt with. There is a vast difference between the problems that arise as a consequence of legitimate business activity and the problems that arise as a consequence of the conduct of illegal, informal transactions. The relationship between the citizen and the informal sector, between local business and the informal sector and government and the informal illegal sector, is totally different from the relationship between the citizen, business, government and the official economy.

The actors in the former are different and have a different life style and *modus operandi*. The rewards and rate of return that accrue to each sector are different. The returns on investment in the parallel economy are staggering. That was why private investment companies, that had asked the public to invest in them, were able to offer a 50 per cent return over a six-month period only to vanish with the invested funds within six months to a year. Thousands, who did not understand that such high rates of return could only come through criminal activity, removed their savings from legitimate savings accounts and business enterprises to invest in these companies and later, the cooperatives. Very few frauds have been brought to book so far although some investors have been recompensed through the sale of the seized property of some companies and cooperatives.[12] The power of the hidden, or informal economy to influence and distort legitimate business activity should not be underestimated.

In Pakistan, the power of the underworld and the informal sector, which may operate through legitimate business concerns, either parallels or, in a number of spheres, exceeds the clout of the legitimate political and economic sectors. The notion that respectability and a clean reputation are becoming rare, and consequently more valuable and desirable than power and clout, does not appear to apply to the business community in Pakistan. Examples of the successful operation of shady enterprises abound. The fact that the informal sector is now successfully subverting the very systems that are supposed to keep it in check is common knowledge. It is also common knowledge that the informal economy plays an active role in pushing through policies that promote and protect its activities. Its largesse knows no bounds when interests have to be protected and policy makers are hungry.

Contrary to popular belief, the informal economy is not of recent origin; at the time of partition, trucks were hired to bring Muslim refugees from East Punjab to Pakistan. While men, women and children were being slaughtered like animals, contractors used these trucks to bring animal hides to Lahore, instead of refugees.[13] The perpetrators of this crime made a fortune, got away scot free in the confusion of the moment and later became politicians. Another lucrative enterprise at that time was the filing of false claims for property left behind in what had become Indian territory. Many princes were born in the period immediately after the partition of the subcontinent. Methods of legitimising ill-gotten gains were already in place long before Dr Haq's 'whitener bonds' as National Saving Certificates were called.

The scramble for wealth and power in Pakistan, after partition and the assassination of Liaquat Ali Khan, was given a new twist through the introduction of women with cosmopolitan tastes, in the political life of the country. When rewarded and pleased they could be trusted to put in a good word where, and when, required.[14] They introduced many of their own ilk into Pakistani society. Until the 1970s, this remained the accepted method of influencing government policy.

During the late 1960s and 1970s, defence procurement entered the picture in a big way. The stakes were high but the criminal element did not enter the picture in a big way until just before the Afghan War. Earlier, smuggling through the Afghan transit trade route was confined to the Northern areas and in 1964-1965 there was even a proposal that a free trade zone be established in the North of Pakistan since the tribals had no other source of income.[15] The reasoning was that it would be better to allow them to trade legitimately rather than declare them all criminals.

Between 1977-1979, in a bind due to the cutting off of US assistance, the government is believed to have made a number of pacts with the devil. Prominent underworld figures of those times were given amnesty for gun running and other services. Many disappeared from the scene thereafter but, apparently, still reside in Pakistan.[16] Many Pakistanis who were serving the government at that time, are fiercely protective when the names of these people are mentioned. It is common knowledge that some government agencies, within every country, are considered above the law and may do anything and permit anything they deem necessary if they consider it to be in the interest of the State. Unfortunately, some elements within such agencies, work in their own interest and that is when such discretionary power becomes dangerous for the public as well as the State.

The Afghan War made Pakistan rich in all kinds of deviant activities that allowed its economy to drift while the influx of arms, money and relief goods for refugees made a select coterie rich through the spillover of assistance. The spillover was deliberately arranged to enrich a number of families who would later be used in the political arena.[17] This was the stage at which Western secret service agencies were operating freely through the BCCI (Bank of Credit and Commerce International). Drug refining techniques were introduced into the Northern areas and these refined drugs became freely available inside the country en route to foreign destinations. Earlier governments had declared that as long as drugs did not circulate in Pakistan, they did not care where they went. The new government was not so scrupulous and as a consequence there are now at least four million known drug addicts in Pakistan.

While the rapid expansion of the informal economy cannot be laid entirely at the door of the managers of the Afghan War and Afghan transit trade, a number of practices originated as a consequence of the thinking that emerged at that time: too many short cuts were approved and malpractices were ignored since the government appeared to have accepted the idea that some kind of undeclared emergency existed. Direct foreign assistance to non-governmental organisations in Pakistan was permitted for the first time. A blind eye was turned towards the streams of illegal immigrants, who came not only to the North from Arab countries but also to Sindh and Punjab from Bangladesh, Burma and elsewhere, and were absorbed into the underworld.[18] Economic policies that created local shortages of various commodities were a boon for traders with vested interests.

An example of poor regulatory practice from the 1990s is the Pakistan government's policy of heavy taxation of locally produced tyres which led to smuggling of all kinds of tyres. Smuggling filled 76 per cent of the local demand for tyres and led to a loss of tax revenue of about Rs. 650 million during 1993-1994. Heavy excise duty and sales tax on local manufactures discouraged investment in the industry.[19] This is one of the markets in Pakistan that the parallel economy has successfully cornered. Similarly, the dumping of silk cloth in Pakistan by foreign countries has made the smuggled silk cheaper than local cotton. According to the Pakistan Silk and Rayon Mills Association, raw material supplied by local yarn manufacturers is both costly and sub-standard and therefore competitive material can no longer be produced in the country.[20]

At another level, a niche in the informal sector has been created by the tradition of presenting a two line defence budget to parliament on national security grounds. On national security grounds, defence procurement enjoys fairly comprehensive immunity from accountability. This encourages financial irregularity. Just about every other retired army officer with access to defence procurement cadres is a commission agent for foreign arms manufacturers. As a result, indigenous defence production has been discouraged and the local production of arms and weaponry is generally considered an unfeasible, eccentric idea. The list of domestic markets cornered by the parallel economy in Pakistan is endless. It is interesting that the government's economic policy appears custom made to perpetuate the situation.

The stagnation of the economy and the presence of powerful criminal elements in the business culture of the country perpetuate an environment in which there is poverty, unemployment and disinterest in legitimate business. As a result, the economic opportunities available for the majority of the population are limited and large numbers are marginalized. Such marginalized elements are a source of recruits for militant organizations promising social and political change.

REFERENCES

1. Elgin, Peter. 'Corruption in a Globalized World.' *SAIS Review* Vol. 22, No. 1. Winter/Spring 2002: pp. 45-59.
2. *The Financial Times (London)* Reuters. 27 April 2002.
3. *The Pakistan Times (Rawalpindi)*. 25 April 1954.
4. *CIDA. Audit Report on Non-Government Organizations Coordination Council (NGO-CC) for Population Welfare.* 15 December 1989.
5. Scott, Bruce R. 'The Great Divide in The Global Village' *Foreign Affairs*. January/February 2001: pp. 160-170.
6. *The Economist.* 'Business and Personal Classified Advertisements'. 2-8 November 2002: pp. 94-95.
7. *International Herald Tribune.* 'Classified Advertisement Section': *High Life* (British Airways inflight magazine). 'Classified Advertisements': *The Economist*. 'Classified. Advertisements Section'. Ibid., 6 and 7 above.
8. Ibid., 6 and 7 above.
9. National Saving Scheme. State Bank of Pakistan.
10. Brzezinski, Mathew. 'Re-engineering the Drug Business' *New York Times Magazine* 23 June 2002: pp. 24-29, 46, 54-55.
11. 'City Page/Special Report'. *The Nation*. 24 July 1996
12. 'Special Report'. *The Nation*. 20 February 2002.
13. Shah, Col (Retd.) Sultan Ali. Conversation with the Author. 8 September 1965. see Appendix; Mahbubal Haq, economist, a (former) Finance minister of Pakistan.
14. See Appendix for further details about the foreign wives of Pakistan's Heads of State and government.
15. 'Editorial.' *The Khyber Mail*. 5 October 1966.
16. 'Special Report'. *The Pakistan Times* (APP). 18 August 1979.
17. 'Special Report'. *Nawai Waqt* (Lahore) 15 June 1987: *The Muslim* (Islamabad) PPI. 27 June 1994.
18. *Jang* (Karachi). APP. 24 September 1994.
19. 'Special Report'. *The Muslim*. 20 June 1994.
20. Ayaz, Babur. 'Smuggled Goods Worth Rs. 100 billion Cause Rs. 50 billion Loss in Government Revenues'. *The News (Business Review)*. 19 March 1994.

14

WEBS OF CORRUPTION

The globalisation of business and commerce,[1] as well as the privatisation of state enterprises in many parts of the world, has led to transactions between corporations and financial institutions in industrialised countries and their counterparts in the private and public sector in developing countries like Pakistan. Foreign investment in power projects in Pakistan was given government guarantees on returns over a period of time. Such investors, generally referred to as Independent Power Producers (IPP), were given a captive market: the entire electricity-using population of the country, as well as a ready-made distribution network. When the deals were being struck, questions were raised about the ability of local consumers to pay for such expensive electric power and the ability of domestic industry to achieve and sustain levels of growth that would allow it to do the same—government projections did not appear to be realistic. Planners and analysts were surprised at the kinds of concessions being provided to foreign investors. It is, therefore, not surprising that allegations of kickbacks and commissions surfaced and were subsequently investigated.[2]

Rising levels of foreign direct investment worldwide have seen corruption emerge as a global practice subverting integrity systems and sound business practice across the globe. Many industrialised countries and their institutions rationalise doubtful business practices and advise dealing with them on a case by case basis: a UK Minister for Trade and Industry once remarked that kickbacks are illegal in the United Kingdom and businessmen would not dream of resorting to such practices at home but there are parts of the world where kickbacks are standard practice for them. Dr Mahathir Mohammed, then Prime Minister of Malaysia, was deeply offended by these remarks and protested against them.[3] With limited success, a number of organisations in different parts of the world have initiated steps to control corruption among those over whom they can exert some influence.

The International Chamber of Commerce is working to revive its Code of Conduct by encouraging compliance. The Council of Europe plans to evolve an anti-corruption convention that will be binding on its members. The Organization for Economic Cooperation and Development recommended that member states take a serious view of the practice of bribing foreign officials by the nationals of member states. At a Summit of the Americas, thirty-five heads of government of Western industrialised countries launched a regional plan to combat a high degree of corruption. In Africa, a regional group was established in late 1994 to monitor and contain corruption.[4]

The World Bank (WB), the International Monetary Fund (IMF) and bilateral assistance agencies have been supporting initiatives to curb corruption in the economic development programs that they are financing. These attempts to curb corruption are relatively new developments that have emerged after the end of the Cold War. Prior to that, such agencies could not have cared less about corruption. The decisions of such development assistance agencies were known to be as political as they were economic and 80 per cent of their activity was geared towards information gathering and influencing decision-making. The control of fraud and corruption was confined to fulfilling the mandatory requirements of regulatory and audit agencies and covering their own employee's activities. After the formal end of the Cold War, development assistance was replaced by the slogan, 'trade not aid'.[5] International business became another instrument of foreign policy in countries previously covered by development assistance agencies that were transacting directly with political elements in recipient countries.

The field offices of international, multilateral and bilateral development assistance agencies and financial institutions had always been notorious for not just looking the other way when local authorities manipulated programs to benefit specific elite groups and satellites in a position to influence political decisions, they were also known to partake of payoffs to such groups in a variety of ways. The conflict of interest clause in the regulations of bilateral, multilateral and international agencies is easily manipulated. Some national professionals who proved to be useful to such organisations over the years were accommodated at their head offices. They did not really need to struggle with national realities and such employment opportunities came their way during the performance of national service. Since equally efficient and qualified government officials were not picked up when they were, there will always be a question about the real reason for their selection for lucrative appointments with the foreign agencies they had dealt with during their tenure with the government.

Many different forms and levels of corruption exist, but just a few have captured the attention of international agencies, the media and the public. It is questionable whether corruption can be dealt with selectively for many activities are interdependent: corruption in business feeds on corruption in government and administration, which in turn, supports social and moral corruption that distorts the fabric of society by promoting questionable values. Corruption at the highest executive level undermines trust in political institutions and public servants[6] while the misuse of public office undermines confidence in the democratic processes that lead to the delegation of authority to elected representatives of the public.

Corruption has been so lucrative for ruling elites in developing countries that to decry moral, political, economic or administrative corruption is generally considered unrealistic and an admission of powerlessness. In Pakistan, the rot began to spread through all national institutions during the 1960s when commissions on defence procurement deals became standard practice and they enriched members of both the civil and military establishments dealing with suppliers. At the time, the President of Pakistan is reported to have said that all those who had not acquired wealth during his tenure were 'fools'. He was not talking about businessmen but public servants. Many of the silver spoons that second and third generation Pakistanis claim to have been born with, were acquired through corrupt practice during that period and thereafter. Over the years, corruption has been institutionalised, creating well known dual compensation systems: public servants hired and assigned by government to perform certain jobs routinely expect and demand additional payment from the public for performing those tasks.[7]

There are many forms of corruption, covering the entire range of human activity. In its various manifestations, corruption has not just crippled the administration but it has also put a stop to productive activity and destroyed public confidence in democratic institutions. It has destroyed the moral base of social transactions and given rise to new criteria for measuring human worth and dignity while simultaneously creating intense resentment amongst those who have few opportunities for upward mobility. At the institutional level, there is some confusion about what is permissible and what lies beyond the pale of correct business practice. As a result, there is a tendency to rationalise and condone sharp practice.

The products of such rationalisation are instruments such as government 'whitener' bonds[8] and the retrospective registration of smuggled vehicles,[9] which signal that the manner in which wealth is acquired is not important but the fact of possessing it is. This undermines the very concept of accountability and proper business conduct. Accountability is based on the assumption that certain types of transactions, methods of conducting business and unfair business practices are illegal even if they are productive and yield profit to some, or all, parties involved. For instance, international trafficking[10] in prohibited drugs and substances has occasionally been rationalised on the supply and demand principle. That does not make it acceptable business. Most civilised countries legislate against certain drugs and substances that are harmful to life and society and subject to misuse if their sale and purchase is left unregulated. Propriety in business does not refer to some kind of unrealistic, archaic value system that cannot be applied in practical life. It is merely a way of ensuring that the interests of all parties in a business transaction are protected.

Official agencies that seek to reclaim national wealth from the corrupt continue to be ineffective because new rationalizations for corruption emerge with the rise and fall of governments and the institutions that control them. The task of such anti-corruption agencies is further complicated when such wealth has been transferred abroad. The work of anti-corruption agencies has been complicated by the globalisation of economic systems, the promotion of free market principles that may disguise sharp practice and modern information technology, which facilitates international financial transactions. Each successive government expects to investigate the previous one but turns a blind eye to the activities of its own establishment.[11] The mechanisms for conducting inquiries, processing complaints as well as prosecuting those against whom there is proof of corruption, may need to be further streamlined in order to deal with charges of witch hunting. Reform after public debate is necessary in order to remove loopholes in systems of governance at all levels. During 1998, in Pakistan, public representatives were reluctant to allow a debate on allegations that the rates the previous government had negotiated with International Power Producers were too high. The management of International Power Producers said, more or less, that this was an example of the manner in which national governments milk foreign direct investment and international transactions that are up for investigation.[12]

The globalisation of business and commerce, as well as the privatisation of state enterprises in many parts of the world, has led to transactions between corporations and financial institutions in industrialised countries and their counterparts in the private and public sector in developing countries like Pakistan. In this *laissez faire* environment, foreign capital will go to great lengths to get a foothold in new markets.[13] French law does not forbid various forms of bribery as a means of securing business, British law is silent on the subject but under United States law, companies offering bribes to secure business, both at home and abroad, are subject to prosecution. This puts the French and the British at an advantage vis-à-vis American business, if they actually toe the line. On behalf of the US government, a senior US State Department official urged support for an international treaty outlawing bribery of foreign officials by transnational companies (26 November 1998). At the same time, in order to secure lucrative deals and political advantages, new methods were being used to pay off corrupt civil and military officials and political decision makers in some of the poorest countries of the world.

The US government is faced with allegations of bribery affecting international contracts worth almost US$30 billion by foreign firms, which are not bound by anti-bribery laws in their home jurisdiction. On the other hand, under the US Foreign Corrupt Practises Act, all US firms are criminally barred from participating in the bribery of foreign government officials in international transactions making corruption an impediment to the American business abroad. Pakistan's Agosta submarine deal with France caused a great deal of heart burning both at home and abroad. It is significant that three middlemen in uniform in Pakistan were identified, tried, convicted of bribery, sentenced and immediately pardoned, while those who were reported to have taken the lion's share in commissions, were not even formally charged. This raises serious doubts about the fairness and effectiveness of the 'Ehtasaab' or accountability, process in Pakistan.

The United States government, the super power in world affairs, which has a controlling interest in multilateral financial institutions that dripfeed weak economies, is uniquely positioned to secure advantageous deals for its business constituency. One of the more convenient ways to do this is to get in on the decision making process in other countries. During the tenure of the military government 1999-2002, this has been done through foreign consultants and special assignees, who were funded by multilateral and international agencies in many cases, and assigned to practically every government department. A case in point was the appointment of an expensive Chairman, Central Board of Revenue who was supposed to out-perform all previous Chairmen in revenue collection besides reorganising the department itself. After a reshuffle of finance departments, he was quietly allowed to leave. But not before the government had spent tens of millions on him.

Foreign consultants, usually funded with development assistance monies, are sitting in Pakistani banks that do not have any funds to work with, in airlines that do not have any aircraft to fly and government offices that do not have any function, or work, to perform. The water supply to Rawalpindi is being put in place by a Japanese firm as if local engineers could not do the job, and another group of foreign consultants has been working in the city with the Board of Secondary Education, as if there were no educationists in the country. Some foreign consultants are working on sewerage projects in Lahore and Karachi. Then there is the deserted Lahore-Islamabad motorway, which sent a major portion of the government's ready cash to South Korea immediately after the Pakistan Muslim League (Nawaz) government came to power. Now law enforcement and deweaponising has also been passed on to foreign consultants. Balochi fishermen were told to surrender their fishing rights to foreign commercial fishing contractors and the strategic Balochi coastline contiguous with the Gulf was given to Forbes, an American group, which was to give 10 per cent of proceeds from business to the federal government but nothing at all to the provincial government, thus disinheriting the local population, which will watch activity in their area without participating in it: an intolerable situation. The terms were not revealed to the provincial government when the agreement was being negotiated.

Naturally the foreign consultants who are in place may be expected to decide how existing and expected future resources should be utilised. They will be watching their own interest while doing so, but they are certainly not in a position to judge, or set, national priorities. Thus the practise introduced by the previous governments has been taken a step forward: the Pakistan People's Party government gained notoriety for appointing consultants from among the party faithful and not according to need or merit. In response to a question by a PML-N member, the National Assembly was informed on 21 June 1995 that the government had appointed twenty-eight individuals as consultants to various government Ministries, departments, and autonomous bodies, including banks. Out of these, twenty-one were assigned government grades, six were on fixed salaries and one was on a special contract. The military government that took over in 1999 broke all previous records in Pakistan by hiring consultants through non-governmental organizations that are receiving funds for their fees from foreign agencies. These consultants have been placed in key government departments to oversee reform processes. Foreign consultants are also at work reforming the government of Pakistan and representative national institutions. It is not possible for such inputs to produce people friendly policies and clean government. It is sad but true that this is where corruption pays best and flourishes most. The injustice and oppression that is a part of such systems breeds unrest and dissatisfaction, thereby sowing the seeds of revolution.

According to estimates[15] provided by international financial institutions, about US$500 billion in proceeds from criminal activity find their way into legitimate businesses around the world annually. This provides criminals with the wherewithal to maintain luxurious lifestyles in the most exclusive surroundings. The business of money laundering is growing at the healthy rate of ten per cent each year and is set to become the single largest economic activity in the world within the next decade or so. Intermediaries conduct multiple transactions with money acquired through illegal or criminal activity in order to disguise the origin of funds. Those performing this service used to charge a commission of about 5 per cent to do the job. Now that a number of countries are investigating suspicious multiple transactions, the standard commission has risen to 15-20 per cent of the total amount handled.

It is likely that instead of helping the economy of developing countries, the investment of funds of dubious origin will expose them to criminal activity they are not equipped to deal with. It will also weaken the economy in the long run: criminals are not likely to make a commitment to further the economic interests of any particular country. Capital investment through stock markets has also been used to introduce black money into the formal economies. In 1996, Pakistan's Corporate Law Authority confiscated irregular applications for the shares of new companies and confiscated millions in funds that were never reclaimed.

As long as proceeds from criminal activity can be legitimised and eventually used in the regular economy, it is difficult to prevent a web of complicity from evolving to protect criminal activity, corruption and organised crime in civil society. The nature of such activity and the severity of transgressions may vary from society to society and economy to economy and time to time. The bulk of earnings from criminal activity continue to come from the drug trade. Links between drug dealing and instances of international terrorism are suspected but have yet to be substantiated. In the United States alone, annual drug sales are in the range of 80 to 120 billion dollars.

Hard drugs began to be sold openly in Pakistan during the 1980s. Heaps of drugs of various qualities are piled before roadside shops in the tribal belt along the Afghan-Pakistan border, much like spices and condiments are in the settled areas of the country. After the fall of the Taliban, who had imposed severe penalties on poppy growers and reduced the area under cultivation substantially, Afghans are growing poppy again. There was a substantial increase in the movement of drugs from the area again in 2003. Money from the drug trade is known to have financed large enterprises and successful political campaigns that have put legislators sympathetic to the trade in positions of power.

The illegal arms trade which provides weaponry to terrorists and sub-national guerrilla organisations is another source of large sums of black money. Such money has also financed conflict and has also been used to stall peace-making to ensure that arms sales remain brisk. After the disintegration of the Soviet Union, both weapons and radioactive material from government stocks became available in the black market.[16] Bribes, graft, kickbacks, so-called commissions, systematic siphoning of government funds through mismanagement, are other sources of black money. Another source is organised crime that may deal in anything from prostitution, smuggling, counterfeit currency to extortion and terrorism.

Regardless of knowledge that criminal activity is introducing large amounts of funds into the economy, there continues to be some ambivalence about the wisdom of enacting legislation at the national and international level to control money laundering. It is feared that rigorous supervision of financial transactions may not be compatible with economic liberalisation that is being promoted by the International

Monetary Fund (IMF) and the World Bank (WB). Commercial banks assert that if serious measures are taken to report substantial transactions, as they are in the United States, valuable customers may go to competitors. Civil rights groups are concerned about privacy. When Germany set about putting in place a series of tough measures to fight organised crime, money laundering and corruption in June 1996, civil rights activists protested that certain measures, such as bugging the homes of suspects, would be an infringement of individual liberty guaranteed by the German constitution.

Since the methods of slipping funds acquired through criminal activity into the official economy are within the knowledge of employees of financial institutions and corporations, there is no reason why the primary responsibility for reporting suspicious transactions should not be placed on them. This will need to be done through appropriate legislation. The basic principles adopted by a committee on banking regulations and supervisory practices instituted in December 1988, identified four areas in which banks and other financial institutions such as DFIs[18] could be prevented from participating in money laundering. These included effective customer identification, strict compliance with the law, adherence to stated rules of business with which all employees of financial institutions should be familiar and cooperation with law enforcement agencies. Efforts being made to deal with the problem at the international level have not been very successful but they forced organised crime to use more sophisticated money laundering techniques. Funds have now begun to move into the global financial market in a big way through legitimate 'front' businesses. This is also how money used to finance militant groups and terrorist activity moves across international borders. Aware of the problem, financial officers from forty Commonwealth countries have prepared recommendations that have been considered by the Finance Ministers of the Commonwealth. Strengthening of regional cooperation in tracking and monitoring money laundering is necessary in order to fight the criminal activity from which it flows, as well as the criminal activity it can finance.[19] Since they must remain hidden, terrorist resource bases are part of this underworld of international finance.

REFERENCES

1. Elgin, Peter. 'Corruption in a Globalized World.' *SAIS Review*, Vol. 22, No. 1, Winter/Spring 2002: pp. 50-53.
2. 'Special Report'. *The Nation*. 21 July 1995.
3. Dr. Mahathir Mohammed. *The News* (Reuters). October 1995.
4. Ibid., see 1, above.
5. Prahalad, C.K. and Allen Hammond. 'Serving the World's Poor Profitably'. *Harvard Business Review*. September 2002: pp. 48-57.
6. 'Statement on the establishment of the Ehtasaab (Accountability) Bureau'. *Pakistan Muslim League, Nawaz Sharif group* 1997: 'Statement on the establishment of the National Accountability Bureau'. *Government of Pakistan*. 1999.
7. 'Special Report' *The Nation*. 18 September 1998.
8. *The News* (AFP). 20 November 1998: Diamond, Larry. 'Democracy and Economic Reform: Tensions, Compatibilities and Strategies of Reconciliation' ed. Edward Lazear. *Economic Transition in Europe and Russia: Realities of Reform*. Stanford CA. Hoover Institution Press. 1995: pp. 107-158.
9. 'Statement'. Pakistan Muslim League-Nawaz Sharif Group: 'Corruption Ranking'. *Transparency International*. Washington DC. 21 October 1999.
10. *The Nation* (APP). 28 March 2001.
11. *Annual Development Plan 2000-2001*. The Planning Commission,: 'Minutes of the weekly meeting'. *ECNEC*. Ministry of Finance, Government of Pakistan. Islamabad. 7 May 2001.
12. 'The price per unit of electricity'. Water and Power Development Authority (WAPDA). *The News*. 15 August 2001.
13. 'Agosta submarine deal'. *The Nation* (Lahore). September 2001.
14. Ibid., see 7 above.
15. 'Report'. *The Nation* (Lahore). November 2002: 15 June 2003. See Appendix for details of alleged corruption by holders of public office in Pakistan.
16. Ibid., see 1 above, see 7 above.
17. Collins, Tom Z. and Jon B. Wolfsthal. 'Nuclear Terrorism and Warhead Control in Russia'. *Arms Control Today* Vol. 32, No. 3. April 2002: pp. 15-19.
18. Development Finance Institutions.
19. Diamond, Larry. *Promoting Democracy in the 1990's—Actors and Instruments, Issues and Imperatives*. Report to the Carnegie Commission on Preventing Deadly Conflict. Carnegie Corporation: New York. December 1995.

15

GREAT DEVELOPMENT GAMES

Until the early 1990s, discussion about the interdependent nature of politics and economic development was frowned upon. Consultants from the World Bank, Harvard and elsewhere, considered it a dangerous transgression by unorthodox, ill-educated dabblers in economic analysis. Although economic theory and politico-economic concepts have changed as a result of experience, consultants with a traditional approach still dominate conferences set up by Pakistan's numerous private and official institutes for the study of economic and political issues. They were always ruthless in suppressing those who dared examine the relationship between the two at the national and international level. It was thought that this would imply that concessionary development assistance was tied to the political objectives of the major shareholders of multilateral financial institutions (MFIs).[1] Those economists, who raised the question of such interdependence, were treading on the turf of power brokers whose activities were protected by both the aid giving countries and agencies as well as the recipients of development assistance.

In Western intellectual circles, it was no secret that the covert politicisation of all kinds of international development activity began at the very outset, after the Second World War, when the Marshall Plan sought to put the war battered countries of Europe on their feet so that they could combat communism on the European continent. A while later bilateral and multilateral assistance was extended to other parts of the globe. In 1952 it arrived in the fledgling Pakistan.[2] The political objectives of the international community, including the desire of various countries to establish a political presence and obtain access to policy level bureaucracy, were curbed by nationalist elements, even in countries like Pakistan. Negotiations between donors and the government remained confined to the upper echelon of national policy makers and senior representatives of bilateral development agencies for a period. These activities were largely benevolent during the 1950s although they were dominated by the domestic compulsions of aid givers even then: grain and cereals brought in from the United States were dumped into the Arabian Sea. They were exported by the United States government in order to appease American farmers and charged to Pakistan's PL-480 account. Some veterans of the Marshall Plan who came to Asia at that time had scruples, even if they did not have the expertise to benefit the region they were entering. Assistance and relief supplies were provided from time to time. Such supplies often consisted of low-grade commodities and expired foodstuff unfit for human consumption. During the early 1970s, a shipment of American biscuits to be distributed to flood victims through a UN agency were found to be full of weevils and unfit for human consumption: however the only official report published in the country about the matter merely states that relief supplies had been received by Pakistan.

Assistance provided for institution building was critical in more ways than one: it allowed for the vetting of government servants and scholars. Those known to have independent and nationalist views were ignored for selection to higher echelons in government departments. Those who were compliant and ready to follow the guidelines provided by assistance agencies were placed in key positions in institutions such as the Pakistan Institute of Development Economics (PIDE) that was supposed to provide background research for economic planning. It is only recently that such institutes in the field of economics and agriculture have been exposed to indigenous, as well as Asian and South American research. This has helped liberate both their Boards of Governors and their mindset.[3] Earlier, all such institutions were staffed by American scholars working under various quid pro quo schemes of the US government and private foundations. Pliant educated men and women, from a certain background, were targeted for cultural and special leadership through exchange programs that exposed them to Western thinking and often served to cut them off from their roots. In other cases, these programs served as a discreet joyride provided to oblige those already in leadership positions. A list of names of political leaders, former ministers and ambassadors who participated in such exchanges makes interesting reading. It is an illustration of how systematically foreign assistance in every sphere of activity, from economics to education to healthcare has been made available by foreigners to those who were selected for leadership positions in Pakistan.[4]

Foreign experts and consultants, employed by the government under various bilateral assistance arrangements with a technical assistance component, had access to government documents and all research material produced in the institutes to which they were assigned. They would pinpoint a few personnel and help 'the chosen few' develop their theses as well as their careers. They even assisted in the write up of final documents presented to the boards of the institutes and at critical government meetings. This two-pronged effort saw to it that key academics and those who approved of development policies being promoted by bilateral and multilateral agencies, including the World Bank, filled government policy positions.[5] Such personnel were provided with lucrative scholarships, and towards the end of their careers, with employment opportunities with the multilateral agencies themselves. A cadre of people who did not owe their security and prosperity to their own country was thus created in Pakistan. In the presence of such a cadre, it was not surprising that the World Bank was able to issue reports that increased bitterness between East and West Pakistan during the 1970s over the utilisation of resources, instead of presenting the government with workable and creative alternatives that would vitiate bitterness.[6]

During the 1980s, the emphasis by both multilateral and bilateral concessionary aid-giving agencies shifted from the provision of assistance for development programmes to the provision of assistance conditional on structural adjustments in fiscal and development programmes. The scope for interference in policy making increased enormously. At about the same time, two long term (6-15 years) programmes with enormous potential for influencing policy formulation and decision making were devised. One program was designed to provide both short and long-term higher education to serving government officials in Pakistan, provided they could supply the US government with a certificate from their supervisors stating they would be promoted on their return from their stint in the United States. This letter of assurance was not listed on any application form as a requirement, but it was what guaranteed a scholarship. Thousands of government servants in key positions today sport degrees they acquired in this way. Most have acquired degrees in subjects that are of little practical use in service.

The second scheme was more audacious. It sought to establish a direct link between the district administration of the government of Pakistan and bilateral and multilateral development aid agencies. Under this scheme, it was proposed that aid would go directly from the agency to the commissioner or deputy commissioner of a district, depending on the assessment of the aid giving agency as to who, and which area, 'deserved or needed' it most.[7] The needs assessment would come from the aid-giving agency. The aid-giving agency would, in effect, become the overlord of what is generally called the 'lord' of the district in Pakistan. This scheme was rejected by the government despite great pressure from foreign agencies.

Subsequently, a modified scheme was developed, introduced and accepted, albeit reluctantly. This scheme released all aid agencies from the formality of giving funds to non-governmental organisations (NGOs) through the Economic Affairs Division (EAD) of the government of Pakistan. Since the EAD generally did not refuse to allow the transfer of funds to bona fide NGOs that bilateral and multilateral agencies were keen on, the real need for such a move remained obscure until after the government approved it: a variety of new NGOs emerged overnight and were awarded substantial funds as direct grants.[8] This direct link between foreign governments and local non-governmental agencies, often run by the relatives of prominent citizens was invaluable for information gathering and infiltration. A number of NGOs deny that they accepted either local, or foreign, official assistance, but they did receive substantial amounts for various activities.[9] In a number of cases the funds were not subject to usual audit.

All this was done in the name of development, the uplift of the poor and the downtrodden including women and children. Someone has rightly said that some work has been done at enormous cost, as a front for the utilisation of large sums by organisers. There should be no confusion about the role of local NGOs in development: they are the trusted eyes and ears of the agencies that pay them. A number of organisations of good repute, such as the Edhi Foundation tend to avoid foreign assistance and prefer local, voluntary funding.

Given this brief history of the evolution of the methodology of disbursement of development assistance in Pakistan, it is not surprising that the last Pakistan People's Party government hit upon the idea of using more or less the same techniques that foreign agencies use in order to extend its own political base through the Social Action Programme. Through the District Social Action Boards constituted under the People's Programme, the PPP government supplied funds to its nominees, who were either elected or non-elected representatives of the party. These representatives were provided with discretionary funds, in addition to development funds that were made available to legislators so that they may provide facilities and basic services to their own constituents. This was done regardless of whether such funds were urgently required for other purposes in other areas. In many cases, this violated the terms of reference under which assistance was provided for various social uplift programs by the World Bank and the Asian Development Bank. Both institutions regularly evaluate the utilisation of development assistance, and from time to time, demand the return of funds used for purposes not authorised under agreements signed with the government.

In such situations, the real sufferers are the people, ordinary citizens who ultimately carry the burden of all development debt without being the beneficiaries of assistance activity. For the people of Pakistan, the real crunch will come when local government schemes are actually implemented: plans have included the installation of governors and mayors, referred to as 'nazims' (administrators) under the latest local government scheme, who are bound to have political interests to protect. In the past, Mohallah (neighbourhood) committees and officially nominated Imams installed in neighbourhood mosques have created problems for those who were apolitical.[10] In such an environment, it is local criminals who become active, making mosques their headquarters. There is little or no supervision or monitoring of such activities by the district administration; once political elements are involved in the development process, the nexus between criminals and political elements becomes institutionalised at the local level. As a result, the weakest sections of society are marginalized in much the same way that states with weak economies are marginalized, at the global level.

The crisis of marginalisation of states within the global economy, and entire sections of the population within states, cannot be considered a purely economic one. There is a political basis for this crisis and there are political implications for the future. It is, therefore, understandable that the response to such marginalization is also political. Both domestic and international political forces are shaping the future of national economies. In a dialogue that took place in May 1997, George Soros, whose Quantum Fund[11] has the best performance record of any investment fund over a period of twenty five years and who was accused of manipulating Malaysia's currency market thereby leading to the collapse of its booming economy, admitted

'...What global competition has done has been to benefit capital at the expense of labour and to benefit financial capital to the detriment of fixed investments...financial capital is the most mobile of all, more mobile than direct investment...' The balance of power within and between regions and states alters as a result of economic adjustment and change. Changes in the status quo have an impact on strategic interests. Attempts to 'correct' such trends are seen in the form of the currency crisis created in East Asia, particularly Malaysia, and the destruction of the environment in Indonesia, which affected the environment of the entire region. It would be naive to assume that national governments and their advisors are not aware of the implications of global policies that have contributed to impoverishing their economies.

There is no doubt that entire regions, as well as states within regions and cross-sections of society within states, are being marginalised as a result of globalisation and deregulation regimes that have made it mandatory to allow international capital access to national markets.[12] There is also no doubt that as a result of astute leadership and management of external influences, including international credit, trade regimes, policy measures and foreign direct investment, among other things, some states have done better than others. For instance, a number of states have been able to establish people-friendly economic priorities, control corruption and restrict current expenditure to what they can spend without resorting to unnecessary borrowing.

The countries that multinational financial institutions and international trade regulation bodies are dealing with on a regional basis are not all at the same stage of economic development and certainly not at the same stage of social and political development. This would imply that the approach to dealing with problems in one country may not be quite as successful in a neighbouring country. Nevertheless, the relentless march of free enterprise with broad based deregulation continues. This has exhausted the reserves of the middle classes in fragile economies.

Privatisation and integration in the global economy does not mean that government intervention in order to protect national interest at one level, and consumers at another level,[13] is no longer necessary. Where strong consumer protection laws and appropriate associations and watchdogs are not in place, the government should not abdicate its responsibility to watch over the welfare of those who are likely to be marginalized in a market economy. It has also become clear that a number of problems that consumers face are caused as a result of official policy.

The marginalization of entire cadres of workers and entrepreneurs is evident where economies have been suddenly exposed to deregulation under international regimes. The public rightly questions the legitimacy of such programs in view of real as well as perceived, present as well as future, threats to their interests. At this point it is important to review the meaning of the term 'marginalization' in view of its popularity in modern social science terminology: in the context of this chapter, it means the transfer of entire social groups to the fringe of society, rendered superfluous and outside the active economy. This is what happens when the products of small enterprises become redundant as a result of the import of cheaper mass produced goods. The closure of such enterprises makes various categories of labour and entrepreneurs redundant, pushing them towards poverty.[14]

Unemployment is just one form of marginalization. It can create the deepest and most enduring resentment, leading to anti-social and militant reaction. There are millions in countries like Pakistan, with the potential to be productive workers, who cannot find any work at all; there is no market for their skills. For a scholar or research scientist, marginalization could be the withdrawal of opportunities for research, lack of access to information and opportunities to participate in the on-going dialogue on a subject of study. Many developing countries are being subjected to a traumatic era in which their economy has bypassed several stages of economic development to a post industrial scenario. In this scenario patterns of employment and support systems have changed beyond recognition and traditional social guarantees no longer hold. The political and social leadership in countries like Pakistan has failed to design new guarantees.

In order to devise viable alternative guarantees, understanding of the imperatives of the new economic environment, alongwith creativity, enterprise and good management, are required. Privatisation of public enterprises and utilities highlights the problem: large numbers of state employees pass into the hands of the private sector. The private sector watches the bottom line in dealing with staff and customers. Those who do not possess marketable skills are marginalized. Opportunities to acquire such skills are limited and expensive. Those who cannot pay for education are marginalized. Poverty reduction schemes, initiated with foreign assistance and channelled through non-governmental organisations, are not a sustainable alternative. An economy in recession, as a result of its own weaknesses and the impact of the slowing global economy, is not likely to have a market for semi-skilled labour; the products of semi-skilled labour are unlikely to be suitable for an export market. MFI recommendations to reduce subsidies[15] on the meagre social services being provided to less privileged economic groups, such as the proposed introduction of higher fees in government educational institutions in Pakistan and increases in token payment at rudimentary health centres, compounds the misery of the majority.

As the benefits accruing from the state decrease, as affiliations with state institutions are reduced, citizens shift allegiance to powerful new entities controlling resources. These could be national or transnational organisations engaged in legitimate business. They could just as easily be organisations engaged in criminal activity.[16] Such organisations tend to seek out and accommodate marginalized individuals and groups, offering them another kind of security. This gives rise to an entirely new set of social problems for all those who are marginalized and cannot be accommodated in the legitimate economy. Only state entities can be expected to take responsibility for the welfare of all its citizens. The private sector is not interested in servicing marginal communities at the grassroots level and private sector affiliations cannot deliver the same degree of security that the public sector does.

It is common knowledge that privatisation of public utilities and the social sector leads to a rise in prices which has a direct impact on the poorest sections of society. Even when wisely planned and when the long-term prospects are carefully calculated, the short-term impact is disruptive and cannot be ignored. If the private sector cannot create employment opportunities for workers with a variety of skills and government cannot shield small entrepreneurs and agriculturists, who form an important constituency, from the negative impact of privatisation and globalisation, there is likely to be a very small market for its policies. Some governments are seeking a way out by offering a proportion of shares in public enterprises to employees and transferring ownership of small units of state lands to landless peasants. This is a method of privatisation that has been successfully used in some parts of Pakistan recently. There is a need to guard against making it a form of political patronage thereby creating one constituency in a community but alienating another.

REFERENCES

1. Williamson, John. and Stephen Haggard. 'The Political Conditions for Economic Reform'. John Williamson ed. *The Political Economy of Policy Reform*. Institute for International Economics. Washington D.C. 1994: pp. 566-567.

2. Agreement 1952. Government of Pakistan and the US State Department: *Economic Survey 1965-1966*. Planning Commission, Government of Pakistan. 1965.

3. Easterly, William. 'The Cartel of Good Intentions'. *Foreign Policy*, Vol. 131, July/August, 2002: pp. 40-49.

4. 'List of Participants USAID training programme 1984-1994.' *Economic Affairs Division, Ministry of Economic Affairs, Government of Pakistan.*

5. The Harvard Group 1964-1969. *The Planning Commission, Ministry of Finance. Government of Pakistan.*

6. Ibid., 4 above.

7. Legal Advisor. *USAID Pakistan Office*. Economic Affairs Division. Government of Pakistan. 1987-1988.

8. Ibid., 7 above: Editorial. *The Nation*. 26 May 1997.

9. 'USAID NGO Program, 1986-1992'. *Economic Affairs Division, Government of Pakistan.*

10. *The Nation* (APP). 30 May 1997.

11. 'Fraternity Fund Ltd. Newsletter, August 17, 1999'. *Soros Fund Management (SFM)*. 1999.

12. Rosenberg, Tim. 'The Free Trade Fix'. *New York Times Magazine*. 18 August 2002.

13. *The Nation* (APP). 20 November 1997.

14. Scott, Bruce R. 'The Great Divide in the Global Village'. *Foreign Affairs*. January/February, 2001: pp. 163-170: Kritz, Neil J. 'The CSCE in the New Era'. *Journal of Democracy*, Vol. 4 No. 3, July 1993: p. 125-126.

15. Ibid., see 3. above.

16. 'Editorial'. *The Nation*, 26 May 1997.

16

ISSUES OF GLOBAL CHANGE

Profound changes in the international economic and security environment make it imperative that adjustments be made in existing international and multilateral organisations dealing with security, finance and economic matters. An assessment of the impact of such changes on policy decisions should be based on in-depth research. Policies adopted after such an exercise could set the trend for bilateral, regional and multilateral cooperation for several decades to come. Adjustments in the relative power of states across the globe will not be confined to regions now that the global economy is relatively more interdependent than it was in the past. The scope and outreach of a number of organisations dealing with international cooperation in specific fields will need to be extended.[1] These organizations and their offshoots have multiplied to the extent where it is difficult for states with a limited budget to ensure representation even where their vital interests are involved. The viability and raison d'etre of a number of international and multilateral regimes as well as organisations that have proved to be ineffective, or powerless, to prevent deterioration in the areas of activity they cover, requires re-examination. A fundamental and far-reaching development is that it is now difficult to contain conflicts within national borders because the diaspora of combatants in one area may be able to retaliate in another area.

Developments in international relations over the past forty years have shown that states with clear strategic objectives and negotiating skill can retain their sovereignty while deriving benefits from the web of economic and security arrangements that exist worldwide. States with leaders who are unaware of the implications of association and without the will and the skill to manoeuvre, have become so-called failed states. This should encourage the public to take an interest in deliberations on the future of bilateral and multilateral pacts (WTO, CTBT, NPT etc.) in order to influence governments to exercise caution before acquiescing to conditions of association that may not be in their national interest.

The link between economic and security issues is well illustrated by the fact that developments within the North Atlantic Treaty Organisation (NATO) were taking place just as the Treaty on the European Union was being formalised.[2] Turkey initially made active support of NATO dependent on the grant of EU membership: it did not get on the membership list but has behaved, as the international community puts it, 'responsibly' in the face of disappointment. It was compensated thereafter by substantial economic assistance and business from the United States. Turkey has been encouraged to play a more active role in West Asia to counter extremist tendencies there and may, in future, be in a position to associate with the more moderate states in the region in its own derivative of NATO's 'Partnership for Peace' initiative. Turkey is an active member of the International Security Force in Afghanistan, which is moving towards an extension of operations covering the whole of Afghanistan through NATO. This, however, is no guarantee that the guerrilla war that is being fought in Afghanistan will be brought to a conclusion speedily. Militants who are active in the country could shift their base to neighbouring countries. The nuclear potential of Pakistan continues to be an important equaliser in the Middle East and West Asia.

Eleven of the sixteen members of NATO took part in the formalisation of the European Union at which point the idea of a European defence for Europe emerged; the concept was endorsed in the Maastricht Treaty, and within NATO it is known as the 'Common Foreign and Security Policy'.[3] This has led to the activation of the Western European Union (WEU) as the defence arm of the EU. The WEU has been re-activated to take up the task of creating a common defence policy for European states. The WEU has accepted East and Central European countries as associates but without vital security guarantees. Steps have been taken to create policy alternatives in Europe but direct control of WEU forces by the EU will be resisted by a number of states within the European Union itself.

Through NATO, the Europeans are determined to keep the United States involved in the region at the level of presence that the United States expects to maintain in the Pacific. Europe's long term contribution to the organization and NATO'S ability to act as a stabilizing force in the region due to an established command structure and ability to mobilize, are cited as reasons for maintaining NATO while a cautious approach is adopted towards involvement in the WEU. The importance of the US as an influential third party in disputes is evident from European inaction during the Bosnian crisis several years ago, and continuing importance is evident from subsequent requests for intervention and help in the resolution of the Kosovo crisis.

The membership of a large number of international and multilateral organizations has expanded rapidly in the past decade as newly independent states of the former Soviet Union find it advantageous, even necessary, to join up now. Parity membership has not been forthcoming for the weaker states. A number of countries are, nevertheless, keen to join and expect, in the future, to be able to secure more favourable terms of association in established economic, political as well as military alliances, such as NATO. Changes in NATO's mandate will lead to the formalisation of its political initiatives, which, in the final analysis, seek to keep the communists out of power in Russia and the states of the former USSR, and promote the creation of a market based economy there. Political initiatives do not imply the absence of military capability or possibilities of military action.

The initiatives of the fifty-five member Organisation for Security and Cooperation in Europe (OSCE), which works on the basis of consensus, have been well received. The organisation works in the field of preventive diplomacy and crisis resolution. It has been associated with the implementation of the civilian aspects of the Dayton Agreement on Bosnia; the OSCE has provided advice on political institution building to Russia, Hungary and Czechoslovakia and sent mediators to Georgia, the Ukraine and Chechnya. In Eastern and Central Europe, its good offices are sought in preference to the intervention of individual states.

In the Pacific,[4] Japan is keenly aware of the profitability of cooperation with Central Asian states in the exploitation of their oil and gas reserves and has sponsored the membership of a number of them in the Asian Development Bank (ADB). The likelihood of stable, long term security arrangements between these states, as well as Russia and China is bound to lead to pressure on East Asia to abandon the bilateral approach to crisis resolution in the area and convert the Asian Regional Forum (ARF) into a 'hard' bloc with regional security on its agenda. This may lead to a drawing of lines in the region which may not be a healthy development. The creation of an organisation similar to the OSCE in Europe would be a more acceptable alternative.

A number of international and multilateral financial organizations are facing criticism of past performance at every level of operation. The World Trade Organisation (WTO) may have been formally accepted by governments, but it has already attracted criticism for ignoring protectionist measures adopted by the larger economies and the discrimination against weaker economies that is inherent in its policies. Two of the most powerful multilateral financial organizations involved in providing assistance to the weaker economies of the world, the International Monetary Fund (IMF) and the World Bank, are facing criticism of their theories and performance.[5] Their policies have contributed to economic crises worldwide, with many poor countries following their guidelines on the brink of bankruptcy, facing civic unrest and political upheaval. These institutions are also being criticised for poor, internal management and well heeled bureaucracies that have no knowledge of grass root realities in the poorer parts of the world.

Such bureaucracies regularly overestimate the capacity of leadership in the less developed countries to control political and social unrest when economic policies create pressure on the weaker sections of society. Several cases in South America can be cited but that of Venezuela is a classic example: following the imposition of IMF adjustment measures in 1989, inflation soared to 81 per cent and in 1994, stood at 71 per cent, the highest in South America. In 1991, 80 per cent of the population lived in relative or critical poverty. From 1988-1991, the share of national income going to the richest 10 per cent increased from 30.3 to 40 per cent and the share going to the poorest declined from 2.3 to 1.8 per cent. A movement against their activities is gaining ground in the countries of South America in which MFIs have been active.[6]

Peacekeeping and peacemaking were the themes during the tenure of the last UN Secretary General Boutros Boutros Ghali. Operations expanded in the post Cold War period and the number of forces deployed under the UN flag increased from 10,000 to between 60,000 and 70,000 at various points in time. The goodwill enjoyed by the United Nations was seriously dented by its alliance with the United States in its excursion into Somalia where a contribution by African states or an Organisation of African Unity force, if such a force had existed, would have been more appropriate. Subsequently, such a force was formed by the Organisation of African Unity (OAU). Although the nature of missions being undertaken under the UN flag has changed, necessary fundamental changes in policy have not taken place. As a consequence, neither UN peacekeeping nor peace making policy initiatives taken in recent years, have worked.[7] The common perception that gained ground, damaging the institution immeasurably, has been that the United States is using UN sanctions as a cover to further its own strategic objectives such as the creation of a permanent military presence in the Persian Gulf.[8] The UN Secretary General's efforts to resolve the 1998 Iraq-UN arms inspections crisis has contributed to restoring confidence in the ability of the world body to act in such eventualities. However, precedents of unilateral NATO intervention have been set by military action in Kosovo and Afghanistan.[9] As a result, the role of the United Nations in conflict prevention and resolution has been curtailed. One view is that a proposed expansion of the Security Council (SC) may help create an institution that is more representative of the expanding community of nations and the global distribution of power at this time. This, however, will depend on the criteria for acceptance of members for a larger Security Council. There is general agreement that this will be meaningless without a discussion on limiting the veto powers of the permanent members.

The impact of the eastward expansion of NATO on Russia and the near abroad added a new dimension to the political and strategic environment of Eurasia[10] during 1997-1998. The reach of NATO now extends to West, Central and even South Asia, through its East European members and Turkey. The forces of NATO member states are already well established in the Persian Gulf, and the United States has made it clear that it does not intend to draw down in the region despite counsel to re-consider the 'containment-plus' policy that included efforts to change the government in Iraq. A parallel development has been the expansion and consolidation of the European Union. Regional integration measures have created a body of legislation that is being implemented, but at the same time remains under review and discussion. This has created new models of inter-state cooperation. A significant development is increased cooperation between Greece and Turkey. The draft resolution co-sponsored by Greece and Turkey at the UN General Assembly 1999, regarding the establishment of a joint Stand-by Disaster Response Unit, urges the international community to create mechanisms to mount prompt and effective rescue operations in the aftermath of natural calamities.[11] This joint effort in an international forum is indicative of a thaw that may well ease Turkey's entry into European institutions once human rights issues, including the impact of its 'Kurd' policy on a large section of the population, have been resolved.

Elsewhere the situation is somewhat different. On 23 December 1998, the Russian Prime Minister had warned of a further cooling of US-Russia relations as a result of a change in the approach of the US and Britain towards the management of international crises. This change in the approach of both countries was characterised by the bypassing of the UN Security Council in authorising the December 1998 air strikes on Iraq. This act was the precursor to NATO's response to the situation created in Kosovo by Serbia. This change in approach has not been well received by both Russia and China. The 23 December 1998 remarks on US-Russia relations had been made during the Russian Premier's two day official visit to Kazakhstan where agreements were signed to further boost economic cooperation and trade relations between the two countries in a bid to consolidate Russia's influence in the region.

In a joint statement issued on 23 April 1997, Moscow and Beijing had opposed a unipolar world order and signed agreements for the establishment of concrete mechanisms for consultation and increased cooperation in international affairs. Mechanisms for technology transfer and bilateral cooperation in the political and economic spheres were already in place. The April 1997 treaty to limit troop presence on borders between Russia and China as well as the Central Asian states of Kazakhstan, Kyrgyzstan and Tajikistan led to the cutting of troop levels by about 15 per cent along the 7300 kilometre border shared by the five states. This is an indication of the stabilisation of territorial boundaries in the region. Eventually, this should reduce military spending in the region, allowing participating states to divert resources to other national priorities.[12]

Understanding between Russia and China on key issues has created a powerful combination of forces in Asia that are bound to affect the outcome elsewhere. Adjustments in security arrangements and strategic alliances have created a situation that is of interest not just to the industrialised West and the larger states of the region, but also to smaller, less powerful states.[13] The impact of these adjustments is likely to spill over into the political, economic and social spheres and will have an impact on bilateral relations. An inquiry into the political history of the region is necessary to determine likely future trends. Meetings between the leaders of Japan and China have revived interest in possibility of trade via the Pacific for land-locked Central Asia. Although the potential of the region continues to be blocked by limited access to the south and east at the present time, improvement in Sino-Japan relations[14] will eventually change this situation.

After the return of Hong Kong and Macau to China, the question of the terms of Taiwan's return to the PRC assumed added importance. In anticipation of a stand-off on the issue, which would have an impact on it's global strategy, the United States announced a major policy change in its missile deployment regime. A Nuclear Missile Defence system is being set up. Initially, this affected arms control talks with Russia, but by early 2002 substantial mutual reductions in arsenals had been agreed upon. There is an ongoing process of consultation between Russia and China and several Central Asian and regional states collectively and on a bilateral basis. For instance, the government of Tajikistan and Islamist militants signed a power sharing agreement in the Iranian city of Mashad on 22 February 1997, and thereafter, peace talks took place in Moscow. In late February 1997, the Defence Ministers of Russia and the Central Asian republics of Uzbekistan, Kyrgyzstan and Kazakhstan met to discuss ways of boosting border security in view of the continuing strife in some parts of Afghanistan. Cooperation between Russia and China has helped in the resolution of border disputes.

Easy movement across national borders and enhanced cross border trade activity increases the possibility of the spill over of political as well as associated militant movements. In the south-western Chinese province of Xinjiang, bordering Pakistan and Afghanistan, political unrest has been associated with religious revival. The Western perception is that contacts between the people of predominantly Muslim states in the region and orthodox groups from other countries act as a catalyst in the promotion of Islam in general and radical offshoots of Pan-Islamism in particular.[15] In China, there is concern about increased interest in religion and ritual in general and in the practise of Islam in particular. The government is extremely sensitive to the political repercussions of socio-cultural developments, hence the recurring crackdowns on the Fulangong movement. Following the fall of the Taliban, the United States and its allies have not been able to quell unrest in Afghanistan, and this has far reaching implications for theocratic political movements worldwide. In October 2003, the US government renewed contacts with Taliban leaders through the interim administration led by Mr Karzai. With theocratic militancy ascendant in Pakistan and the conservatives in Iran in reasonably good shape, such developments could seal off a large and important area of West Asia for modernist intervention.

Militants based in Daghestan launched a campaign to seize control of Chechnya early in 1999. They were, reportedly, inspired by the Afghan experience. Russia viewed this as a new attack on national integrity that was bound to have repercussions in the neighbouring Caucasian republics as well. Despite severe economic constraints, Russia launched a full scale military and air campaign to regain control of the Caucasus. This was Russia's second campaign in Chechnya within this decade. According to some Russian analysts, instability in the northern Caucasus has been encouraged by the United States to influence regional development, such as the laying of new pipelines for Caspian Sea oil—this oil has traditionally moved by pipeline across the Caucasus through Chechnya to the Black Sea. If this view is correct, it may be difficult to bring peace to the region especially now that a protocol to move Caucasian oil through pipelines running through Turkey has been signed with the blessing of the United States. The signing ceremony took place during the OSCE summit in Istanbul (18 November 1999). However, it will be difficult to consolidate new routes for oil in the face of Russian hostility. The heavy peripheral damage caused by Russia's 1999 campaign to reclaim Chechnya from militants has drawn protests from Western capitals, particularly because Russia refused to allow OSCE monitors into the theatre of war. The subject dominated the proceedings at the OSCE summit in Istanbul.

Apart from emerging patterns in power sharing in the region, socio-cultural and political developments are taking place there. The significance of these developments is obvious and tangible in the new strategic scenario. Associations and consultative groups attached to official regional cooperation and development entities have evolved into substantive organisations and emerged as important players in international affairs. In practical terms, these organisations represent the alternative to official intervention in a broad range of activities at both the national and international level. They are in a position to operate in ways that may not be appropriate or possible for governments.

The heads of state and government of the 55 members of the Organisation for Security and Cooperation in Europe (OSCE) who met in Istanbul, 18 November 1999, signed four documents including a political declaration, an assessment of the political and security situation in the Euro-Atlantic region and a review of the main activities and issues it is facing. Guidelines for future activities, operations, consolidation and the efficiency of its mechanisms and institutions were also reviewed. The OSCE has been asked by the EU and NATO to send monitors to review the situation in the Caucasus and expects to present a report on the condition of refugees in Southern Russia. The talks about the situation in Chechnya that took place between the Presidents of Russia and the United States at the OSCE summit in Istanbul are a long way from the informal consultations of its predecessor organisation, the CSCE. This is another indication of moves to establish regional institutions that provide an alternative to United Nations activity in strategic areas.

During the 1990s, festering territorial and ethnic tensions became full blown conflicts leading to the large scale displacement of populations on several continents and resulting in great human suffering. During every single day of 1992, almost 10,000 people in various parts of the world were forced to flee from their countries. As a result, the total number of refugees who had crossed international borders by the beginning of 1993[16] was 18.2 million. Even more disturbing was the fact that 24 million others were forcibly displaced during the period: these people were forced to leave their homes but still remained within the borders of their own countries, and therefore, were not classified as refugees. They were called displaced persons. The number of such persons has remained relatively constant as new conflicts emerge almost as soon as old ones are resolved. On the basis of these statistics it is estimated that one out of every 130 persons on the face of the earth had been forced to flee their permanent place of residence at one time or other.

The traditional focus of the activities of the United Nations High Commission for Refugees (UNHCR) has been, and continues to be on securing the right of refugees to asylum. The agency acknowledges, however, that countries that were traditionally proud to grant asylum to those seeking refuge from persecution, are now less keen to do so. Many of these countries say that they want to guard their frontiers from what they perceive to be 'economic' rather than political refugees. They believe that it is becoming more difficult to differentiate between those under political pressure and in physical danger and those who are merely the victims of social and economic injustice. The latter, according to the books, do not merit asylum. Regardless of how well they are treated, refugee status creates deep personal and communal insecurity that may take decades to resolve, even when peace returns.

While insisting on the right to asylum for all those in danger, UNHCR is now also involved in trying to protect internally displaced people by seeking to remove, through negotiations with national governments, the causes of their displacement. These negotiations include efforts to pressure national governments to enforce human rights within their borders and to take the responsibility for maintaining law and order where groups of the population are pitted against each other. This new strategy aims at containing displaced people within their country of origin in an effort to prevent them from becoming refugees in the technical sense of the word.

Often, this kind of operation requires the provision of a full range of services to displaced persons, a clear understanding that they are in danger, and therefore, under the protection of the United Nations. It may well involve negotiation on their behalf with other governments as well. In 1995, after bombing Bosnian-Serb targets for two weeks, the US negotiator was able to persuade the Balkan leadership to end the Bosnian war, creating a loose federation that has been kept in place since, despite tension. In a more recent case it took NATO and the United States seven months to act after hostilities had broken out in Kosovo.[17] It was said that a specific Security Council resolution was needed to give intervention a legal basis while Russia was likely to obstruct such a resolution. Thereafter, it took threat of violence to get the Yugoslav President to allow NATO air surveillance and the deployment of 2000 international observers to ensure compliance on UN demands in Kosovo. It was some time before NATO acted, on its own authority, to deal with the humanitarian crisis arising out of the scorched earth policy of the Serbian forces that led to the displacement of over a quarter million of the population of Kosovo.

The Serb government repeatedly urged NATO to tell the displaced ethnic Albanians of Kosovo to return to their homes. These homes, including farms and livestock, had been burnt or destroyed by Serb forces as part of a policy, according to UNHCR's analysis of the situation, to subdue, impoverish and socially depress the ethnic Albanian population. This represents a classic example of the systematic economic subjugation of communities. Thousands of families look refuge in forests, surviving in makeshift shelters that were so well concealed that it took UNHCR months to find them. Others crossed international borders to seek safety. Many of those who were persuaded to go back after the Serbs had given assurances to NATO and UNHCR that they would be safe, were killed on their return. The government said they were killed by renegades in the police service, not on government orders.

Forcible repatriation of victimised and disadvantaged communities is an issue of global dimensions: Germany is a case in point. Both the Rumanians and the Germans reached an agreement to repatriate about 60,000 gypsies.[18] The gypsy community voiced resentment over the agreement that was arrived at without consulting them. One opinion is that the basis for determining the ethnic identity of those so-called gypsies whom Germany wished to send back to Rumania was questionable. Gypsies form about 1.8 per cent of the Rumanian population. While their elders state they are not persecuted in Rumania there is, nevertheless, discrimination as a result of increased competition for economic opportunities due to the deterioration of the economic situation in Rumania. An estimated one million people are jobless there. Economic recession rebounds on those who may be temporarily displaced as well as on refugees.

Thousands of Afghans routinely flee from Kabul and other urban areas of Afghanistan towards sanctuary in Pakistan when clashes break out between various militant groups in the country or, when coalition bombing intensifies.[19] The situation has eased somewhat in urban areas, especially Kabul, since ISAF troops arrived and a government was installed in Kabul. These troops have now been replaced by NATO forces. Sometimes the Pakistan border is closed not just to prevent the movement of genuine refugees but criminal elements that use refugee status as a cover. UNHCR began enforcing its policy of containment of displaced persons within national boundaries to the confusion and dismay of thousands who had previously just walked across to safety in Pakistan. Safe areas have now been designated within Afghanistan, near Jalalabad, and UNHCR and the International Committee of the Red Cross (ICRC) began operations inside Afghan territory in an effort to contain fresh waves of refugees. Coalition forces allege that many Al-Qaeda members and Taliban have moved into Pakistan's tribal belt. American and Pakistan forces have raided the area repeatedly, without success. Local inhabitants of this area resent these search operations.

Pakistan is no stranger to the kinds of crises and political upheavals that produce refugees. Long before the Martial Law of 1977 that led to the flight of hundreds from the country, there was the East Pakistan crisis which resulted in the death of thousands, the flight of many more, and later, the internment of prisoners of war in India. What began in the 1950s as a movement to protect a unique cultural heritage in the face of a changing political milieu, was transformed by brutal insensitivity into a full-scale insurgency in East Pakistan, now called Bangladesh. The freedom movement there was supported not just by India, but also by many Western capitals. The remnants of that movement are the nationless Biharis who consider themselves citizens of Pakistan, since they migrated to Pakistan at the time of the partition of the subcontinent. These are the people who have lived in a terrible limbo in shantytowns, rather than refugee camps, for neither Pakistan nor Bangladesh will accept responsibility for them.[20] The situation is untenable and should be resolved through negotiation between both countries.

At the time of the crisis in East Pakistan, an unnecessary confrontation was created between the traditions and the cultural heritage of the people of the area and what was perceived to be the religious heritage of the Muslims of the subcontinent as a whole. Many felt they were expected to choose between the two and did not feel inclined to do so. A review of events will reveal that cultural dissimilarities were exploited and used to create an ethnic rationale for the movement that led to the disintegration of united Pakistan. This created the problem of ethnic Biharis, who insist they are Pakistanis, and whose third generation is now growing up in camps in Bangladesh. The Biharis of Bangladesh and India's Bengal have become symbolic of the ethnic divide in the region. Routinely, the Indian states of Assam and Bihar expel ethnic Bengalis to West Bengal. Many are then pushed into Bangladesh because they are Muslims. There does not appear to be any end to this vicious cycle of non-acceptance.

In February 1994, about 200 delegates attending the Human Rights Conference called by the United Nations Human Rights Commission in Geneva, met with representatives of the Mohajir Qaumi Movement (MQM, now known as the Muttahida Qaumi Movement) representatives. Meanwhile, Pakistan sought world support for the cause of the Kashmiri people. The MQM representatives handed over substantial dossiers documenting alleged human rights abuses committed by Pakistan's law enforcement agencies during 'Operation Clean Up' in Sindh. A large number of MQM activists sought, and were granted, political asylum abroad.

Why and how did this situation arise? It is the usual story, beginning with the systematic attempts of various power brokers to exploit ethnicity for political purposes. It culminated in official operations to control and dissipate a movement that is now out of control and infiltrated by criminal elements. There is a need to identify and separate criminal elements from political ones and contain terrorist activity. Cultural biases in society also need to be tackled: for instance, the word 'Mohajir' (refugee) cannot really apply to any person who migrated to Pakistan when it was created in 1947. Indeed, it is a misnomer as far as the movement of Muslims of subcontinental origin to Pakistan is concerned. This is not a question of semantics, but a matter of fact. Indian Muslims and others who moved towards Pakistan on its creation were merely entering their own homeland, a homeland they had helped create. It is self-destructive to make them refugees in their own home. Their alienation from their socio-political environment has helped create a hard core of militants among them, who are exploited by the establishment and sections of the political leadership from time to time.

REFERENCES

1. Key, Sean. 'American Strategies Towards the Enlargement of European security Institutions: Partnership or Cold Peace'. cited in *NATO Enlargement and Russia*. Stephen J. Cimbala. *Strategic Review*, Vol. 24 No. 2. Spring 1996.

2. Nelson, Daniel N. 'Transatlantic Transmutations'. *Washington Quarterly*, Vol. 25 No. 4. Autumn 2002: pp. 51-66.

3. De Witte, Bruno. 'Anticipating the Institutional Consequences of Expanded Membership of the European Union'. *International Political Security Review* Vol. 23, No. 3, July 2002: pp. 235-248: USIS Backgrounder: Karl Kaiser. 'Reforming NATO'. *Foreign Policy*, No. 103. Summer 1996: pp. 129, 131: Alexander Moens. 'European Defense and NATO: the Case for Good Governance'. *International Journal*, Vol. 56, No. 2: pp. 261-278.

4. Pyle, Kenneth B. 'The Context of APEC: US-Japan Relations'. *NBR Analysis*, Vol. 6, No. 3, November 1995.

5. Locke, Mary. 'Funding the IMF: The Debate in the US Congress'. *Finance and Development,* Vol. 37, No. 3, September 2000: pp. 56-59.

6. Ibid., see 5 above.

7. Diehl, Paul F. and Others. 'UN Intervention and Recurring Conflict'. *International Organization*, Vol. 50, No. 4. Autumn 1996: pp. 683-700 : Maurice Strong and Edward Cornish. 'Reforming the United Nations'. *Futurist*, Vol. 33, No. 5, September/October 2001: pp. 19-25: Harriet Hentges and Jean-Marc Colcaud. 'The Economies of Peacekeeping: Dividends of Peace'. *Journal of International Affairs*, Vol. 55, No. 2. Spring 2002: pp. 333- 349.

8. Report. *The Nation*. (AFP) December 23, 1998: 'Proceedings'. *The United Nations* New York. 23 September 1999.
9. 'News Report'. *The Nation* (AFP). 23 April 1997.
10. Brad and Roberts and Others. 'China: the Forgotten Nuclear Power'. *Foreign Affairs* Vol. 76, No. 4, July/August 2000: pp. 53-63.
11. 'News Report'. *The Nation* (AFP). 22 February 1997.
12. M. Ehsan Ahrar. 'China, Pakistan and the 'Taliban Syndrom'. *Asian Survey*, Vol. 40, No. 4, July/August 2000: pp. 658-671.
13. 'News Report'. *The Nation* (AFP/APA). 18 November 1999.
14. 'News Report'. *The Nation* (AFP/Reuters). 20 November 1999.
15. Ibid., see 10 above.
16. *UNHCR 1993*. Report to the Secretary General, United Nations. New York. December 1993.
17. Rubin, James. 'Countdown to a Very Personal War'. *FT Weekend* (London). September 30- October 01, 2000: p. 1: John Esposito and Vali R. Nasr. 'Rethinking US Foreign Policy and Islam After Kosovo'. *Georgetown Journal of International Affairs*, Vol. 1, No. 1. Winter/Spring 2000: pp. 1-10 : 'News Report'. *The Nation* (AFP/APA). 10 November 2001.
18. Ibid., see 16 above.
19. 'News Report'. *The Nation* (AFP/APP). 15 November 2002.
20. *The News* (AFP-Reuters). 28 February 1994: 'The Biharis'. *The Nation* (APP). 29 July 2002.

PART III

A GLOBAL PERSPECTIVE

17

EUROPEAN SECURITY

NATO's 'Strategic Concept' was approved by the heads of state and governments attending the meeting of the North Atlantic Council in Washington D.C., on 23-24 April 1999.[1] It needs to be studied carefully to determine the future shape of the strategic environment of the world rather than impact of NATO policy on Euro-Atlantic security alone. Reassessment of the political, institutional and security network in place in Europe at this time has contributed to the broadening of the scope and conceptualisation of policy. The situation in south east Europe, regional instability, the proliferation of weapons of mass destruction and availability of dual use technology through unofficial sources, have had an impact on the thinking behind this document. The threat of instability as a result of sub-national militant activity has also influenced its conceptualisation.

The Alliance is keen to protect its forty year investment in peace in Western Europe, and this has led to an unprecedented level of institutionalised cooperation.[2] This institutionalised cooperation takes place through the European Union (EU), the Organisation for Security and Cooperation in Europe (OSCE), the Western European Union (WEU) as well as NATO, which oversees the defence dimension of Euro-Atlantic cooperation. There is increased intra-European activity in the private sector as well, although traditional rivalries, such as those in the defence and aviation industries, continue to exist. However, there appears to be a concurrent realisation that a number of new challenges to regional peace have emerged and will have to be addressed.[3]

These challenges include ethnic conflict and political oppression. Political oppression was associated with non-representative political systems that were supposed to have been replaced by democratic institutions after the collapse of the Soviet Union. Pockets of acute poverty, organised crime and the collapse of civil society continue to be major threats to stability and were not eliminated on the European continent, merely kept out of Western Europe. Large-scale emigration is a problem. Facing difficult conditions at home, in just one decade (1980-1990), about 400,000 young Albanians, 10 per cent of the total population of Albania, migrated to Greece. The uncontrolled movement of large numbers of people, such as the displaced of Kosovo, is a threat to regional stability. Those displaced continue to be at grave risk of exploitation by criminals and other elements until they can return to their homes with guarantees of security.

As early as 1992, Serbia was informed that '...in the event of conflict in Kosovo caused by Serbian action, the United States will be prepared to employ military force against the Serbians in Kosovo and in Serbia proper'. A similar warning was issued in March 1993 when the despatch of US troops to Kosovo was seriously considered. The Republic of Kosovo was announced in November 1995,[4] almost seven years after its autonomy was stripped away by the government in Belgrade. Thereafter, the US government pledged to establish an 'official presence' in the capital of Kosovo. This gave rise to fears that Albanians in Macedonia, Montenegro and Greece would be encouraged to create a so-called 'Greater Albania'. This did not happen.

In 1999, over six million Albanians lived as citizens of three European countries, where the average size of a country's population is 1.5 to 4 million. This makes the Albanians one of the largest ethnic groups in the Balkans. Albania, with a population of over 3.2 million, has some ethnic Greek communities in the south of the country. About 750,000 ethnic Albanians live in the west of Macedonia. They have been given representation in government and state institutions. Of the two million ethnic Albanians of Kosovo, who formed 98 per cent of the total population, one million had been driven out by Serb forces by 30 April 1999[5] and more were either being killed or pushed out every day. This temporarily altered the ethnic balance in south-east Europe. The economic and social conditions prevailing there are poor compared to Western Europe. In 1997, an international force of 7000 troops led by Italy (Operation Alba) was sent to restore order in Albania where emergency conditions prevailed and where the government had been struggling to rebuild institutions after a series of fraudulent saving schemes created economic chaos. There was concern that criminal elements and carpetbaggers from various parts of the world would take advantage of the refugee crisis.

US designed military, rehabilitation and national reconstruction programs put in place after the Dayton Accord on Bosnia, were considered the forerunners of a network of alliances between the United States and the states of East and Central Europe, rather than an Alliance initiative. These were expected to halt further destabilisation of the region. East European states were, traditionally, outside the sphere of influence of NATO and considered of secondary importance to the security of Western Europe. This view did not take into account the implications of Serbia's ambitions. In Bosnia, the NATO Implementation Force assisted civilian reconstruction through the provision of logistic support. Military training programs were designed for Hungary, Rumania, Macedonia and Albania to prepare them for action in NATO's 'Partnership for Peace' activities. The Croatian and Bosnian Muslim armies were equipped and trained to provide a military power base to statehood. Later NATO took over coordination of humanitarian relief efforts for Kosovar refugees. States burdened with the majority of refugees were promised, and given, immediate economic aid and long-term development assistance for the rehabilitation of their economies.[6]

Serbia's vision of the future continued to be in direct conflict with, and intolerant of, assimilation of the aspirations of multi-ethnic non-Serb communities in the region. So far moderate elements have not been able to manoeuvre a real change of government policy. The crisis is bound to have an impact on the future status of areas at risk, such as Kosovo, within the Alliance. The paper dealing with the Alliance's 'Strategic Concept'[7] Part I-The Purpose and Tasks of the Alliance, reiterates that, '6. NATO's essential and enduring purpose... to secure a just and lasting peaceful order in Europe...' The effort to achieve this goal does not confine Alliance activity to North America and Europe alone.

Of interest to Pakistan, India, and a number of other states, is the concern of the Euro-Atlantic Alliance about the vision of regional security and terms for power sharing in areas on the periphery of the Alliance and in other regions. In defining potential security risks and challenges, the Alliance's 'Strategic Concept' takes note of '21. The existence of powerful nuclear forces outside the Alliance (China? etc.,) also constitutes a significant factor which the Alliance has to take into account if security and stability in the Euro-Atlantic area is to be maintained.' Concern is expressed about, '22. The proliferation of NBC weapons and their means of delivery...Some states, including some on NATO's periphery and in other regions, sell or try to acquire

NBC weapons and delivery means. Commodities and technology that could be used to build these weapons of mass destruction and their delivery means are becoming more common...prevention of illicit trade...difficult...' It is observed that, '24...Alliance strategy must also take account of the global context...'

> In Part IV, 'Guidelines for the Alliance's Forces' there are statements of (p. 5 ctd.) the Principles of Alliance Strategy. Besides observing that, '41. The security of all Allies is indivisible: an attack on one is an attack on all...' and it is stated that '53. b... geostrategic considerations within the Alliance will have to be taken into account, as instabilities on NATO's periphery could lead to crises or conflicts requiring an Alliance military response, potentially with short warning times... a limited but militarily significant proportion of ground, air and sea forces will be able to react as rapidly as necessary to a wide range of eventualities...It must take into account the possibility of substantial improvements in the readiness and capabilities of military forces on the periphery of the Alliance. Capabilities for timely reinforcement and resupply ... with a resulting need for a high degree of deployability, mobility and flexibility.'

At the time, negotiations were on for setting up a US base in Yemen, fairly close to targets in Iraq, as well as potential targets in Afghanistan, Pakistan and India. Since then the base has been established and used in the war on Iraq. It is not surprising, therefore, that a statement of significance to states with nuclear capability, like Pakistan and India, is the statement that, '56...the Alliance's defence posture against the risks and potential threats of the proliferation of NBC weapons and their means of delivery must continue to be improved, including work on missile defence. As NATO forces may be called upon to operate beyond NATO's borders...' NATO forces replaced ISAF troops in Afghanistan in August 2003.

The institutions that are evolving in the Euro-Atlantic strategic environment pose a challenge for the international community as a whole and the United Nations in particular. A number of crises have led to the streamlining of procedures for consultation and response within these organisations. Their effectiveness was tested at several levels in dealing with the Kosovo crisis. Public response within NATO member states, those directly involved in dealing with the crisis in the Balkans, as well as official and public response in states that were not directly involved, was monitored and analyzed. Analysis was expected to provide policy guidelines and planning support for similar initiatives for the resolution of crises in the Euro-Atlantic region and other parts of the world. In the presence of a number of effective, official transnational institutions, the role of the United Nations in international management is bound to diminish further as a result. In fact, United Nation's conflict resolution activity may be confined in future to specific, low priority areas of the world, where the major alliances do not feel the need to intervene directly. In post-war Iraq, the United States has confined the UN to secondary development work.

This has implications for states that do not belong to major alliances and continue to depend on United Nations support and intervention for the resolution of bilateral and multilateral disputes. Since indications of these trends in the development of international security systems have been there for a decade, they should not come as a surprise. Meanwhile, administrative reform at the United Nations has not produced results that meet the expectations of major donors and support for the expansion of peacekeeping operations has been limited. This is one of the consequences of diminished standards in leadership cadres and internal management, poor understanding of field conditions and incorrect intelligence. The responsibility for this state of affairs rests equally on present leadership within the organisation as well as on the member states that put such leadership in place, through a nomination process.

Internal reform at NATO led to the building of a European Security and Defence Identity (ESDI)[8] within the Alliance and the creation of a Combined Joint Task Force (CJTF) with arrangements for the rapid deployment of forces from European bases. The development of the ESDI as well as moves within the EU for consensus on important foreign policy issues has increased the importance of consultation and dialogue. Efforts have been made to create a multinational political executive representing a range of European interests and capable of undertaking different kinds of missions on the direction of the North Atlantic Council. For actual implementation, an easily deployable and mobile force has been placed at three European headquarters. These have been used in air strikes against Iraq.

The Euro-Atlantic Partnership Council (EAPC) provides the framework for cooperation with members of the Partnership for Peace (PFP) program,[9] which is now the principal mechanism for creating practical security links and conducting joint operations such as those envisaged with the WEU (Western European Union). There are plans to increase the role of such members in decision-making and planning.

The failure of UN efforts in Bosnia,[10] as well as a number of other developments,[11] led to the re-evaluation of the existing nature of the Euro-Atlantic Alliance and the form it would take in the future. The understanding that responsibility for peace in East, Central and South Europe would have to be actively shared by Europe with the United States, and negotiated with the Russians, has led to changes in the institutional and command structure of NATO as well as the level of dialogue with potential members and associates. It has affected decisions on the acceptance of new members of NATO and the EU. For instance, one of the arguments given by Hungary for the feasibility of its full membership of NATO was that it would provide the Alliance with access to the Balkans in crisis situations. Hungary participated fully in NATO's peacekeeping mission in Bosnia. In the first week of May 1999, Bulgaria provided NATO with an air corridor for strikes on Serbia.

The realisation that the threat of force would have to be used to support diplomacy has influenced the transformation of NATO's command structure.[13] Efforts have been made to create a multinational political executive representing a range of European interests and capable of undertaking different kinds of missions on the direction of the North Atlantic Council. For actual implementation, force structures to meet NATO's objectives and to provide adequate response, have been put in place at the strategic locations. Afghanistan has become the testing ground for some of the strategies that have been put in place to deal with sub-national threats outside NATO's traditional area of operation.

REFERENCES

1. North Atlantic Council. *Proceedings of the Meeting held in Washington D.C 23-24 April 1999*: issued by the Office of Public Affairs, US Embassy. Islamabad.
2. Ibid., see 1 above.
3. Marshall, Andrew. 'Future of Europe's Foreign Policy'. *The Independent* published by special arrangement in *The News*, 7 July 1995.
4. Rubin, James. 'A Very Personal War'. *FT Weekend*. 30 September 1 October and 7-8 October 2000: John Esposito and Vali R. Nasr. 'Rethinking US Foreign Policy and Islam After Kosovo' *Georgetown Journal of International Affairs* Vol. 1 No. 1. Winter/Spring 2000: pp. 1-10: 'Report'. *The Nation* (APA/Reuters). 28 November 1995: *The Nation* (APA/Reuters). 21 February 1996.

5. 'Report'. *The Nation*. (APA). 30 April 1999.
6. 'Report'. *The Nation* (Reuters). 22 September 1999.
7. 'Strategic Concept'. Text of US State Department Document issued by the *USIS, Office of Public Affairs US Embassy Islamabad*. 30 April 1999.
8. Moens, Alexander. 'European Defence and NATO: the Case for Good Governance'. *International Journal*, Vol. 56, No. 2, Spring 2001: pp. 261-278.
9. Ibid., see 8 above.
10. 'Report'. *The News* (AFP/Reuters). 15 May 1993.
11. Pincus, Walter. 'Iran Arms for Bosnia: US Explored Other Options'. Dawn-IHT-WP News Service. *Dawn*. 27 April 1996.
12. 'A Dual Act By Europe and America (dateline: Brussels)'. *The Economist* (London). 3 June 2000: p. 27.
13. Brzezinski, Zbigniew. 'Living With A New Europe'. *The National Interest No. 60*. Summer 2000: pp. 17-29.

18

WEST ASIA AND THE MIDDLE EAST

The political and economic environment of West Asia and the Middle East is overshadowed by a number of unresolved issues. Developments in various fields of national activity are inter-related. In a number of cases, issues related to domestic politics have had an impact on external affairs, and vice versa. The delimitation of borders in the region has also been a painfully slow exercise requiring the consensus of all states that are a party to various disputes. For instance, Yemen has had territorial disputes with the Saudis over the oil rich southern provinces of Asir, Najran and Jizan. The final settlement of this territorial dispute between Saudi Arabia and Yemen is a good augury for peace and prosperity in the region.[1] Such settlements can serve as a guide for negotiations taking place elsewhere in the region. Arbitration by third parties may provide a solution but direct, bilateral negotiations are likely to be more stable and fruitful.

There is a need to remember, however, that such disputes are not just about rights over a few barren islands near the coast, a few oil wells near a border, or a few hundred square miles of uninhabited desert; they are about fundamental issues of sovereignty that have been held in abeyance for decades while decolonised areas dealt with more urgent matters of state. Understanding of the historical background and roots of contention makes it easier to assess the likely course of events when these issues are finally taken up by the concerned parties.

Contrary to the view of a number of Western observers, who see it as relatively static, there has been a discreet ebb and flow in political and intellectual development in the entire West Asia and Middle East region. Without intellectual and managerial capability, the Iranian Revolution could not have moved to its present stage of democratic reform, the Palestinians could not have launched the Intifada, Hezbollah could not have liberated southern Lebanon and economic transition would not have been possible in the Gulf States.[2]

An underlying concern in leadership cadres in West Asia and the Middle East appears to revolve around the patterns of interaction between Muslim states, Arab and non-Arab, issues of national sovereignty and the power of common Arab identity in the creation of a regional security order that will support national economic development. According to one view, 'In Arab politics a shared Arab identity has long been associated with various political projects at odds with a regional order, premised on sovereignty and exclusivity...' To explain, the author states that,

A recurring debate in Egyptian politics has been the relationship between the Egyptian national identity and the Arab national identity, and related obligations that Egypt had, if any, to other Arab states. Such debates generally spring up around seminal events, including the Arab Palestine Revolt in 1936, the creation of the Arab League in 1945, the defeat in the 1948 Palestine War, and Anwar Sadat's path to Camp David...

But Egypt is just one of many Arab states, and each state has a history of interaction with the world that has led to the evolution of a national character influencing reaction to events and crises.

To understand the genesis of political thought and the character of relations in the region, and between the regional powers and the West, it is necessary to go back in time. Decolonisation after the Second World War led to the creation of states and the strategic regrouping of those that already existed. A constant element, directing the course of events in one area and influencing events in other areas, has been the presence of the British, Americans, and the Europeans in the oil rich region. Their official establishments have jealously guarded the commercial interests of their citizens and multinationals, by supporting national leadership they considered favourable towards them.

A clear picture of the evolution of the political environment in West Asia and the Middle East, and its relationship with the industrialized West, emerges when we glance through the contents of just a few newspapers published in the subcontinent during the early 1950s. *The Statesman* (English daily published simultaneously from Calcutta and New Delhi) in its issue of 21 February 1952,[4] highlighted discussions taking place at the United Nations between the representatives of Arab countries and others, over the future of Tunisia.

Pakistan was reported to have called for a meeting of the Security Council to discuss the matter.

In the same issue of *The Statesman* there was a report that King Faisal II of Iraq had called on the new Queen of England (London, Tuesday, 18 February 1952)[5] as King George, who had recently passed away, lay in state in London. Meanwhile, another report on the front page of the same newspaper (dateline: PTI/Reuters, 18 February 1952) provided details of an Anglo-Iraqi 50-50 profit sharing agreement between the Government of Iraq and the Iraq Petroleum Company, ratified by the Senate, which would give the country Pounds Sterling 31 million during 1952.[6] A successful general strike had been called on 18 February by the leaders of the Istaqlal, National Democratic and United Popular Front parties to protest against the ratification of the agreement by Parliament. Obviously, resistance to the commercial policies of the incumbent leadership was well established in the larger countries of the region.

Political resistance was also an established element of regional culture. A few days later, the front page of *The Statesman* (21 February 1952)[7] carried a report about Iran:

Twelve Opposition Deputies of the Persian Parliament who have been taking sanctuary in the Majlis building for over three months came out of refuge as the 16th Majlis ended...synchronising with the closing of the Majlis, large groups of students paraded Tehran streets peacefully today shouting "Long Live Mossadeq"...The International Bank mission after their meeting with Dr. Mossadeq this morning were lunching at the Pakistan Embassy prior to their scheduled departure tomorrow...

National character in the region has evolved, but remains recognisable. It is noteworthy that while the Muslim world has been moving towards the assertion of sovereignty through state-specific economic and security policies orchestrated by the West and requiring its cooperation, the industrialised countries have re-grouped and moved into a phase of effective regional economic integration (EU, NAFTA, etc.) that is leading to close interaction on security and foreign policy issues as well. Multilateral diplomacy and multilateral force have become effective instruments of global strategic management. This has been seen in the hammering out of a settlement of sorts for the Palestinians and its subsequent abandonment by consensus and during the Gulf War, which created new dynamics in the Muslim world, particularly in the Middle East and West Asia.

The strengthening and institutionalization of sovereignty as the basis of inter-Arab relations in the aftermath of the Gulf War (Damascus Declaration, March 1991)[8] was seen as a recognition of the legitimacy of Arab state's borders, the right of each to arrange its security and the exclusive claim of each to its resources (Secretary General of the Arab League, 15 December 1992) '...We should basically assume that there should be no interference in any country's security. We must acknowledge and proceed from this principle...').[9] This shift was seen as the end of the Arab Collective Security Pact. It has not been possible to access the comments of independent analysts in the region on the subject. However, it is known that a subsequent phase of discussion, initiated in Cairo, dealt with inter-Arab re-conciliation and the strategic need for maintaining a unified approach in international forums at least on issues of common interest. A parallel development has been the use of the concept of 'jihad', variously interpreted as a way of life, for the resolution of crises in the Muslim world. These developments have had a profound impact not just on the Arab world but also on non-Arab Muslim countries, such as Pakistan, Bangladesh, Indonesia and others, and have affected their relations with the rest of the world.

There is an enormous amount of literature available on the first Gulf War, the UN Security Council Resolution 687 (3/4/91)[10] that led to a ceasefire, various interpretations of the contents of the Resolution, subsequent UN Resolutions as well as events and engagements including Operation Desert Fox (December 1998),[11] that was triggered by a negative UNSCOM report. The departure of weapons inspectors from Iraq was followed by almost daily bombardments of military targets in Iraq and has led to substantial peripheral damage over time.

There is little doubt that over the years there was an erosion of support in the region, as well as in Europe and the United States itself for the US policy of dual containment of Iran and Iraq. Nevertheless, trade sanctions against both countries, imposed through the United Nations and bilaterally, continue to be strictly enforced. The failure of sanctions against Iraq to achieve desired objectives has raised questions about the effectiveness of trade sanctions as a tool of foreign policy. As a result, and because of the declared intent of the United States to bring about regime change in Iraq, the impact of harsh economic sanctions on domestic politics and the morale of citizens in Iraq was of interest to Western analysts and strategists.

In West Asia and the Middle East, the internal dynamics governing domestic politics have to be seen in conjunction with other issues, such as national sovereignty. The domestic milieu in Iraq, ten years after the imposition of trade sanctions, was a revelation. After February 1998, the Royal Institute of International Affairs commissioned several briefing papers in which the situation was discussed. One of these briefing papers emerged as the result of a visit in connection with a research project on 'Regional Policy and the Development of a New Arabic-Middle Eastern System' (V. Perthes, Royal Institute of International Affairs).[12] The author of the paper reported that both official and private sector representatives were of the view that the political consequences of economic sanctions and other measures taken, were obvious and that the young generation, which had grown up under sanctions, was not likely to forget what had happened to them because of the USA and the West. What concerned him and his colleagues, as well as traders and entrepreneurs, was that before the last war and the embargo, they might have engaged in unambiguous 'remarks' about Saddam Hussein—'remarks' meaning criticism or opposition to the official position but not any more. As a result of the intense hardship caused by the sanctions regime and Western attitudes, the authors of the report noted, 'everyone now stands behind the regime'. The relationship between the private sector and the regime also improved because the embargo and foreign currency crisis led to the liberalisation of the economy. This did not bode well for any Western intervention in Iraq.

These observations were substantiated by events following the occupation of Iraq by US troops in May 2003, after a war that went on longer than expected. There have been daily skirmishes between US forces and elements amongst the local population, resulting in casualties as well as fatalities amongst US forces and local citizens. Daily public demonstrations against the war, against occupation by US troops, against dislocation of services, economic hardship and the poor law and order situation, have made it clear that running Iraq is going to be a difficult proposition. Pipeline sabotage has become routine and US commanders acknowledge that they are now fighting a guerilla war in Iraq. The profits that were expected to accrue to the United States from the control of the oil wealth of Iraq are going to be difficult to reap under the circumstances.[9] Meanwhile, intense resentment and hostility, in a vast country, has led to the creation of yet another sub-national and elusive militant force in the world.

REFERENCES

1. 'Report'. *The News* (AFP). December 16, 1997: Shahwar Junaid. 'Possibilities of Regional Cooperation and the Erosion of National Sovereignty'. *Strategic Perspectives*, Vol. 3, No. 3. Summer 1995: pp. 85-98.
2. Gule, Nilufer. 'Snapshots of Islamic Modernities'. *Daedalus*, Vol. 129, No. 1. Winter 2000: pp. 91-118: Jack Miles. 'Theology and the Clash of Civilizations'. *Cross Currents*, Vol. 51, No. 4. Winter 2002: pp. 451-458.
3. Barnet, M.N. 'Regional Security After the Gulf War'. *Political Science Quarterly*, Vol. III, No. 4. Winter 1996/1997: pp. 597-618.
4. 'News Report'. *The Statesman*. 21 February 1952.
5. 'News Report'. *The Statesman*. 18 February 1952.
6. Ibid., see 5 above.
7. Ibid., see 5 above.
8. 'Damascus Declaration'. *The News* (AFP/Reuters). March, 1991.
9. 'Statement of the Secretary General, Arab League-December 15, 1992'. (AFP/ Reuters) *The News*. 16 December 1992.
10. *United Nations*. 'UN Security Council Resolution 687 (3/4/91)': 'Report'. *The News* (AFP/Reuters). 4 April 1991.
11. *The Nation*. (AFP/Reuters). 23 December 1998.
12. Perthes, V. 'Regional Policy and the Development of a New Arabic-Middle Eastern System' and related briefing papers, February 1998 the *Royal Institute of International Affairs*.

19

THE REGION AND A
NUCLEAR INDIA

During the 1990s, an international campaign was launched to contain the development of nuclear capability in states other than the nuclear five, Israel and Japan. France continued testing prior to declaring a moratorium. The United Nations First Committee examines and approves resolutions before they are put up to the General Assembly for voting. In mid-November 1995,[1] the Committee took up a resolution deploring nuclear testing and called for its cessation.[2] The resolution was sparked off by test explosions carried out by France and China during 1995. The general public in a number of countries expressed strong resentment against these tests. The resolution carried with a vote of 62 to 5 in favour of the resolution. Lobbying by France persuaded fifteen countries to change their mind and they either did not vote or cast abstentions. Representatives from twenty-five countries left the room during the vote while another forty-five countries abstained; abstentions included the United States, Spain, Pakistan, Germany and Russia. In fact, none of the nuclear states voted in favour of the resolution and French diplomats were pleased with the moderate response to their test explosion.

Nevertheless, strong public revulsion against nuclear weapons was expressed[3] in many parts of the world, particularly in the Pacific region, near the test site. It could not be ignored. This, however, worked to the advantage of the nuclear states against which it was directed. These states drew attention to international public opinion when they sought to draw the less developed countries of the world into the Non-Proliferation Treaty (NPT), an unequal partnership. Under this Treaty, five of the signatories, the US, Russia, France, Britain and China, are permitted to keep the nuclear weapons they possess, while the other signatories undertake never to acquire them. One hundred and seventy countries of the world have already accepted the terms of this Treaty regardless of the implications of such acceptance on their sovereignty.

India is not a signatory to the NPT and has maintained a vigorous nuclear programme over the past twenty-nine years since its first test explosion of a nuclear device in 1974. During this period, India has been able to conclude defence pacts with a number of countries including its traditional ally, Russia, the successor state of the Soviet Union, as well as the United States, traditionally an ally of Pakistan. For Pakistan, the development of nuclear capability was never easy; although the effort was motivated by genuine security concerns, the international community expected these concerns to be tackled on different terms. During the 1990s, when India carried out a series of nuclear explosions that yielded the data to make nuclear devices, it already had reliable delivery systems. India continues to refine and upgrade missile technology through frequent testing. India's nuclear tests, obviously for the purpose of perfecting weapons, changed the security environment in South and West Asia and a review of the depth of alliances in the region became necessary. It became necessary for the United States and allied advocates of non-proliferation to consider the provision of firm security guarantees to states likely to be affected. Credible guarantees were not forthcoming.

It is noteworthy that in a speech on 14 May 1998,[4] the Indian Prime Minister said that India would not hesitate to use nuclear weapons if attacked. The President of the BJP, with reference to Kashmir, stated in a TV interview that his Party has always said it '...does not covet the territory of others but it will not allow anyone to retain what (it considers) its own...' It is also noteworthy that while on a number of occasions, the Indian Defence Minister said that China could be considered an adversary of India, implying that the country's defence capabilities must be sophisticated enough to deter aggression from the North, rather than from smaller Pakistan. After rapprochement with China, over the status of Tibet in 2003, the situation can be said to have changed. However, it remains to be seen whether this will have an impact on Indian plans for the development of defence capability.

After conducting test explosions in May 1998, Pakistan came under unusual pressure from the international community. Economic sanctions were imposed on Pakistan when it conducted nuclear tests in order to refine technology. Since it needed IMF support in order to manage its economy, it stood to lose much more than India, which had a vibrant economy. However, the option of defaulting on loans was always open to Pakistan. Default by even one debtor state was likely to be a tremendous blow to international financial regimes and could have had a domino effect, triggering default by a large number of other debtor states.

Since the global security environment has changed, West Asia and the Middle East are in a state of flux and have not received appropriate assurances, Pakistan needs to keep its own security options open and maintain a credible nuclear deterrent. Betrayed time and again, this is what Pakistan must do, not just in the national interest but to maintain a strategic equilibrium in the region. Pakistan needs to do so until it can determine whether the United States and its allies are willing and able to come up with robust regional security arrangements that can guarantee the sovereignty and territorial integrity of member states. This is not likely to happen in the near future in view of the situation in West Asia after US intervention in Afghanistan and Iraq, and its extraordinary interest in promoting political change in Iran. In 1995 advocates of the American line were urging the government of Pakistan to sign the CTBT (Comprehensive Test Ban Treaty). If it had done so, the international community would not be taking any interest in the future of Pakistan and the causes it upholds, today.[5] Decisions about the level of nuclear capability Pakistan needs to maintain can be taken after consideration of India's nuclear program and the development of its missile capability in a historical perspective. The contribution of Pakistan's traditional allies, such as Canada and the United States, to the development of India's nuclear program and past experience of the ability of international institutions and multilateral alliances to provide security guarantees to state entities need to be considered.

In December 1995,[6] the United States revealed that India might be preparing to explode another nuclear device. Reports that a test explosion may take place were based on analysis of satellite pictures. The Congress government was warned not to go ahead with the experiments and they desisted. It is interesting that before the nuclear test explosions actually took place in 1998, no prior reports of unusual activity near Pokhran, the site of the tests, were leaked to the press and satellite surveillance data was not available. It was later revealed that by 1998 India had the capability to manufacture up to eighty nuclear bombs. This was not news for many knowledgeable observers. It was also meaningless data for one nuclear device is as good as eighty in most scenarios.

In 1985, the incumbent US Under Secretary for Defence is reported to have said that the United States' '...long term interests could be served by providing India with enough advanced weapons technology to turn it into a military power strong enough to play a major role in global security in this century...' This is the key to long term US policy in South Asia. The pursuance of this policy has led to investment in the SAARC initiative by the international community and insistence that Pakistan expand trade ties with India rather than with other states in the region. Between 1985 and 1989, India was the third largest Third World recipient of defence technology. In 1987, 13,000 Indians were studying in US universities and working in science and technology institutions. They were also introduced to space, missile and solid fuel technology.[7] A new era of defence and security cooperation between India and the United States began after 11 September 2001. Developments in September 2003 saw the consolidation of these trends.

The Indian Space Research Organisation (ISRO) signed an agreement with the International Telecommunications Satellite Organisation (INTELSAT) for the lease of transponders to be used for various purposes. US firms also showed interest in collaborating with the launch of 500-1000 kg satellites using the Polar Satellite Launch Vehicle. The US government did not interfere in such commercial arrangements planned and eventually reached, between Indian and American organisations. Assistance was also provided to India in the nuclear field: according to a report published in March 1995,[8] the United States supplied heavy water for India's Cirus reactor. Heavy water is what enabled India to manufacture plutonium for its first nuclear explosion in 1974. According to another report, India obtained US technology that will enable it to make air-delivered laser guided bombs. The trials of these bombs were held in September 1994 at Pokhran in Rajasthan. The refinement of missile technology is an ongoing process.

The response of the United States to the test explosions carried out by India needs to be considered in view of this record of decades of cooperation with the Indian establishment. It is not surprising that the Senate Foreign Relations Committee reacted sharply at the time and asked the Clinton administration to '...refuse to allow India to paper over its actions by signing the CTBT...not agree to any treaty which would legitimise de facto India's possession of these weapons, just so long as there is no further testing...' Senator Jesse Helms was sceptical about promises of no further testing in view of the fact that, '...two tests were clearly intended to fall below the seismic threshold, a clear indication that India intended to remain a nuclear power at all costs...demonstrates the intent to exploit the verification deficiencies of the CTBT by testing new designs in an undetectable fashion...' This was the view of a politician. Concern was also expressed over the threat to US territory in view of India's development of missile capability. This should underscore the legitimate security concerns of the states of West Asia, the Middle East and Central Asia as well as China that are within easier reach than the United States.

For well over ten years, the United States focused its attention on two accords in an attempt to prevent countries it considered unreliable from acquiring nuclear capability: the Nuclear Non-Proliferation Treaty (NPT) and the Comprehensive Test Ban Treaty (CTBT) which came into effect in 1996. Efforts to enforce both regimes were intensified during the 1990s. Nevertheless, China and France continued to test during the 1990s. The attitude of the United States towards non-proliferation regimes remained ambiguous as evident from its reaction to a historic Treaty on non-proliferation that was signed by ASEAN states at their fifth summit in Bangkok. The Treaty was negotiated between member states over a period of ten years. It banned the acquisition, deployment, use, testing and stationing of nuclear arms in the ASEAN zone. Cambodia, Laos and Myanmar also signed the Treaty.[9]

The Bangkok Declaration urged the five nuclear powers to implement '...more vigorous measures to reduce and eliminate all nuclear weapons...' None of the countries signing the treaty were nuclear powers, therefore it was only of symbolic significance.[10] Nevertheless, the US refused to accept the treaty on the basis of its concern that the movement of its nuclear military vessels may be restricted in the Pacific and they might not be able to access the Indian Ocean and Persian Gulf, where its reconstituted Fifth Fleet is now located. A statement insisted that '...the right of passage and other issues are very important...' although the Treaty provided for the passage of foreign nuclear warships and submarines on peaceful missions. That is how keenly vigilant independent nations guard their interests.

It is in this kind of international security environment, which has only changed on the surface since Pakistan joined the so-called, US War on Terror, that the government of Pakistan must negotiate. The

Pakistan government has been facing flak from a number of quarters within the country for initiating a relatively high profile dialogue with the Indian government on issues that need to be resolved. One of the reasons for discomfort in Pakistan has been the unwillingness of the Indian government to speak of, let alone discuss, a legal settlement of the Kashmir dispute on the basis of United Nations resolutions and in the light of India's historical acceptance of the right of self-determination of the Kashmiri people. India has campaigned in world capitals for international pressure to control, what it is calls 'cross-border terrorism' that is allegedly sustained by Pakistan's help.[11]

During 1999-2000, the British government declassified many post-Partition, official documents, including some related to the Kashmir issue. These confirm that at the time, the leaders of both countries agreed that the only appropriate method of dealing with the dispute was to resolve it in accordance with internationally accepted legal precedents set at the time of the partition of the subcontinent and the UN resolution on the subject. Some foreign governments, including that of the United States, have expressed pleasure at the initiation of a formal dialogue between the two countries and a return to bilateralism. This has raised suspicions that the dialogue, unlikely to yield results on Kashmir, will be used as an excuse to neutralise Pakistan's position on Kashmir in the United Nations. From time to time, the United States has been asking the UN to wrap up the UN Military Observer Group monitoring the Line of Control. Prior to 9/11, this was one of the measures conditional to the release of arrears of its contribution to the United Nations.[12]

After one round of bilateral diplomatic initiatives, a hot line was installed, with great fanfare, connecting the Prime Ministers of both countries. After the conclusion of another round of Foreign Secretary level talks in Islamabad, a statement was issued and the formation of a joint working group (JWG) was announced. However, on his return to New Delhi, the Indian Foreign Secretary stated that, '...yes, we have agreed to discuss, not (the) Kashmir dispute but issues related to Jammu and Kashmir in the JWG...' Elaborating further, he said that the issues he was referring to included the return of Azad Kashmir to India which, according to him, is '...under Pakistani occupation by force...' and not the status of Indian Held Kashmir. The Pakistan government may have been embarrassed by this volte-face but the Pakistani public was furious. A spokesman of the Pakistan Foreign

Office expressed disappointment at the statement of the Indian Foreign Secretary and called it mere propaganda. Actually it is not propaganda. This has been the Indian position for several decades now and Pakistan needs to face this reality. Pakistan also needs to take stock of factors in the global geo-strategic environment that may help bring about a change in India's position.

Now that India's policy on the settlement of outstanding issues, including Kashmir, has been clarified once again Pakistan needs to take stock of its own position and develop appropriate policies. Some insight into the formulation of foreign policy and the mechanics of its implementation in Pakistan is necessary in this context. Analysts need to remember that instructions to Pakistan's embassy in Washington and the High Commission in New Delhi do not go from, or through, the Pakistan Foreign Office.[13] The ambassador in Washington, the High Commissioner in New Delhi and the representative at the United Nations are neither selected for appointment by the political government in the country nor are they under the control of the political government. The Foreign Office is neither informed nor consulted regarding instructions transmitted to these posts. It is not involved in policy formulation for these three posts. The Foreign Office and the political government are in the unique position of acting as a front for a coterie of 'official' and co-opted grand strategists of Pakistan. The services of the Foreign Office spokesman are, however, utilised to cover up any foreign policy fiascos. Given this kind of situation, it will not be possible to develop an integrated foreign policy in which manoeuvring on one front bolsters the position of the country on other fronts as well.

The individual contribution of a number of Pakistan's representatives to the United Nations towards the consolidation of Pakistan's case with regard to Kashmir has been remarkable: the original UN Resolutions regarding Kashmir form the bedrock of Pakistan's Kashmir policy. Unfortunately, subsequent governments were not able to secure substantive progress despite the existence of such clean and uncompromising UN Resolutions. In recent times, given the existing chain of command, the Pakistan Foreign Office and the political governments of the country cannot be held responsible for foreign policy failures, or successes. They are, of course, responsible for losing control of the policymaking and implementation processes and need to make determined efforts to get back in action and in charge. Before this can happen they will have to first deal with the corrupt and incompetent elements in their ranks who have destroyed their credibility. Under existing circumstances what can be done about Kashmir and who will do it?

Kashmir has been disputed territory since the very moment of independence of the subcontinent and the creation of India and Pakistan. In October 1947 Lord Mountbatten observed that '...the question of the state's accession should be settled by a reference to the people...' On 5 January 1949, the United Nations passed a resolution granting the right of self-determination to the people of Kashmir through a free, fair and impartial plebiscite. On 6 January 1949, the details of the proposal for holding such a plebiscite were released by the United Nation's Commission for India and Pakistan and were accepted by both the governments.[14] According to the proposal, the Secretary General of the United Nations would, in agreement with the Commission, nominate a plebiscite administrator of high international standing and commanding general confidence, who would be formally appointed to the office by the government of Jammu and Kashmir. After the conclusion of the plebiscite, the Commission was required to certify to the Security Council whether the plebiscite '...has or has not been free and impartial...' While the Simla Agreement sought the resolution of the dispute through bilateral negotiation, it has always been understood that the UN resolutions would remain effective and relevant until they are implemented and the issue resolved.

At the present time, the interest of some major powers in the resolution of the Kashmir dispute is a cause for concern, reflection and analysis, particularly in view of their insistence that an economically weakened Pakistan deal with the matter bilaterally.[15] In this case, serious measures to enforce United Nations resolutions have never been considered an option by world powers. The promotion of this option could have included the imposition of sanctions and the extreme, but logical, step of declaring Kashmir a protectorate of the UN in order to give respite to the people prior to the holding of a plebiscite there.

There is need to take stock of the changing geo-strategic and economic imperatives in the South Asia region that could affect the status of the Kashmir dispute now. Talk about the region being a flashpoint stems from the knowledge that both India and Pakistan have nuclear capability and the Indian fear that the Taliban, active in Afghanistan, could be diverted to Kashmir once they have, again, secured their position in Afghanistan. The Taliban have stated in interviews with the press that they do not believe their jihad can be, or should be, confined to one area.[16] This approach to global strategy stands, despite the events of 11 September 2001, the war in Afghanistan and the political process that led to the installation of the Karzai government. The entire region, from Iran to China and Central Asia, has been alienated by Pakistan's past association with the Taliban and regional powers believe that it may still not be easy to contain those elements among the Taliban that have survived, in Afghanistan.[17] This has proved to be correct.

The disintegration of the Soviet Union was of special significance for South Asia. India gained substantial benefits through its longstanding 'Treaty of Friendship and Cooperation' with the former USSR. The collapse of the USSR may have made India relatively vulnerable in the international forums, including the UN, but it also made India more aggressive in the pursuit of its objectives. It is, therefore, not surprising that India is lobbying for an expansion of the UN Security Council and expects to be included as one of the new permanent members when this happens. In the meantime, Soviet supplies of defence technology, products and oil at subsidised rates have dwindled, and for the first time in their history, technology transfer deals between Russia and India have been informally scrutinized by the West-the cryogenic engines deal for example. An alternative supplier of critical technology is Israel.[18] However, conventional weapon superiority, as a strategic determinant, is becoming redundant in the region for both Pakistan and India have achieved a critical degree of competence in nuclear weapons technology and are believed to have the political will to use it.

A significant change in the region is the revolutionizing force of the economic expectations of the people of both India and Pakistan as well as the fading away of the image of India as a secular state subsequent to the desecration of the Babri Mosque in Ayodhya, anti-Muslim riots in Bombay and the emergence of Hindu revivalist political parties and politicians as a substantial force in public life.[19] After years of protecting and nurturing its economy, India has opened its doors to foreign investment and long-term liberal economic policies have been put in place. A market of relatively prosperous 220 million middle class Indians, who are gainfully employed and upwardly mobile, has emerged. This market is of great interest to Western manufacturers. In Pakistan, there is impatience with delays in the judicious re-ordering of the economy. Both countries are facing major crises arising from a breakdown of values in public life.

The stabilisation of the Iranian revolution and the holding of peaceful Presidential elections in that country is equally significant in view of the fact that Iran has developed substantial naval power and carries influence in the region. The emergence of China as a major economic force in the world is of enormous significance for South Asia in general, and Pakistan in particular.[20] China is now in a position to manipulate western, in particular the US, economy. There are indications that steps are being taken to contain its influence in the South Asia region through the creation of a belt of neutral, if not hostile, states that will be under the influence of the West. Its south-western provinces have been infiltrated and its Central Asian neighbours are under pressure from some sources while others are courting them. This is where Kashmir comes in as an issue of strategic concern for the region. Formulas for resolution of the Kashmir dispute that are obviously designed to serve the long term interests of countries which seek to contain the power of the region, must be effectively countered with integrated, indigenous policies that protect the interests of the people of South, Central and West Asia.

REFERENCES

1. 'Report'. *The Nation* (AFP). 16 December 1995.
2. Ibid., see 1 above.
3. Cirincione, Joseph. 'The Asian Nuclear Reaction Chain'. *Foreign Policy*, No. 118 Spring 2000: pp. 120-136.
4. *The News*. (AFP/Reuters). 18 May 1998.
5. *The Nation* (APP). 23 December 2001.
6. *The News* (APA/Reuters). 12 December 1995.
7. M. Ali. 'Special Report'. *The Muslim*. 28 December 1994: Richard F. Grimet. 'Conventional Arms Transfer to Developing Nations 1994-2001'. *US Congressional Review Series*. August 2002.
8. Ibid., see 7 above.
9. Ibid., see 3 above.
10. Pyle, Kenneth B. 'The Context of APEC: US-Japan Relations'. *NBR Analysis*, Vol. 6, No. 3. November 1995.
11. Schaffer, Teresita C. 'Building Confidence in India and Pakistan'. *Center for Strategic and International Studies*. August 2002.
12. *United Nations*: New York, 30 October 1995.
13. *The Nation* (APP). November 1998.

14. 'Special Report'. *Dawn* (APA/Reuters). 5,6,7 and 8 January 1949.
15. 'Talking and Killing in Kashmir'. *The Economist* (London). 3 June 2000: p. 63: 'Lessons Learned: India Pakistan Crisis of 2002'. Proceedings of Consultations. *Henry L. Stimson Center.* September 2002.
16. 'Report'. *The Nation* (APA/Reuters). November 18, 1999: Jennifer Stern. 'Pakistan's Jihad Culture' *Foreign Affairs* Vol. 70, No. 6. November-December, 2000: pp. 115-126.
17. M. Ehsan Ahrari. 'China, Pakistan and the 'Taliban Syndrome'. *Asian Survey* Vol. 40, No. 4. July/August 2000: pp. 658-671.
18. Collins, Tom Z. and Jon B. Wolfstaal. 'Nuclear Terrorism and Warhead Control in Russia'. *Arms Control Today* Vol. 32, No. 3. April 2002: pp. 15-19.
19. *The News.* (Reuters). 15 March 1991.
20. Brad et. al.. 'China: the Forgotten Nuclear Power'. *Foreign Affairs* Vol. 76, No. 4. July/August 2000: pp. 53-63.

20

EURASIAN ALLIANCES— BEYOND 2002

During the year 2001, a number of dramatic changes took place in the economic and strategic environment of the world. Although many changes were impending, the world was not really prepared for them. As a result, response to events has been ad hoc, rather than considered. Many rituals of civilized conduct have been set aside and accepted standards of civilized behaviour have become irrelevant to the conduct of international affairs. It has been, and continues to be, a dirty fight between unequal forces with many unsuspecting, innocent people, who do not even know that they are at war. Their spirits have been destroyed, and they have been maimed or killed in combat because of imaginary threats that haunt Western society and culture. The CIA has admitted (CNN Online, 17 December 2001)[1] that it has used, and continues to use, anthrax as a weapon of biological warfare in peacetime. The world really knew that all along. We have also been aware that the establishments of some other countries use biological weapons in covert operations. In Pakistan, targets of such operations have been the educated intelligentsia, people with limited resources who like to read books and magazines and who are known to scour roadside stalls and second-hand bookshops for suitable reading material in which the spores of such biological weapons are easily concealed. The knowledge that this cannot be done without the cooperation of the national establishment makes such incidents all the more horrifying. The United States in particular, and the Western nations in general, are not interested in making allies amongst the hard core of intellectual nationalists in other countries. Those who fall in this category would, therefore, be well advised to burn second hand periodicals and books that they may have picked up and avoid cans of cola, in case they have been doctored with salmonella, which is still in the biological warfare arsenal[2] of some of the most advanced military machines in the world, as well as some of the most primitive. This is all the more unfortunate because such educated people are the natural allies of liberal forces worldwide.

In such an environment, hopes for progressive economic alliances with the industrialized countries are likely to come to naught. The US economy shrank at a seasonably adjusted 1.1 per cent from July to September 2001. This represented a significant downward trend likely to have an impact on consumer spending, investment and saving. The Japanese economy, closely linked to the United States and East Asia, a major engine of growth during the 1980s, has been in full recession, with high unemployment levels.[3] Europe is beginning to feel the pinch as major US corporations begin to retrench and downsize operations there. Existing trends have been reinforced by the psychological impact of the events of 11 September. It is not difficult to see that the inconclusive US war in Afghanistan and now Iraq, has not revived confidence in the ability of the world to cope with the challenges to global security that emerged after the end of the Cold War. This is the environment in which the United States has withdrawn from the Anti-Ballistic Missile Treaty (ABM) of 1972 with a view to launching its Nuclear Missile Defense program while making adjustments in its strategic priorities worldwide.[4]

Russia has reacted sharply to the US pull out from the ABM because of fears that this could spark a nuclear arms race in Asia, with showdowns in China, India and Pakistan, as well as the Middle East, where Israel could change the existing delicate balance in security arrangements with Arab states. Russia is reported to be reconsidering existing strategic arms reduction treaties (START) with the United States in order to safeguard its interests.[5] Russia has also accepted that the United States is within its rights to abrogate what has been called a Cold War era pact (ABM). There are concerns within the United States about the timing of the administration's decision to go ahead with the Nuclear Missile Defense program, the influence the defense industry may have had in prompting its initiation and the repercussions for other security initiatives. Democrat Biden (US Senate) has criticized the Bush administration's decision because he feels it will not help Washington in achieving nonproliferation goals. These were actually abandoned soon after the present US administration (Republican/George Bush II) took office, along with a number of other policies that had prompted significant foreign policy initiatives, including the Middle East peace process. Significant new patterns in power sharing have been evolving for some time. They are likely to be given formal shape in the near future. This is of significance at the regional as well as the international level.

The impact of the eastward expansion of NATO on Russia and the near abroad added a new dimension to the political and strategic environment of Europe and Asia as early as 1997-1998. The outreach of NATO now extends to West, Central and even South Asia, through NATO's East European members and Turkey.[6] The forces of NATO states are well established in the Persian Gulf and it has been obvious for some time now that the United States will not be drawing down in the region although it had promised to hand over power to the representatives of the people of Iraq by 30 June 2004. The situation in the Pacific is similar where North Korea is the focus of attention. As a parallel development, the expansion and consolidation of the European Union that began using its uniform currency, the Euro, on 1 January 2002, has been important. Regional integration measures have created a body of legislation that is being implemented, but at the same time, remains under review and discussion, creating important new models of international cooperation. A significant development in the region is cooperation between countries such as Greece and Turkey, that have disputes to resolve, but are nevertheless cooperating in a number of spheres.[7]

Alliances that were forged in Eurasia during the past decade have tried to correct the shift in the balance of power between nations as a result of the dissolution of the Soviet Union. During this period, Russia's position as a Eurasian power, and counterweight to the United States, has been reinforced by treaties that include the broad ranging declaration of mutual cooperation signed with China in 1996 and updated at meetings of heads of state in 1999, 2000 and 2001. During 1999, when the original cooperation agreement was first updated, Russia's war to reclaim ascendance in the Caucasus was being condemned. China was reiterating its claim on Taiwan and protesting moves to consider the island for membership of the World Trade Organization. Today, both China and Taiwan are WTO members, the issue having been eclipsed by events in West Asia. At that time both countries reiterated the need for a multipolar world. These calls were not just a reaction to the dominance of US strategic systems but also reflected concern about the desire of the United States to install an anti-ballistic missile defense system to protect the American mainland

and a global theatre missile defense, of which Taiwan was expected to be a part. This theatre missile defense system was expected to cover the rest of the world, protecting US interests.

At the time, in a joint declaration signed by the Russian and Chinese Presidents, during the visit of the former to Beijing on 9-10 December 1999, these issues were covered. It was stated that '...Both sides are against the use of placing human rights higher than state sovereignty and using human rights to harm an independent country's sovereignty...' This was a rebuttal of criticism from Western countries against the Russian military offensive in the Caucasus as well as a re-statement of Sino-Russian policy towards crises such as that witnessed on the disintegration of Yugoslavia. Unanimity of views on such issues paved the way for a long-term 'strategic partnership' between Russia and China.[8] Details are not available but it is believed to encompass technological, economic as well as political and military cooperation. Both nations have been coordinating policy on matters of mutual interest and have moved towards a unified stand on critical strategic issues in international forums. For a while this was seen as an expression of Russia's annoyance with the North Atlantic Treaty Organization (NATO) for including East and Central European countries in its Partnership for Peace program. Now this coordination is acknowledged as part of a long term policy aimed at consolidating Russia's position as a world power and asserting its ability to influence world events. Treaties to strengthen defense and military cooperation signed with the Central Asian republics of Kazakhstan, Uzbekistan, Tajikistan, Turkmenistan, Kyrgyzstan and Belarus provide for joint action to fight international terrorism and militants believed to have been trained in Chechnya and Afghanistan. Militants were being held responsible for a series of attacks that led to large numbers of casualties in the states of the region. The treaties, which have been mentioned above, were in effect when the United States was supporting the Taliban authorities in Afghanistan through US/Saudi corporations and the government of Pakistan. As a result, it is not surprising that the United States had to ask Russia to use its influence with the wary Central Asian states that are contiguous with Afghanistan to secure bases for forces that they now wanted to send to Afghanistan. Although it has been providing substantial development assistance in the region, the United States has been able to secure only limited cooperation for its war in Afghanistan.

Among other things, alliances are for mutual benefit against common threats. We may speak in grand technical terms but the truth is that some of the most powerful strategic alliances that shape world events and transform the world community originate and exist at the community and the national level. Reinforcement of interests is then sought through alliances with external forces and interests. The public and national governments are locked in a strategic alliance of fundamental importance to the world community. The formal terms of such alliances, between the people and the state, are contained in power-sharing charters, such as constitutions that are the result of national consensus. The priorities that are set as a result of such alliances within national boundaries have a profound impact on alliances at other levels, weakening or strengthening national institutions, as the case may be, in their dealings with the world community. Vital strategic alliances exist at the regional as well as international level. Again, such alliances may be formal, covering specific areas of activity through clearly enunciated programs of action, or they may be informal. The rise of terrorism as a tool of negotiation is one result of the failure to acknowledge the importance of power groups with diverse interests that exist and operate at various levels in the global hierarchy and the need for forging mutually beneficial alliances with them. Information that is available to the public confirms that attempts to use such power groups against each other, to serve the interests of state entities, tend to backfire.

One of the most profound strategic alliances of our times has been forged between national governments and multilateral financial institutions. A review of developments over the past decade or so shows that economic and political power has been centralized within institutions and within specific states in regions. A number of economic objectives of the more influential industrialized states have been achieved with the cooperation of multilateral trade regulation bodies and financial institutions active in the poorer countries of Asia and Africa. Power over nations that have become dependent on foreign assistance and credit has been centralized within multilateral financial institutions and sources of commercial credit. The power of economic factors to shape the political environment is well illustrated in the case of Argentina,[9] where multilateral financial institutions have been supervising a broad-based structural readjustment of the economy for decades but the economy shrank by 11 per cent between July and December 2001. Measures taken to enable compliance with multilateral financial institution conditionalities led to a breakdown of law and order, change of government (22 December 2001) and subsequent suspension of foreign debt repayments in order to ease the situation of the people. Today, in Argentina, one child in every six is severely malnourished. A number of economic relief measures are now expected. The default by Argentina was bound to lead to repercussions in Asia. South Korea, for example had been an important lender and business partner of Argentina and was affected. Earlier, during the decade of the 1990s, the Mexican economy fell apart. Its proximity to the United States, US business interests there and plans to create NAFTA led to a fiscal package that rescued Mexico and helped in the rehabilitation of its economy.

It is feared that developments in Argentina could have a domino effect and lead to defaults by hard-pressed countries in other parts of the world. In Pakistan, the government has been under pressure to secure economic concessions from the international community and multilateral financial institutions. The view that such concessions can be obtained is based on the assumption that Pakistan can provide valuable assistance to the international community in its drive against global terrorism. The fact of the matter is that the US war in Afghanistan and the installation of an interim government there marked the end of a phase of military activity and a mere reversal to the situation that existed prior to the emergence of the Taliban in 1992-1993. It certainly does not mark the end of global terrorism. It is unfortunate that the interim administration in Afghanistan does not have the manpower to create civil order in the country, and as a result, after endeavoring to do so for two hundred years, the British are finally in Kabul. However, Mr Karzai has conducted himself well and he has also spoken well—he has mentioned the need to move from an economy of war to an economy of peace and prosperity. It is not going to be easy. There are already demonstrations on the streets by people looking for jobs—as we all know, there is a difference between a job and work. The alliances the interim setup is able to create within the country, among those who desire peace, must be a match for those who profit from war. The kind of money that can be made during wartime is not easily made in times of peace, or even during a phase of reconstruction. The kind of funds that are required for a decade of reconstruction are not likely to be forthcoming from the United States which has already spent US$40 billion on the war in Afghanistan and has begun to count the cost.[10]

The priorities of the United States government in the reconstruction of Afghanistan are understandable and entirely appropriate and in line with the interests of its own people—an anti-drug program, contractual work and the building of an Embassy and related facilities for its staff there. It is not likely to invest further in Afghanistan at the cost of interests elsewhere. Instead, the United States has now called upon its allies to share the cost of any time lag in the return on their investment in Afghanistan. This news should spur the Afghans to examine their options and take stock of the possibility of using the resources of their diaspora for national reconstruction. Given the situation that exists in the region, Pakistan can expect some unusual, and unwelcome, 'windfalls'.

The first casualty of the US decision to dislodge the Taliban in Afghanistan, Pakistan's strategic partners in the region, was Pakistan's Kashmir policy and its stand that the people of the valley and Jammu must be given the right of self-determination. It would be self-deluding to assume otherwise. Obviously the government of Pakistan was also aware of the repercussions of its decision when it allowed the United States to establish military bases on Pakistani territory. US forces expect to maintain a substantial presence in Dalbadin and Pasni for an extended period of time. However, Pakistan has not been able to secure arrangements that would guarantee its sovereignty and territorial integrity in return for such facilities. In case of an attack on Pakistan, US bases would be evacuated immediately. On the other hand, Pakistan will no longer be able to control surveillance over large tracts of its own territory and the territory of its neighbours. This is bound to have an impact on Pakistan's interaction with states in the region.[11] The armed forces have done what they would have killed a civilian government for doing.

Far-reaching decisions that have an impact on the sovereignty and territorial integrity of the country are being taken by a small group of men who are seeking legitimacy for a government they have installed for themselves. Such decisions should be taken by a national government in full control of policy formulation after all aspects have been considered and debated by elected public representatives. They have obtained that legitimacy in the form of joy rides, photo opportunities and handshakes.[12] But photo opportunities and handshakes do not necessarily represent, or lead to, enduring strategic alliances that are based on common, shared interests, perceptions and objectives that have the support of the population of a country. This should not be construed as an endorsement of the claims of those corrupt political elements that have had several opportunities to forge strategic alliances for Pakistan but have merely used such opportunities to secure personal interests.

The alliance between the wealthy industrialized states and multilateral financial institutions acting as their intermediaries in the economic management of poorer countries, represents one element of present global financial strategy: hands off, long distance management. States that are recipients of assistance and financial support from multilateral financial institutions constitute the other element in the system. The interests of international capital have always been an important consideration in the formation of foreign policy by world powers. The management of such interests has been considered critical to the success of foreign policy. In Europe, after the Second World War, the Marshall Plan could not have achieved the desired results without the cooperation of the private sector. Subsequently, economic cooperation in Europe fostered peace and an unprecedented level of regional integration sanctioned through democratic institutions at the national level. Despite reservations, the meshing of financial systems and facilitation of the movement of people and goods across national boundaries has already yielded substantial benefits to the population of the region. During the 1990s, the European experience raised hopes that similar movements could be duplicated in other parts of the world. This led to a resurgence of regional alliances, such as ASEAN, and expectations from groups such as the Commonwealth of Independent States (CIS).

REFERENCES

1. 'News Online'. *CNN*. 17 December 2001.
2. Pearson, Graham S. 'The Protocol to the Biological Weapons Convention is Within Reach'. *Arms Control Today*, Vol. 30, No. 5. June 2000: pp. 15-20.
3. 'Statistics issued by the Government of Japan'. *BBC World*. 30 June 2002.
4. Payne, Keith B. 'The Case for National Missile Defense'. *Orbis*, Vol. 44, No. 3. Spring 2000: pp. 187-1996: John Deutch and Others. 'National Missile Defense: Is There Another Way'. *Foreign Policy*, No. 119. Summer 2000: pp. 91-100.
5. *Strategic Arms Reduction Treaty*. Moscow, July 2002.
6. 'Kid Gloves Needed for Turkey'. *Swiss Press Review and News Report* Vol. 37, No. 15. August 12, 1995: 'EU tries to Calm Turkey's Anger'. *The News* (AFP-Reuters). 16 December 1997.
7. *Communique on Joint Draft Resolution Regarding Humanitarian Assistance/ Greece-Turkey*. United Nations. 23 September 1999.

8. McFaul, Michael. 'Why Russia's Politics Matter'. *Foreign Affairs* Vol. 74, No. 1. January-February 1995: pp. 98-99: Starr, S. Frederick. 'Making Eurasia Stable'. *Foreign Affairs*. January-February, 1996.
9. Hartlyn, Jonathan and Arturo Valenzuela, 'Democracy in Latin America since 1930' ed. Leslie Bethell. *The Cambridge History of Latin America* Vol. VI: *Latin America Since 1930: Economy, Society and Politics* (Cambridge University Press).
10. *The Nation* (AFP/Reuters). 24 September 2002.
11. 'Report'. *The Nation* (APP) 19 August 2002: see Appendix.
12. BBC World News, 29 November 2002.

21

PALESTINE AND MULTILATERAL INITIATIVES

Once the Intifada began in December 1987, Palestinian protesters maintained a tempo of resistance to Israeli presence that led to the imposition of a modern day scorched earth policy in the area by the Israelis: curfews sealed Palestinians within their homes while fields of ripe crops rotted within sight of the farmers of Gaza and the West Bank because they were not allowed to leave their homes to harvest them. Even when the curfew was not in places, travel to and from the area became practically impossible because of intense security and the 70,000 Palestinians, who commuted to work in Israel every day, were helpless. Palestinians who were pushed out of Jordan and Lebanon and the PLO had to establish its headquarters in Tunis. This allowed a group of American backed moderates to emerge as the future negotiators of an agreement with Israel. The influx of Palestinians displaced from Lebanon, Jordan as well as Syria led to further deterioration in the economic situation of the occupied territories since many families in the area had been dependent on their remittances. The population of 750,000 swelled to over a million and the Palestinians faced starvation; their hospitals were without medicines, their schools were closed and their houses were often destroyed as punishment.[1] After the PLO voiced support for Iraq during the first Gulf War, a number of Arab countries providing assistance to Palestinian refugees stopped doing so. By that time the long-term ally of the Palestinians, the USSR, had disintegrated and another source of support disappeared.

A confluence of events had pushed the PLO towards a peace accord that remains tragic in the context of events that preceded it and inadequate in the context of events that followed. The substance of the accord was lost in the rhetoric and ceremony surrounding its signing in Washington. Three generations of Palestinians were lost for a cause that was signed away with the flourish of a pen. Instead of an equitable settlement and the creation of an independent state for the Palestinians, the accord, in fact, marked the real birth of Israel and the establishment of a state for the Jewish people which was envisaged as a 'final solution' to the Jewish problem, by the West.[2] This was what had been proposed at the Zionist Congress of 1897[3] that took place in Basle. Within twenty years (1917), of that Congress, the British government had indicated that it viewed the proposal favourably and would use its good offices to facilitate the achievement of the objective.

Thirty years later (1947), the United Nations General Assembly passed Resolution 181 dividing Palestine into an independent Arab and an independent Jewish state with specified boundaries. It was then agreed that the city of Jerusalem be administered separately under a UN resolution passed the following year. It was only after the British mandate terminated that Egypt, Jordan, Iraq and Syria acted and by then it was too late: they not only lost their own territories in the wars that followed but over three million Palestinians, whose land was seized by the Israelis, had to flee to other countries. To this day many of these refugees carry the keys to homes they were forced to abandon at that time. What do the Palestinians look forward to today, as a consequence of the peace accord between the PLO and Israel and subsequent developments?

To begin with, there was further splintering within and between Palestinian organisations and a loss in its (PLO) bargaining power both within the Palestinian community and at the international level. The PLO's tacit acceptance of demands that the group reorganise on lines acceptable to the United States and Israel, led to the rise of hardline organisations that see the achievement of a pre-1948 status for Palestine as their objective. As a consequence of its decision to compromise in the hope that the long-term multilateral negotiation process will produce results, the PLO became Israel's first line of defence against dispossessed Palestinians.

Subsequently, elections were held for a Palestinian self-governing council that is responsible for municipal and administrative arrangements in the towns from which the Israelis have partly withdrawn. Promises of investment and assistance for economic development on the West Bank by those brokering the multilateral peace process did not materialise. There was little improvement in the lives of the majority of people on the West Bank and in Gaza even before the renewal of the Intifada. Withdrawal of forces from 80 per cent of Hebron, the seventh such town, took place over eighteen months after it was due. In each town from which troops have been withdrawn, a pocket of Jewish settlers, with the potential for creating trouble and the likelihood of sudden expansion in numbers on one pretext or other, remained. Meanwhile, there was no sign of the withdrawal of the Israeli army from villages, where 900,000 of the 1.3 million Palestinians on the West Bank live. The bulk of the population, therefore remained under Israeli control.[4] A wall is being built on Palestinian land (2004) as a barrier between Israeli and Palestinian territory. The International Court of Justice passed a judgment against this on July 09, 2004.

The basic problems seen in the Palestine-Israel peace accord, arise from the form and nature of multilateral peace processes in which the concerns of the parties involved remain far apart: the Israelis want peace on their own terms, they also want consolidation of their claim on territory while the Palestinians seek part of that territory and independence for themselves. As a result, only a very vague agreement, or understanding, could be pushed through with the proviso that the concerns of both would be addressed through side agreements to be negotiated later. The two warring parties could not be separated as they occupied parts of the same disputed territory. There was, originally, no neutral force on the ground[5] to enforce peace and, subsequently, to implement various aspects of the accord. An agreement was signed for the deployment of an expanded, unarmed, six-nation observer force on the border between Palestinian and Jewish areas. However, there are areas in which Jews are surrounded by Arabs and other areas in which Arabs are surrounded by Jews.

Detailed side agreements flowing from peace accords could only have been hammered out by equally skilled, motivated and empowered negotiators of the parties concerned. Such negotiators need the backing of a substantial moderate constituency in favour of the terms of settlement between the warring parties. Such a constituency did not, and does not, exist amongst the Palestinians and the Israelis. The original Palestinian negotiating team was without sufficient support and influence at PLO headquarters and lacked experience of the situation in Gaza. It did not command the respect it needed at the negotiating table in order to make demands on behalf of the Palestinian people. It was also not in a position to guarantee the enforcement of side agreements that were to flow from the peace accord. The weaknesses inherent in multilateral initiatives for the resolution of crises and problems of this nature[6] are well represented in this case.

The US brokered Rabin-Arafat peace agreement did not bring peace and stability to the Middle East in general and the Palestinians and Israelis in particular. It was accepted by, and has affected, a minority in the area in which it was implemented. It was, nevertheless, expected to bring in big dividends through the normalization of ties between the rich Gulf States and Israel. Shortly after the conclusion of the agreement, an attempt was made to introduce Israel into the region as an economic partner. At the OIC summit in Morocco[7] a proposal to establish the Middle East Bank, on the lines of the World Bank, was tabled. Thereafter, a number of Arab states, including Morocco, Oman and Qatar, were persuaded to relax restrictions on trade with Israel. After the accord on Hebron, a bid to revive these trends has been made. Since the Middle East is still unstable, the strategy appears to be to allow traditional rivalries and border conflicts to dissipate the economies of the region while projecting Israel as everyone's friend. This strategy is in line with the increased independent manouvering of Israel across the globe through the transfer of defence technology it has received from the United States. South Africa, China, India and Turkey have been beneficiaries of such technology transfer, broadening the sphere of influence of Israel.

There has been talk of 'Oslo-type' negotiations for the resolution of the Kashmir issue since 2002. A multilateral initiative has also been suggested. Attempts have been made for the past several years, through a number of foreign foundations, to create public opinion in influential circles in both countries in favour of some kind of peace initiative that would allow formal trade on a larger scale between India and Pakistan. If such efforts were directed towards persuading India to hold a plebiscite in Kashmir under UN auspices, according to UN resolutions, they would be welcome. The spontaneous hostility towards Muslims, Muslim culture and Pakistan that is evident in sanctions of the official establishment in India and 50 per cent of the population that votes for the Hindu revivalist BJP, negates unofficial efforts to create an environment conducive to the peaceful resolution of differences and is reminiscent of the hostility between the Palestinians and the Israelis.[8] Their experiences with multilateral initiatives enjoin caution.

Israel's most vicious attack on institutions of the Palestinian Authority took place on 9 March 2002, while the foreign ministers of

Arab League states were meeting to discuss a peace proposal broached by Saudi Arabia's Crown Prince. US special envoys were in the area while the attack was taking place. The US Vice-President was already on his way to the region to shore up support for an attack on Iraq. During this attack, the headquarters of the Palestinian Authority were completely destroyed. The Israeli attack on the headquarters of the Palestinian Authority stopped short of eliminating the President of Palestine. As such, it must be seen as an attempt to convert the Palestinian nation into a leaderless population without institutions, which could be intimidated and hounded out of the area.

The timing of the attack confirmed suspicions that Israel was trying to scuttle the endorsement of the Saudi peace proposal by states holding consultations at the Arab League meeting. If the peace proposal were to be endorsed, in principle, it would be difficult for Israel to refuse to negotiate on substantive issues with a view to honouring earlier commitments that were made to members of the international community overseeing the Middle East peace process.[9] Israel's attempts to scuttle the Saudi proposal for peace in the Middle East, which is based on earlier peace proposals with the added incentive of Arab recognition of Israel, and Israel's drive to destroy symbols of Palestinian nationhood, need to be frustrated. Action needs to be taken on several fronts at one and the same time.

It goes without saying that a united Palestinian response in the face of Israeli aggression is a prerequisite for successful negotiations and the creation of a Palestinian state. Through various means, the US and Israeli leadership has tried to create dissension amongst Palestinian groups. The Palestinians need to consider establishing a second line of shadow leadership so that negotiators will, under no circumstances, be able to cite the absence of a Palestinian leader as the reason for not dealing with them as a nation. Muslim states that are allies of the United States need to consider disassociating themselves from active cooperation in its so-called anti-terror coalition, that is fighting shadows in Afghanistan, until the United States takes serious steps to persuade Israel, its closest ally in the Middle East, that aggression against the Palestinians must stop and serious steps must be taken to negotiate a peace on the principle of 'land for peace'.

The governments of some Muslim states may not be inclined to actively support the Palestinian cause because they feel they have something to gain by toeing the American line in this matter. The government of Pakistan, for instance, is religiously toeing the American line at this time because the military regime has gained a measure of international legitimacy due to the travails of the United States, which stands behind Israeli policy on Palestine. In such an environment and in the absence of representative national institutions in Pakistan, public demonstrations of solidarity with the Palestinians have indicated what a wide gulf exists between government policy and public sentiment. Such demonstrations of public concern may well have persuaded the government to adjust a foreign policy bias that does not enjoy the support of the people.[10]

Target killing of alleged militants and the destruction of homes is standard Israeli policy now. International peace activists from various cultures have an important role to play in mitigating the suffering in Palestine. Their presence on the scene, in substantial numbers, could act as a deterrent to military operations by Israel. Institutions of the international community, such as the OSCE, must seriously consider stationing neutral observers in the area in order to obtain accurate reports on the situation. During negotiations under the Middle East peace process, an agreement was signed for the deployment of an expanded, unarmed six-nation observer force on the border between Palestinian and Jewish areas. On several occasions, the United Nations Security Council has been asked to approve the deployment of a neutral force to separate the warring parties. Each time the proposal has been shot down by the United States. In view of escalating violence in the area, and the absence of any other proposal for the restoration of peace, the United States needs to reconsider its position on the matter. Those elements of the Jewish diaspora and those moderate Israelis who yearn for peace, and demonstrate for rapprochement between the Palestinians and the Israelis from time to time, need to work systematically and seriously in order to expand their constituency both within Israel and abroad. Without a serious and committed constituency for peace, on the basis of a fair and viable settlement of outstanding issues, enduring peace is not possible.

A constituency for peace in the disputed area has not always been active at the official level in the states of the region. The Saudi peace initiative must, therefore, continue to be treated seriously and with respect. It is not going to be easy for Arab states to win domestic support for concessions for Israel. However, the basic idea can be refined in accordance with suggestions made by Muslim countries. Syria has rightly suggested that the offer of 'complete normalization' with Israel be changed to 'complete peace' which promises government to government ties rather than people to people ties. A just and comprehensive peace in the region is expected to promote normalization of ties at every level, in due course of time. Saudi Arabia had presented a full written version of its initiative at the Arab Summit scheduled for 27-28 March 2002, in Beirut.[11] Basically, Israel was being asked to do precisely what was required by international law and under UN Security Council resolutions 242 and 338, in line with precedents set by the 1991 Madrid accords and arrange a complete withdrawal from Arab lands. The Madrid talks were sponsored by the United States and the Soviet Union. Israel, Syria, Lebanon, Jordan and the Palestinians had participated with a view to negotiating on the establishment of two states under the land for peace resolutions 242 and 338.

Apart from official endorsement by concerned governments, any successful peace initiative in the Middle East must enjoy the support of the general public in the area. A number of Arab commentators have rightly pointed out that it is not correct to assume that the rulers of states in the region are in a position to take steps on such emotionally charged strategic issues without consensus in the upper echelons of government and support of the people. The Saudi offer of recognition of Israel by Arab states will hinge on the resolution of three issues. These include the return of millions of Palestinian refugees who had to flee from their homes in what became Israel in 1948, a complete pullback of Israeli forces from Palestinian territories occupied in 1967 and the status of Jerusalem, which was accepted as part of Palestine in earlier initiatives. No peace initiative can be successful without the closure of Jewish settlements on Palestinian territory. These settlements are no more than listening posts and high frequency surveillance units that serve to harass the local population. An issue that needs to be discussed at the outset is the control and status of routes that lead from one part of Palestinian territory to the other, via Israeli checkpoints.

Earlier attempts to bring peace to the Middle East failed for a number of reasons. Fundamental problems arose as a result of the form and nature of multilateral peace processes in which the concerns of the parties involved remained far apart. Each party wanted peace on its own terms and those facilitating the process wanted quick results that could be translated into political capital. During earlier attempts to achieve peace through multilateral efforts, only a vague, settlement of key issues could be pushed through with the proviso that the concerns of both parties would be addressed through side agreements to be negotiated later. They never were. Recognition of Israel by Arab states is of such fundamental importance that it should only be granted when matters of equally fundamental importance for the Palestinians have been settled with Israel and the method of implementation of agreements defined and guaranteed by the United Nations, the European Union as well as the United States. The United States and Israel stand to gain substantial strategic advantage from peace in the Middle East for this would facilitate the building of the Middle East hub of the US Nuclear Missile Defense (NMD) system in Israel.

REFERENCES

1. 'News Report'. *The Muslim.* (AFP/Reuters). 28 December 1987.
2. Tickle, Ian. 'Peace in Gaza: Implications and Aftermath'. *Swiss Press Review and News Report,* Vol. 34, No. 22. 8 November 1993.
3. 'Protocols of the Zionist Congress'. See notes: Walter Lacquer. 'Postmodern Terrorism'. *Foreign Affairs,* Vol. 75, No. 5. September/October 1996.
4. 'Editorial: A Bad Peace in Exchange for a Good Cause'. *The Muslim.* 23 January 1996: Avi Shlaim.
    'The Oslo Accord'. *Journal of Palestine Studies,* Vol. 23, No. 3. Spring 1994: pp. 24-25: 'Israel Demolishes Palestinian Homes' (Reuters. Occupied Jerusalem). *The News.* 16 December 1997.
5. *The News* (APA-Reuters). 13 October 2001': *Proposal for the Deployment of Observers.* United Nations Security Council. 2001.
6. Ibid., see 2 and 4 above.
7. Ibid., see 2 above.
8. 'News Report'. *The Nation* (AFP/ Reuters). 9 March 2002.
9. 'News Report'. *The Nation* (AFP/Reuters). 28 March 2002.
10. *The Nation* (APP/NNI). 20-29 March 2002: *The News* (APP/NNI) 20 March 2002.
11. *The News* (AFP/Reuters). 29-30, March 2002.

CONCLUSION

The economic and social fabric of nations, their very psyche, has been irrevocably changed by the failure of national and global security systems and institutions to resolve issues that threaten the peaceful co-existence of nations and peoples. At many levels, as a result, there has been an increase in organized efforts to bring about change. Such organized efforts adapt to the environment in which they seek to bring about change. For instance, a history of suppression of political dissent through a show of force and violence, rather than dialogue, encourages protestors to arm themselves long before any confrontation. Freedom struggles signal the breakdown of political dialogue. Terrorist activity is not so much a rejection of political dialogue and peaceful change as it is the recognition of differences in the relative power of forces within society and an attempt to correct this imbalance through various means. Terrorism is, therefore, a new form of dialogue for charge that involves the use of arms in new formations.

Efforts to find military solutions to terrorism are likely to fail. Recognition of the circumstances and underlying causes that give rise to terrorism, and efforts to remove these causes and change those circumstances, are likely to be more effective. For this to happen, the dispossessed will have to be given their rights and compensated for the injustices they have suffered. The definition of such terms and concepts needs to be debated within institutions that can bring about change and create mechanisms within global systems to achieve the desired ends. This requires international consensus and the political will to strengthen institutions that can do the job. The sooner the better.

The acceptance of such solutions to terrorism and sub-national militant activity, seems a remote possibility at present. By accepting the principle of pre-emptive strike as military doctrine, the United States has created a security environment in which it can expect to be pitched against unequal adversaries: the United States versus regimes and sub-national, or other groups, as well as terrorists. At the same time, the organizations and alliances it controls, such as NATO, can also expect to go to war against unequal adversaries such as sub-national and militant groups in countries like Iraq and Afghanistan. This has increased the possibility of the use of unconventional methods of warfare, including terrorism, or extreme violence, in conflict situations. US intervention in Afghanistan, to remove the Taliban regime and capture members of the Al-Qaeda network, had United Nations cover but there are almost daily attacks on the NATO personnel and the government forces. The Taliban are now regrouping and seizing control of territory in Afghanistan. The replacement of ISAF (International Security Assistance Force) troops by NATO personnel has created a new precedent with its own dynamics in global security.

The occupation of Iraq by the United States has met direct and indirect resistance from the local population. Armed attacks on US forces have become more frequent with the passage of time. By 16 July 2003, the number of US personnel killed after the occupation of Iraq equaled the total number of casualties the United States suffered during the duration of the second Gulf War. Efforts are underway to create a multilateral security force to assist US troops on the ground, in Iraq. Without the cover of the United Nations or an existing security alliance, such efforts are likely to meet limited success. Meanwhile, a new pocket of militancy employing unconventional methods of warfare has been created in the world. It is likely that this second phase of the war in Iraq will set the pattern of response to similar interventions by the United States and its allies, in other parts of the world that they may seek to subdue. Obviously, such situations and such solutions are untenable in the long run and alternative methods of managing global security will have to be considered. Global power systems that have created an environment in which terror and extreme violence have become tools of political, social and economic change, need to be examined and re-ordered.

APPENDIX

Supplementary Notes to References

Chapter 1

Page 6. Ref: 5. In 1894, an Italian anarchist killed French President Sadi Carnot, in 1897 Empress Elizabeth of Austria was stabbed and killed; in 1897 the Spanish Prime Minister, Antonio Canovas was killed; in 1900 the King of Italy, Umberto I was killed by anarchists; in 1901 President William McKinley was killed by an American anarchist.

Chapter 2

Page 12. Ref: 2. Recording of coverage is available from BBC Archives. Transcripts are available from the Office of the Balkan War Crimes Tribunal: The Hague.

Page 13. Ref: 4. Royal Archives, United Kingdom. The school was set up under the patronage of the Royal Household in the United Kingdom. The Duke of Edinburgh took special interest in it. He was assisted by his personal staff and others. Some of them were aware of the experiments with subliminal radio messaging, psychological warfare and nonlethal technologies, others were not. Among those who did not know, was his Equerry, Peter Horsley, This is obvious from the following excerpt from 'Terrorism and the State', Shahwar Junaid, *The Nation*, 1 October 1998, '...In the September 1998 issue of *Harpers and Queen*, a glossy published in England, an article on paranormal phenomenon was published. An excerpt from '*Sounds From Another Room*', the autobiography of Sir Peter Horsley, a distinguished member of the RAF and later Equerry to the Duke of Edinburgh, has been published in this article on paranormal phenomenon. Peter Horsley was a loyal, but astute and perceptive man. However, it is apparent from his lack of knowledge that he did not enjoy the full confidence of his employers. He writes in '*Sounds From Another Room*': 'During my last few years at the Palace I became interested in UFOs, because so many reported sightings came from airmen such as myself. Prince Philip agreed I could investigate the matter as long as I did not involve his office. I was introduced to a General Martin...He arranged for me to meet...I was ushered into a dim room in which there was just one other occupant, a Mr Janus... Here the strangeness of it all began—Mr Janus could read my thoughts, and anticipated my thoughts precisely...He knew much more than he should have done...' It is sad to read this honest and correct recounting of an incident that was designed to throw him off the track of experiments being conducted by the British at the time. Before the two met 'Mr Janus' was told the questions that subliminal messages would persuade Peter Horsley to ask him. And he had been briefed about what to say. It is unfortunate but true that Peter Horsley was being duped and diverted with the knowledge and permission of his own employers. After the job was done the perpetrators laughed at the 'Horse' as they called him. It was an era in which the use of subliminal radio wave messages for various purposes was being tested by the British Secret Service. Such subliminal message techniques, used on television as well in recent years, have since been banned by the United States government for advertisement purposes. For all we know they are still being used by the US and the intelligence services of other countries for various purposes...'.

Page 14. Ref: 11. Remarks attributed to British Prime Minister Tony Blair, on his return to London after consultations with the US President. BBC World. November 2001.

Page 15. Ref: 16. *The Muslim*, Islamabad, PPI, 13 September 1994. Both reports dealt with the economic difficulties of the general population and reported recently released Pakistan's Federal Bureau of Statistics figures on the income differential and unemployment (1.69 million unemployed).

Page 16. Ref: 19. Report. *The Nation* (AFP) Ankara: 15 September 2002. In the 5 November 2002, General Elections in Turkey the conservative Justice and Development Party won 35 per cent of the seats in Parliament, and thereby, the right to form a government. Two weeks later, Mr Abdullah Gule was nominated Prime Minister. He immediately took up a proposal from the United Nations for solving the Cyprus dispute with Greece. It is expected that the resolution of this dispute will pave the way for Turkey's admission to the European Union.

Page 17. Ref: 24. Ismail Khan. Special Report/Peshawar. *The News* 13 May 1996. These comments are substantiated by the results of the 2002 General Elections in which a joint religious political parties alliance moderated its approach and won enough seats at the national level to form a solid opposition in Parliament.

Chapter 3

Page 23. Ref: 2. Deliberations of The Trilateral Commission (United Nations), The Club of Rome, as well as numerous private sector think tanks and government subsidized research groups in Europe and the United States, such as the Rand Corporation and the Aspen Club, contributed to the formation of international policy on economic affairs and global security. These policies, in turn, had an impact on strategic and national security policies that contributed to the rise of militant activity in many parts of the world.

Page 30. Ref: 24. Author's telephone conversation with the Administration. Royal Society for the Prevention of Tropical Disease. 8 September 1979. London. From the author's notes. The conversation took place when she was in London for the Annual Meeting of the International Institute of Communications. Advice on locating medical specialists is often provided by the Royal Society as a courtesy to private persons as well as overseas health and research organizations. The attitude of the Society's administration in 1979 was both unusual and unexpected.

Chapter 4

Page 38. Ref: 10. Records of the Government of Pakistan, Ministry of Information and Broadcasting, Islamabad, Pakistan. Also see notes. When I entered the drawing room at the State Guest House to join the President and the other four already present there, the blood drained from the woman's face. I wondered what had happened. I did not know why she was there, therefore, I made small talk but the woman remained silent, practically refusing to acknowledge me although she had already called on me in my office. I had been asked to receive her through a formal letter sent to me by Mr Masoodur Rauf, Additional Secretary, M /I&B. The letter is in the records of the Ministry of Interior. I had been co-opted into service by the President and was already serving as Communications Media Consultant to the Government of Pakistan, Ministry for Information and Broadcasting. Several minutes after I joined them, the woman abruptly told the General that his old friend and colleague, Col (Retd.) Qayyum was the right person for 'the job'. Col. (Retd.) Qayyum, a Bengali by origin, often claimed in public that he liased with the Bangladesh military for Zia ul Haq and had social and political influence in Bangladesh. He also claimed he had influence in the Bangladesh military. Eventually, a liberally funded research organization called the Institute of Regional Studies was set up under the aegis of the Ministry for Information and Broadcasting and Col (Retd) Qayyum was made its Chairman. He occupied this chair for well over a decade.

Page 38. Ref: 11. Photographs were being snapped while the incident was taking place, which indicated that the incident was pre-arranged to compromise the victim, the author of this book, who was a member of the International

Institute of Communications and attending its 1979 Annual Meeting in London. The meeting was being co-hosted by a number of organizations including the BBC and Reuters. The British Government was, supposedly, responsible for the protection of the delegates to the IIC Annual Meeting. The Director General of the BBC at the time, Lord Trevelyn, was informed of the incident by the security services of a third country, (not Pakistan). On Wednesday, 12 September 1979, he stood in the receiving line to greet members of the IIC who were arriving to attend an evening of Victorian Music Hall hosted by BBC Television Service at the Players Theatre, (173 Villiers Street, London WC2). When he saw the author arrive he came towards her, introduced himself and expressed his deepest regrets at the incident. He then introduced the author to Mr Binn, Chairman Capital Radio, who was standing beside him, and left the venue. However, there was no formal apology from the BBC or the British Government.

Page 39. Ref: 13. Report in *Sairbeen* (a radio magazine program of the BBC Urdu Service). BBC Urdu Service Online. 13 November 2002. Mir Aimal Kansi was executed by lethal injection on 14 November 2002, in Virginia, USA. On 13 November 2002 the BBC Urdu Service (*Sairbeen*) broadcast an interview in which Mr. Kansi said he had shot the two CIA personnel to register his protest against US policy in the Middle East and the attitude of the United States towards Muslims elsewhere. He did not cite any other reason for the act. Earlier reports had suggested he was inflamed by the behaviour of the two agents he killed and had worked with in Pakistan, where they had been listed as USAID employees for the duration of their tenure in Pakistan, (Record of the USAID/Pakistan and Afghanistan, Executive Office, Islamabad, list of official personnel, 1990-1994). Kansi came into contact with the agents at the USAID Liaison Office in Quetta, Balochistan/Pakistan. Throughout the world, USAID has a policy whereby it employs locals as personal services contractors to assist expatriate staff. These locals, technically, are not employees of the United States government and are not covered by the Rules of Business of the State Department or by USG Labor Laws.

Chapter 5
Page 44. Ref: 2. Possony, Stefan. 'Scientific Advances Hold Dramatic Prospects for Psy-Strategy' *Defence and Foreign Affairs*. July 1983. Dr Stefan Possony was a Hoover Institute fellow who was called 'the intellectual father of 'Star Wars' and dubbed 'one of the most influential civilian strategic planners in the Pentagon' (*Guardian*, 1995).

Page 52. Ref: 12. Department of Commerce: Government of India. 'Letter in connection with recruitment No. 71.20 (T)nb; 30 December 1946. Please note: these were top secret experiments. Most of the administrative instructions given were verbal or under cover of other activities. Even cover assignment papers were destroyed. Proof is the duping of Sir Peter Horsley, Equerry to the Duke of Edinburgh, who was thought to be 'too inquistive'(Chapter 2, Ref: 4.). However, part of one document is reproduced below as record of the post World War II movement of personnel and traffic between Germany and New Delhi on special assignment. As mentioned in the letter, it was written because the addressee could not be reached on the telephone. Subsequently, it was revealed to me that he did not take a telephone call because he wanted a documentary record of the offer. The Letter read as follows:

'No. 71.20 (T)nb; Department of Commerce, New Delhi, the 30th December 1946; Confidential;

My Dear Junaid,
You will no doubt recollect Sir Raghavan mentioned to you some days ago about the post of Economic Advisor to the Indian Military Mission in Berlin and enquired whether you would be prepared to accept the post in case it was offered to you. I understand from Sir Raghavan that you wanted some time to make up your mind but that you have not communicated your decision to him so far. As the final selection cannot be delayed much further, I shall be obliged if you will kindly let me know by return whether you would wish to be considered for this post. 2. I tried to get you on the telephone, but without success; hence this letter,

Yours Sincerely,
(signed) B.N.Bannerji-

Dr. M.M. Junaid, M.A.,Ph.D.(Lond.),
Director of Statistics,
Food Department,
New Delhi.'

Chapter 6
Page 61. Ref: 14. As recounted to the author in 1988 by Ms Virginia Stewart, spouse of Jon Stewart, the USIS officer in question. Virginia Stewart was also working at the American Embassy in Beirut when it was first attacked and taken over by Arab guerrillas—she gave the author a chilling account of that experience as well.

Page 63. Ref: 17. Joint Statement on the conclusion of the G-7 Meeting on Combating Terrorism. G-7 Secretariat. 30 July 1996. Sector-wise Working Groups were set up to recommend legislation to be enacted by member states and recommendations to be made to the United Nations General Assembly in September 1996.

Chapter 7

Page 65. Ref: 2. The possibility was discussed at the policy level when the author was Communications Media Consultant to the Government of Pakistan 1977-1979.

Page 68. Ref: 7. The Supreme Court of Pakistan. Proceedings of the Contempt of Court case against Prime Minister Mr. Nawaz Sharif. Islamabad: 1997. On Saturday 23 November 2002 the President of Pakistan issued an Ordinance to further amend the Anti-Terrorism Act, 1997 (second Amendment). This followed an earlier issued under the PCO (Provisional Constitution Order) No. 1 of 1999. The second amendment increased the scope of powers for extra-judicial arrest and confinement of persons on mere suspicion of being involved in, or associated in any way with terror suspects or terrorist activity, among other things.

Page 68. Ref: 8. APP Report. *The News* (Islamabad) 16 February 1996: and BBC World. Documentaries on NATO during the Cold War. October 1994. One covered the circumstances surrounding the assassination of Mr Aldo Moro, former Italian Premier. The alleged assassin, a member of the Red Brigade, was caught in Brazil on 11 November 2002 (BBC World News).

Page 69. Ref: 10. 'Resolving Bilateral Conflicts Through Regional Cooperation'—a Seminar organized by FES, CASAC, SAMA was held 22-23 April 1995 in Rawalpindi (Pakistan). Participants discussed the ramifications of the issue. For details read the proceedings of the Seminar. Transcripts are available at the Friedrich Ebert Stiftung, Office of the Representative Pakistan, 6-A, Street 14, F-8/3 Islamabad, Pakistan.

Chapter 8

Page 79. Ref: 12. Dr Gowher Rizvi, a Bangladesh national, was a Research Fellow at Nuffield College, Oxford at the time (1991-). He was also serving on the Editorial Advisory Board of *Strategic Perspectives*, published by the Institute of Strategic Studies, Ministry of Foreign Affairs, Government of Pakistan, among other things: 'The Role of Think Tanks in US Foreign Policy' was the title of an issue of the *US Foreign Policy Agenda*, an electronic journal of the US Department of State (Vol. 7, No. 3, November 2002)—the articles in this issue provide insight into some of the reasons why US think tanks have failed to provide useful options and alternatives for American policy makers.

Chapter 10

Page 92. Ref: 8. In July 1973, I happened to be in the US INS premises, New York, on personal business and was informed of this by personnel on duty there.

Chapter 11

Page 116. Ref: 12. The Majlis-e-Amal, a coalition of Pakistan's religious political parties, won about a third of the seats in general elections to the National Assembly that were held in October 2002. It also won a majority in two Provinces, the North West Frontier Province and Balochistan.

Chapter 13

Page 121. Ref: 7. *International Herald Tribune.* 'Classified Advertisements Section': *High Life* (British Airways inflight magazine). 'Classified Advertisements Section': *The Economist.* 'Classified. Advertisements Section'. It is necessary to add here that the services offered by those who are advertising are legal in the countries to which access is being offered. It is the source of funds and intent of those seeking access to these countries that has to be scrutinized.

Page 121. Ref: 8. National Saving Scheme instruments are guaranteed by the State Bank of Pakistan. For details of returns on available schemes see National Savings brochures from 1982-1999. Thereafter, the government has systematically reduced the rate of return on government guaranteed investments to discourage public investment in them. For instance, the rate of return on popular 3 year term Special Saving Certificates was reduced from 15 per cent per annum (average) to 8.75 per cent (average) between 1999-2002.

Page 123. Ref: 11. 'Special Report'. *The Nation.* 20 February 2002: 25,000 members of cooperative societies, each with a holding of Re. 100, 000/- or less (USD 1:Pk Re. 61/-), were reimbursed with funds recovered by the government between 1995-2001 from defunct cooperatives.

Page 124. Ref: 13. Shah, Col (Retd.) Sultan Ali. Conversation with the Author. 8 September 1965. Some tanners in the Punjab managed to commandeer trucks meant for transporting refugees: Recollections of Col. (Retd.) Sultan Ali Shah (British Army) of Kohat, NWFP, as told to the author. At the time of Partition, between August-September 1947, Col. Sultan Ali Shah served with one of the groups of military escorts that accompanied convoys of Muslim refugees from India to newly created Pakistan. He was responsible for bringing refugees from East Punjab to West Punjab and often spoke of the horrors he witnessed.

Page 124. Ref: 14. Victoria, later Viqarunnisa Noon, the second wife of Sir Feroze Khan Noon, was a British subject. She was sent to India as a WACI (Women's Army Corps of India): Naheed, the second wife of Iskander Mirza, was Iranian. Naheed introduced Zulfiqar Ali Bhutto to Nusrat, who was also an Iranian, and who became Bhutto's second wife.

Chapter 14
P. 130. Ref: 6. Press statement on the establishment of the Ehtasaab Bureau by the Pakistan Muslim League, Nawaz Sharif group, 1997: Press statement on the establishment of the National Acountability Bureau, by the military government of General Pervaiz Musharraf (1999).

P. 132. Ref: 12. 'The price per unit of electricity' was re-negotiated between Pakistan's Water and Power Development Authority(WAPDA) and independent power producers (IPP) in Pakistan after the military seized power on 12 October 1999. See press reports of negotiations and final settlement of rates (*The News*, 15 August 2001).

P. 132. Ref: 13. Note: In the French Agosta submarine deal between the manufacturers and the Government of Pakistan, it was alleged that about USD 14 million were given as commission to the main accused, former Admiral and Chief of Naval Staff, Mansurul Haq, through middlemen. He was extradited from the United States, where he had settled, at the request of the Government of Pakistan. He was formally charged by the National Accountability Bureau, indicted in Accountability Court and released after a plea bargain settlement in 2001. He agreed to return some of the money he had received as commission. Others accused of aiding him and also receiving commissions have not surrendered to the court, and are proclaimed offenders.

Chapter 15
P. 138. Ref: 2. The Agreement between the Government of Pakistan and the US State Department regarding the terms of development assistance programs is in the Archives of The Ministry of Foreign Affairs, Government of Pakistan. It is also available from the US State Department. According to the 1965-1966 Economic Survey produced by the Planning Commission, Government of Pakistan, in 1965 Pakistan faced '...a reduced inflow of foreign economic assistance and increased burden of defence expenditure on us by the Indian aggression in September last (1965)...' This marked the beginning of a pattern for rationalizing poor economic performance and rising defence expenditure.

P. 139. Ref: 4. A List of Participants in USAID's training programme for employees of the Government of Pakistan (1984-1994) is available with the Academy for Educational Development (AED), a private sector, US-based organization located in Washington DC. One of the pre-conditions for approval of a candidate was a guarantee that the official being sent for training would be promoted on his/her return. Individual officers were recommended by their departments directly and there was no vetting of candidates by the Economic Affairs Division of the Ministry of Foreign Affairs or centralized training programme to further the objectives of good governance.

P. 140. Ref: 5. The Harvard Group of economists, led by the Papanecks, was attached to the Planning Commission, Ministry of Finance, between 1964 and 1969.

P. 141. Ref: 7. Records of the Economic Affairs Division, Government of Pakistan, 1987-1988. The Plan was prepared under the guidance of the Legal Advisor (Spielman) to USAID, Pakistan Office.

P. 141. Ref: 9. USAID NGO Program, 1986-1992. The United States development aid agency, USAID, provided grants to several NGOs in Pakistan: Among others, the Edhi Foundation was given a grant for the purchase of a helicopter (1986-1987), to enable it to expand the scope of its existing ambulance network in Sindh. A Karachi based women lawyer's Legal Aid Project was given a grant to open free legal aid centres for women. Another, Lahore based, legal aid organization was given funds for producing and distributing informative material. The Orangi Pilot Project in Karachi also received assistance for community uplift. At one point or other, people working in these organizations expressed reservations about the motives of external aid agencies in contact with them. For instance, during the Sohrab Goth bloodbath in 1987, which was believed to be ethnic in motivation, workers at the OPP made video films with equipment donated by aid agencies. They were asked to hand over all the cassettes of the video films they had made to representatives of the development aid agency that had donated equipment and had grave reservations about doing so.

P. 142. Ref: 11. The Quantum Fund was what is called 'a fund of funds'. When it was fully subscribed the Soros group set up several others. So did other investment organizations. Another such fund set up by Soros was called the Fraternity Fund Ltd. The Fraternity Fund is described as follows in its newsletter of 17 August 1999: 'Fraternity Fund Ltd. Is a fund of funds that only invests in the Quantum Group of Funds (The investment Portfolio that are either directly or indirectly advised by George Soros or Soros Fund Management (SFM)). We are a specialized offshore investment management organization that allows institutional investors as well as smaller sophisticated investors to invest and participate in the financial world of George Soros and Soros Fund Management etc.' This put enormous amounts of manuvoerable capital at the disposal of one individual and organization, for the sole purpose of maximizing profit from investment.

P. 143. Ref: 13. Household expenses-inflation data is released to the Press by the Federal Bureau of Statistics, Government of Pakistan, on a quarterly basis. Independent sources prepare comparative data to check the accuracy of official figures. *The Nation* (APP). 20 November 1997.

Chapter 16

P. 149. Ref: 4. In mid-November 2002 the United States sent letters to its Allies, including Japan, to pledge troops to the war it expected to fight against Iraq. Among others, Japan declined to commit itself to the US war effort and said it would wait for the results of UNSC efforts for Iraq's compliance with the Resolutions of the Security Council.

P. 158. Ref: 20. In 1985, official estimates of the population in Bangladesh's Bihari refugee camps was 300,000. On the basis of these estimates Saudi Arabian non governmental organizations gave the first tranche of funds for the resettlement and housing of Biharis, to the Government of Pakistan. Some houses were constructed in rural Punjab. Three hundred persons were brought to Pakistan under the program. Since then the population in the Bihari camps of Bangladesh is reported to have crossed the one million mark, despite the unofficial movement of large numbers to Pakistan.

Chapter 20

P. 186. Ref: 5. This has already happened. After receiving assurances on mutual reduction and being invited to join NATO, the latest Strategic Arms reduction Treaty was signed by US President George W. Bush and Russian President Putin, in Moscow, July 2002.

P. 191. Ref: 11. On 22 November 2002, a civilian government was installed in Pakistan. Despite stiff resistance from major political groups, the new Prime Minister, Mir Zafarullah Jamali, who belongs to the pro-establishment Pakistan Muslim League-Q (Quaid-I-Azam) faction, promised to uphold amendments that were made to the 1973 Constitution of Pakistan by the military regime between 1999-2002. The 1973 Constitution was adopted by consensus.

P. 191. Ref: 12. Far-reaching decisions that have an impact on the sovereignty and territorial integrity of the country are being taken by a small group of men who are seeking legitimacy for a government they have installed for themselves. Such decisions should be taken by a national government in full control of policy formulation after all aspects have been considered and debated by elected public representatives. They have got that legitimacy in the form of joy rides, photo opportunities and handshakes.[12] But photo opportunities and handshakes do not necessarily represent, or lead to, enduring strategic alliances that are based on common, shared interests, perceptions and objectives that have the support of the population of a country. This should not be construed as an endorsement of the claims of those corrupt political elements that have had several opportunities to forge strategic alliances for Pakistan but have merely used such opportunities to secure personal interests.

Chapter 21

P. 195. Ref: 3. 'Protocols of the Zionist Congress'. The deliberations at the Congress, generally referred to as the Protocols of the Zionist Congress were never made public. An English language version of the policy recommended and decisions taken by the Elders was published between 1907 and 1910, in a series of booklets. This publication infuriated the Elders who ordered Israelis to seek out copies and destroy them. This was done. The few who still have copies of the original booklets will not reveal their existence. I was shown one of the booklets in the United States in 1975 and merely glanced through the first few pages.

After the Islamic Revolution, the Government of Iran published a version of the Protocols. This version was widely circulated in Muslim countries. I was given a photocopy of this version. Neither the language nor the format resembled that of the original version that I had seen in the United States/ Also read Walter Lacquer, Postmodern Terrorism, *Foreign Affairs*, Vol. 75, No. 5, September/October 1996.

P. 4. Ref: 5. 13 October 2001. A proposal for the deployment of observers was presented before the United Nations Security Council in 2001, but it was vetoed by the United States.

BIBLIOGRAPHY

A. Callaghy, Thomas. *Vision and Politics in the Transformation of the Global Economy, Global Transformation and the Third World*, ed., Slater/Schutz/Dort, Boulder, CO. Lynne Riennet Publishers. 1992.

Adamec, Ludwig W. *Dictionary of Afghan Wars, Revolutions and Insurgencies*. Scarecrow Press. 1996.

Amos, John W. *Palestinian Resistance: organization of nationalist movement*. New York. Pergamon Press. 1980.

Arora, Subhash Chander. *Strategies to Combat Terrorism: A Study of Punjab*. New Delhi. Har-Anand Publications. 1999.

Ben-Menashe, Ari. *Profits of War: inside the secret U.S.-Israeli arms network* New York. Sheridan Square Press. 1992.

C. Schelling, Thomas. *The Strategy of Conflict*. Cambridge. Harvard University Press. 1960.

Chubin, Shahram. *Security in the Persian Gulf: The Role of Outside Powers*. Gower Publishing Company Limited. 1982.

Clausewitz, Carl von. *On War*. edited and translated by Michael Howard and Peter Paret Princeton, N.J. Princeton University Press. 1984.

Diamond, Larry. *Promoting Democracy in the 1990's- Actors and Instruments, Issues and Imperatives*. Report to the Carnegie Commission on Preventing Deadly Conflict. Carnegie Corporation of New York. 1995.

Ezeldin, Ahmad Galal. *Terrorism and Political Violence: an Egyptian perspective*. (translated by Sanaa Ragheb). Cairo. Dar El Houriah. 1985.

Freedom in the World: The Annual Survey of Political Rights and Civil Liberties 1994-1995. New York. 1995.

Fukuyama, Francis. *The Soviet Union and Iraq Since 1968*. Rand (N-1524-AF).1980.

George, Alexander. ed., *Western State Terrorism*. New York. Routledge. 1991.

Geraghty, Tony. *The Irish War: the Hidden Conflict Between the IRA and British Intelligence*. Baltimore. Johns Hopkins University Press. 2000.

Hadawi, Sami. *Bitter Harvest: Palestine Between 1914-1979*. Caravan Books. 1979.

Hartlyn, Jonathan. and Arturo Valenzuela. *Democracy in Latin America since 1930*. The Cambridge History of Latin America Vol. VI: Latin America Since 1930: Economy, Society and Politics Leslie Bethell ed., Cambridge. Cambridge University Press.

India and Pakistan Eyeball to Eyeball. South Asia Monitor. Center for Strategic and International Studies. June 1, 2002.

International Religious Freedom Report. US Department of State. October 2001. Available online.

Keddie, Nikki. *Roots of Revolution*. New Haven. Yale University Press. 1981.

Keller, Konrad. *The Impact of Terrorism on the Federal Republic of Germany 1968-1982*. Rand Corporation (Report R-3438).1987. ISBN 0833007742.

Khalilzad, M. Zalmay. and David A. Ochmanek. eds., *Strategy and Defense Planning for the 21st Century*. Santa Monica. Rand. 1997.

L. Rotberg, Robert. ed., *Creating Peace in Sri Lanka: Civil War and Reconciliation*. Brookings Institute Press. 1999.

Norris, Christopher. *Uncritical Theory: Postmodernism, Intellectuals, and the Gulf War*. Amherst. University of Massachusetts Press. 1992.

O'Ballance, Edgar. *Afghan Wars 1839-1992, What Britain Gave Up and the Soviet Union Lost*, New York. Brassey's. 1993.

Report of the Task Force on the Military Options and Implications of Non-Lethal Technologies. United States Council on Foreign Relations. New York. 1995.

SIPRI. *Military Capacity and the Risk of War, China, India, Pakistan and Iran*. Oxford. Oxford University Press. 1997).

Sterling, Claire. *The Terror Network: the secret war of international terrorism*. London. Weidenfeld and Nicholson 1981. 1981-ISBN 029777929X.

The Nuclear Debate: Strategic Issues No. 3. The Institute of Strategic Studies, Islamabad. March 2000.

The Persian Gulf at the Millennium, Essays in Politics, Economy, Security and Religion. New York. St. Martin's Press. 1997.

The Secret Army: the IRA 1916-1979. Dublin. Poolbeg. 1989. ISBN 185371027X.

W. Pursell Jr., Carroll. *The Military Industrial Complex*. New York. Harper and Row. 1972.

Williamson, John. ed., *The Political Economy of Policy Reform*. Washington DC. Institute for International Economics. 1994.

Willis, Michael Willis. *The Islamist Challenge in Algeria: a political history*. New York University Press. 1997.

Yonah, Alexander. *International Terrorism: national, regional and global perspectives*. New York: Praeger Press. 1976.

INDEX

A

ABM (Anti Ballistic Missile Treaty), 188
accountability, 132
ADB (Asian Development Bank), 142, 149
aeronautics, 109
Afghan War, 125
Afghan, 104, 157, 193
Afghanistan, 13, 17, 62, 69, 70, 74, 75, 84, 88, 90, 94,97, 99-101, 103-104, 115, 148, 151,153, 166, 178, 183, 188, 190-192, 205
Africa, 73, 85, 191; North, 77; South, 62, 198
agricultural income, 113
aircraft, 109, 157
Al Qaeda, 73, 205
Albania, 9, 156, 164
Algeria, 6, 9, 16, 17, 57, 65, 71,84
Al-Jazeera, 98
America Watch, 58
America: North, 165; South, 25, 58, 85, 101, 103, 110, 150
American, 75, 103, 133, 139, 171, 189, 196, 200
Annan, Kofi, 18
Anthrax, 74, 187
Apartheid, 58
Arab Collective Security Pact, 173
Arab lands, 202
Arab League, 171, 200
Arab Palestine Revolt, 171
Arab Summit, 202
Arab, 110, 171, 188, 196, 199-200
Arabian Sea, 139
ARF (Asian Regional Forum), 149
Argentina, 191-192
Arms Export Control Act, US, 86

ASEAN (Association of South East Asian Nations), 69, 180, 194
Asia, 73, 77, 85, 103, 188-189; Central, 29, 149, 152-153, 180, 184-185, 189-190, East, 27, 79, 87, 110, 143, South, 25, 70, 79, 83, 105, 177, 179, 183, 189; West, 70, 79, 105, 148, 154, 170, 172, 174, 177, 178, 185, 189
Asian, 139
Asia-Pacific, 111
Asir, 170
Assassins, 5
Australia, 101-102
Austro-Hungarian Empire, 6
Ayodhya, 81, 184

B

Baader Meinhoff, 61
Babri mosque, 81,184
Balkan, 156,164, 168
Balochi, 133
Balochistan, 70
Bangkok Declaration, 180
Bangladesh, 126, 158, 173
Barter system, 118
Basle, 197
BBC (British Broadcasting Corporation), 38, 39, 44, 98
BCCI (Bank of Credit and Commerce International),125
Beirut, 202
Belarus, 190
Bengali, 158
Biden, US Senator, 188
Bihari, 158
Biological weapons, 187
Biotechnology, 109
BJP (Bharatya Janata Party), 177
Black Sea, 154